Top Auditing Issues for 2005
CPE Course

CCH Editorial Staff Publication

CCH INCORPORATED
Chicago

A WoltersKluwer Company

Contributors

Contributing Editors .... Steven C. Fustolo, CPA
Gary L. Maydew, PhD, CPA
Production Coordinator .... Susan Haldiman
Production .... Lynn J. Brown
Layout and Design .... Laila Gaidulis

This publication is designed to provide accurate and authoritative information in regard to the subject matter covered. It is sold with the understanding that the publisher is not engaged in rendering legal, accounting, or other professional service. If legal advice or other expert assistance is required, the services of a competent professional person should be sought.

ISBN 0-8080-1184-7

© 2004, **CCH** INCORPORATED
4025 W. Peterson Ave.
Chicago, IL 60646-6085
1 800 248 3248
http://tax.cchgroup.com

No claim is made to original government works; however, within this Product or Publication, the following are subject to CCH's copyright: (1) the gathering, compilation, and arrangement of such government materials; (2) the magnetic translation and digital conversion of data, if applicable; (3) the historical, statutory and other notes and references; and (4) the commentary and other materials.

All Rights Reserved
Printed in the United States of America

TOP AUDITING ISSUES FOR 2005 CPE COURSE

Introduction

The purpose of this course is to present current and arising issues in the field of auditing. It begins by covering selected developments, including details on the AICPA's top technology issues and the public's perceptions of the accounting profession. Other items covered concern the issue of fraud and how to deliberate with clients about this topic. There is also discussion on the impact of the Sarbanes-Oxley Act of 2002 on the accounting profession, as well as an examination of federal securities laws.

The use of fair value measurements in accounting has expanded over the past decade. Auditors, in turn, must address the auditing requirements to deal with use of fair value. Chapter 2 of the course reviews SAS No. 101 and offers greater clarification on the use of fair value measures within the accounting model. Additionally, other audit procedures that may provide evidence relevant to the measurement and disclosure of fair values are also discussed.

Chapter 3 contains a detailed overview of a major auditing standard, SAS No. 99. Users and regulators have placed an added emphasis on fraud detection, so knowledge of this standard is crucial to auditors.

The second module of the course, Chapters 4 and 5, focuses on developments affecting compilation and review engagements, such as SSARS No. 8, SSARS No. 9, and recently issued interpretations of SSARS No. 1. It lists the exemptions from SSARSs for engagements, offers information about new opportunities for expanding compilation and review practices, and details what actually transpires in compilation and review engagements. It also incorporates some of the matters discussed in the AICPA's Compilation and Review Alerts, as well as how the Alerts clarify certain existing standards and assist accountants in implementing the SSARSs and related interpretations.

Throughout the course, there are examples and observations to illustrate the topics covered, as well as study questions to test your knowledge. The course is divided into two modules. Take your time and review both course modules. When you feel confident that you thoroughly understand the material, turn to the CPE quizzer. Complete one or both module quizzers for Continuing Professional Education credit. Further information is provided in the quizzer instructions on page 207.

October 2004

COURSE OBJECTIVES

This course was prepared to provide the participant with an overview of important new auditing standards and developments. At the completion of the course, you will be able to:

- Understand the impact of SAS No. 99 on audits of nonpublic entities.
- Comprehend the cause and effect of the Sarbanes-Oxley Act of 2002.
- Understand the requirements of SAS No. 101 as it relates to an auditor's responsibility for auditing fair value measurements and disclosures.
- Understand the definition and characteristics of fraud.
- Identify risks that may result in a material misappropriation due to fraud.
- View the ways in which market forces are changing the compilation and review process.
- Understand the latest developments affecting compilation and review engagements.

CCH'S PLEDGE TO QUALITY

Thank you for choosing this CCH Continuing Education product. We will continue to produce high quality products that challenge your intellect and give you the best option for your Continuing Education requirements. Should you have a concern about this or any other CCH CPE product, please call our Customer Service Department at 1-800-248-3248.

One **complimentary copy** of this course is provided with all copies of the Miller Auditing Guides. Additional copies of this course may be ordered for $25.00 each by calling 1-800-248-3248 (ask for product 0-0912-100).

TOP AUDITING ISSUES FOR 2005 CPE COURSE

Contents

MODULE 1

1 Auditing: Selected Developments 1
Learning Objectives 1
Introduction 1
AICPA's Top 10 Technology Issues: 2004 1
How are Auditors and Business Ethics Viewed by the Public? 3
The Impact of SAS No. 99 on Audits of Non-Public Entities 5
Dealing With the Realities of SAS No. 99 10
The Aftermath of Sarbanes-Oxley 13

**2 SAS No. 101: Auditing Fair Value
Measurements and Disclosures** 29
Learning Objectives 29
Introduction 30
Requirements of SAS No. 101 30
Evaluating Conformity of Fair Value Measurements
    and Disclosures with GAAP 34
Engaging A Specialist 37
Testing the Entity's Fair Value Measurements and Disclosures 37
Testing Management's Significant Assumptions,
    the Valuation Model, and the Underlying Data 39
Developing Independent Fair Value Estimates for
    Corroborative Purposes 42
Reviewing Subsequent Events and Transactions 42
Disclosures about Fair Values 43
Evaluating the Results of Audit Procedures 43
Management Representation 43
Communication with Audit Committee 44

3 Fraud Detection: Understanding and Applying SAS No. 99 45
Learning Objectives 45
Introduction 46
Characteristics of Fraud 46
Overview Of SAS No. 99 47
Importance of Exercising Professional Skepticism 50
Risks of or Potential for Fraud 51
Identify the Risks of Fraud 52
Material Misappropriation Due to Fraud 56
Responding to the Results of the Assessment 57
Evaluating Audit Evidence 63

vi TOP AUDITING ISSUES FOR 2005 CPE COURSE

MODULE 2

4 Compilation and Review: Important and Evolving Issues 68
Learning Objectives 68
Introduction 69
Controversy on the Compilation Front 69
Alternatives to the Traditional Compilation Engagement:
   The Debate Over Assembly, Plain Paper, and Other Alternatives 70
SSARS No. 8, *Amendment to Statement on Standards for*
   Accounting and Review Services No. 1, Compilation and
   Review of Financial Statements 72
Financial Statements Generated Using General Ledger Software 78
Rules for Issuing Management-Use Only Financial Statements 91
Other Issues for Management-Use Only Financial Statements 101
Exemptions from the SSARSs 103
Controllership Issues: What Is Going on in Practice? 110

5 Compilation and Review Update 118
Learning Objectives 118
Introduction 119
SSARS No. 9: *Omnibus Statement on Standards for Accounting*
   and Review Services 2002 119
Selected Information: "Substantially All Disclosures Required By
   Generally Accepted Accounting Principles Are Not Included" 145
Reference to the Country of Origin in a Review
   or Compilation Report 149

Answers to Study Questions **151**

Appendix A **172**

Appendix B **187**

Index **197**

CPE Quizzer Instructions **207**

CPE Quizzer **209**

Module 1: Answer Sheet **225**

Module 2: Answer Sheet **229**

Evaluation Form **233**

MODULE 1 — CHAPTER 1

Auditing: Selected Developments

LEARNING OBJECTIVES

At the completion of this chapter, you should be able to:

- Identify the AICPA's current and emerging top technology issues of 2004.
- Better understand the public's opinions of the auditing profession and its business ethics.
- Understand the impact of SAS No. 99 on audits of nonpublic entities.
- Comprehend the cause and effect of the Sarbanes-Oxley Act of 2002.

INTRODUCTION

This chapter centers around current and arising developments of auditing. The section on the AICPA details a list of its *Top Ten Technology Issues of 2004*, which provides a brief description of each technology issue being discussed. A list of the AICPA's latest emerging technology issues is also included.

Included is a section on the public's perceptions of the accounting profession, posing questions and comparing auditors to other professionals after such auditing scandals as Enron. How to identify fraud, the conditions of fraud, and how to deliberate with clients about fraud are the highlights of the SAS No. 99 section. Lastly, the impact of the Sarbanes-Oxley Act of 2002 on the accounting profession and federal securities laws is examined. The author details the impact of the Act.

AICPA'S TOP 10 TECHNOLOGY ISSUES: 2004

In January 2004, based on the results of a survey of its membership, the AICPA announced its list of *Top Ten Technology Issues of 2004*, which includes seven new items that were not on the 2003 list. To no surprise, information security continued to be the number one item on the list.

AICPA's Top 10 Technologies

Technology	Description
1. Information Security	The hardware, software, processes and procedures in place that protect an entity's systems, including firewalls, anti-virus, password management, patches, and locked facilities

TOP AUDITING ISSUES FOR 2005 CPE COURSE

Technology	Description
2. Spam Technology (new)	Using technology to reduce or eliminate unwanted e-mail with technologies ranging from confirmation of the sender through ISP lookup to methods where the recipient accepts e-mail only from specific senders
3. Digital Optimization (new)	Heading toward the Paperless Office with the process of capturing and managing documents electronically via PDF or other formats
4. Database and Application Integration (new)	The ability to update one field and have it automatically synchronize between multiple databases
5. Wireless Technologies	The transfer of voice or data from one machine to another through the airwaves without physical connectivity
6. Disaster Recovery	The development, monitoring and updating of the process by which organizations plan for continuity of their businesses in the event of a loss of business information resources due to a theft, weather damage, accident or malicious destruction
7. Data Mining (new)	Methods by which a user can sift through volumes of data to find specific answers
8. Virtual Office (new)	The technologies, processes, and procedures that allow personnel to work effectively, either individually or with others, regardless of physical location
9. Business Exchange Technology (new)	The evolution from EDI to greater business transaction and data exchange via the Internet using datasets that are transported easily between programs and databases (e.g., XBRL)
10. Message Applications (new)	Applications that permit users to communicate electronically, including by e-mail, voicemail and instant messaging

Source: AICPA

The survey also addressed Emerging Technologies: those technologies that may not have a current commercial impact, but may do so in the next few years.

AICPA's Top 5 Emerging Technologies

Technology	Description
1. ID/Authentication	Verifying either the identity of a user who is logging onto a computer system or the integrity of a transmitted message
2. Radio Frequency Identification (RFID)	RFID tags, which consist of silicon chips and an antenna that can transmit data to a wireless receiver, and could be used to track the geographic location of anything. Unlike bar codes, RFID tags do not require line-of-sight for reading
3. 3G Wireless	Used for high-speed multimedia data and voice
4. Simple Object Access Protocol (SOAP)	A message-based protocol based on XML for accessing services on the Internet

MODULE 1 — CHAPTER 1 — Auditing: Selected Developments

Technology	Description
5. Autonomic Computers	Tools and strategies to manage and maintain all systems across an entity, including system maintenance, upgrades, automatic patching' and self-healing with a goal toward self-managing computer systems with a minimum of human interface

Source: AICPA

STUDY QUESTIONS

1. One of the AICPA's Top 10 Technology Issues for 2004 is Information Security. *True or False?*

2. The AICPA's list of Top 5 Emerging Technologies includes 3G Wireless. *True or False?*

HOW ARE AUDITORS AND BUSINESS ETHICS VIEWED BY THE PUBLIC?

After the break of the Enron scandal in late 2001, public confidence in the entire business community and the accounting profession dropped to an all-time low. In two recent polls, one by the Wall Street Journal, and the other by The Gallup Organization (the Gallup Poll), it appears as if the accounting profession's image has rebounded.

Wall Street Journal/NBC Poll

Poll question: Based on recent events, some people have said that they feel less certain about the information they receive. For each one, please tell me whether you still feel confident in it or whether you are not really confident in it.

	Still feel confident	Not really confident	Depends	Not sure
Rules governing 401(k) investment accounts	48	31	2	19
Wall Street stock brokerage firms providing solid analysis and recommendations	36	47	5	12
Financial statements and earnings reports from corporations	**33**	**54**	**5**	**8**
Corporate leaders honestly representing their businesses' future	22	65	6	7

Source: Wall Street Journal

Additionally, 57% of the respondents stated that standards and values of corporate leaders and executives have dropped in the past 20 years, as compared with 38% who indicated standards and values are the same or higher. In another poll, it appears that the public has lost confidence in auditors.

In comparing auditors to other professionals, 55% of respondents ranked overall performance of their auditors as being very good or excellent, as compared with a 70-75% mean for other professions. Further, 55% of the respondents said they definitely or probably would recommend their auditors to business colleagues, as compared with 75% for other professional services.

The survey did note some positive comments: The respondents gave high marks to auditors with respect to:

- Being a company to trust
- Having employees committed to personal ethics
- Having a culture of business integrity
- Being committed to maintaining a position of independence as an auditor

Poll question: Do auditors feel pressure to "fudge" the numbers? A recent AICPA poll shows:

Never	24%
Rarely	42%
Sometimes	25%
Often	6%
All the time	2%
Other comments	1%

Source: AICPA Sound-Off Survey

The Gallup Poll

As a follow-up to the Wall Street Journal Poll, in 2003, Gallup published its annual poll of the public image of various professions. In the poll, Americans were asked to rate their overall view of each of 25 industries ranging from very positive to very negative.

The results of the 2003 poll were quite positive for the accounting profession, showing a 14% increase in positive image, while showing a 17% decrease in negative image. Computer, restaurant, and grocery businesses had the most positive images, while the oil and gas, healthcare, and legal industries had the most negative images. A summary of the Poll follows.

Accounting Profession's Image

	2003	2002	2001*
Positive image	45%	31%	47%
Negative image	14%	31%	8%

* 2001 survey published prior to Enron scandal.
Source: The Gallup Organization, August 18, 2003

Comparison of Accountant's Image Versus Selected Professions: 2003

Industry	% Positive	% Neutral	% Negative	Net Positive
Computers	70%	20%	6%	64%
Banking	52%	26%	20%	32%
Internet	51%	25%	20%	31%
Accounting	45%	37%	14%	31%
Federal government	41%	23%	35%	6%
Legal	36%	24%	38%	-2%
Healthcare	42%	12%	45%	-3%
Oil and gas	35%	22%	43%	-8%

Source: Accounting's Image Recovers - The Gallup Organization, 2003

STUDY QUESTION

> **3.** According to the 2003 Gallup Poll, the public image of accountants has deteriorated from 2002 to 2003. **True or False?**

THE IMPACT OF SAS NO. 99 ON AUDITS OF NON-PUBLIC ENTITIES

General

In October 2002, the Auditing Standards Board (ASB) issued SAS No. 99, *Consideration of Fraud in a Financial Statement Audit.* SAS No. 99 was effective for audits of financial statements for periods beginning on or after December 15, 2002. SAS No. 99 supersedes SAS No. 82, *Consideration of Fraud in a Financial Statement Audit,* and establishes expanded requirements for auditors to consider fraud in a financial statement audit. It applies to audits of both public and non-public entities. Specifically, SAS No. 99 does the following:

- Emphasizes that an auditor must exercise professional skepticism during the audit.
- Requires that the auditor conduct a brainstorming session with audit engagement personnel to discuss the risks of material misstatement due to fraud and set the tone of the audit.
- Expands information gathering required to identify fraud risks. The auditor should:
  - Make greater inquiries of management and other personnel within the entity about the risks of fraud.
  - Perform analytical procedures including specific procedures on revenue.
  - Consider fraud risk factors.
  - Consider other information that may be useful in identifying fraud risks.

TOP AUDITING ISSUES FOR 2005 CPE COURSE

- Requires, after the information-gathering phase, the auditor to identify risks that may result in a material misstatement due to fraud.
- Requires the auditor to assess the identified risks due to fraud throughout the audit and evaluate those risks at the completion of the audit.
- Requires the auditor to perform additional procedures to deal with the risk of management override of controls including:
  - Examine journal entries and other adjustments for evidence of possible material misstatement due to fraud.
  - Review accounting estimates for biases that could result in material misstatement due to fraud including performing a retrospective review of significant accounting estimates reflected in the financial statements of the prior year to determine whether management judgments and assumptions relating to the estimates indicate a possible bias on the part of management.
  - Evaluate the business rationale for significant unusual transactions.
- Requires new language to be included in the management representation letter. SAS No. 85, *Management Representations,* is amended to require additional language regarding fraud.

STUDY QUESTIONS

> **4.** SAS No. 99 expands upon SAS No. 82 but does not supersede it. *True or False?*
>
> **5.** SAS No. 99 requires that an auditor maintain a high degree of professional skepticism in conducting his or her audit. *True or False?*

Types of Fraud

There are two types of misstatements due to fraud, misstatements arising from fraudulent financial reporting and misstatements arising from misappropriation of assets (theft or defalcation)

Misstatements arising from fraudulent financial reporting involve intentional misstatements or omissions of amounts or disclosures in financial statements designed to deceive financial statement users where the effect causes the financial statements not to be presented in accordance with GAAP (or another comprehensive basis of accounting, if used). Fraudulent financial reporting is accomplished in several ways:

- Manipulation, falsification, or alteration of accounting records or supporting documents from which financial statements are prepared
- Misrepresentation in or intentional omission from the financial statements of events, transactions, or other significant information, or,
- Intentional misapplication of accounting principles relating to amounts, classification, manner of presentation, or disclosure.

> ### OBSERVATION
>
> Fraudulent financial reporting need not occur as some sort of grand scheme or conspiracy. Instead, it may be the result of management rationalizing the appropriateness of a material misstatement as merely an aggressive, rather than an indefensible, interpretation of complex accounting rules. Or, management might argue that a misstatement is temporary and will reverse or correct itself in future reporting periods.

Misappropriation of assets is accomplished in several ways, including:
- Embezzling receipts
- Stealing assets
- Causing the entity to pay for goods or services not received

> ### OBSERVATION
>
> An auditor is only concerned with misappropriation of asset (theft or defalcation) that results in a material financial statement misstatement. Immaterial theft, for example, is not important to the auditor, per se. However, if an immaterial theft has occurred, the auditor should be concerned about the bigger picture and whether the occurrence of the theft suggests a deficiency in internal control.

What Types of Assets or Transactions Are Susceptible to Fraud?

The types of assets and transactions subject to fraud vary depending on whether the fraud involves fraudulent financial reporting (cooking the books) or misappropriation of assets (theft). It also depends on whether the company is large or small, and closely held versus publicly held. The following table compares the two types of frauds:

Description	Fraudulent Financial Reporting	Misappropriation of assets (theft)
Types of assets or transactions	Inventories, receivables and revenue	Cash: 90%* Inventories and other assets: 10%
Typical perpetrator	Management	All levels of employees and management
3G Wireless	Used for high-speed multimedia data and voice	
Primary reason for actions - Incentive/pressure - Opportunity - Rationalization/attitude	Incentive/pressure	Opportunity and rationalization/attitude
Size of transaction	Usually material to the financial statements	Usually immaterial to the financial statements
Type of entity more likely to be victimized	Larger entity with sophisticated financial management	Closely held businesses with poor internal controls

*2002 Report to the Nation, Occupational Fraud and Abuse (the Report), Association of Certified Fraud Examiners.

STUDY QUESTIONS

> **6.** There is generally only one type of fraud, according to the author. *True or False?*
>
> **7.** Fraudulent financial reporting involves the intentional misstatements or omissions of amounts or disclosures in financial statements. *True or False?*
>
> **8.** Misappropriation of assets involves the theft of an entity's assets where the effect of the theft causes the financial statements not to be presented in conformity with GAAP. *True or False?*
>
> **9.** When it comes to fraudulent financial reporting, cash is the asset most likely to be involved in the fraud. *True or False?*

Conditions Needed for Fraud: The Fraud Triangle

Three conditions usually are present when a fraud occurs. These three conditions are commonly referred to by fraud examiners as the fraud triangle and consist of the following:

- **Incentive or Pressure:** Management or other employees have an incentive or are under pressure (financial or otherwise), which provides a reason to commit fraud.
- **Opportunity:** Circumstances exist, such as the absence of controls, ineffective controls, or the ability of management to override controls, that provide an opportunity for a fraud to be perpetrated.
- **Rationalization or attitude:** Individuals involved in the fraud are able to rationalize committing the fraud. Some individuals possess an attitude, character, or set of ethical values that allow them to knowingly and intentionally commit a dishonest act.

Although the three conditions of the fraud triangle are typically present in a perpetuation of a fraud, there are circumstances when only one, or even two of the conditions may not present. These conditions could, for example, include these scenarios:

- An employee who is under personal financial pressure and is able to rationalize committing a fraud, is able to perpetrate a fraud even though there is a strong system of internal control. The employee can use a narrow breach in the system of internal control.
- A company who has a poor system of internal control is victimized by an employee fraud. The employee, who has no incentive/pressure to commit the fraud and appears not to possess a rationalization/attitude to commit a fraud, perpetrates a fraud because he or she is tempted by ability to commit the fraud from the poor system of internal control.
- A manager/owner has an incentive/pressure to achieve a certain income level to avoid triggering a loan default, where there is no indication of the presence of the other two conditions.

Considering the Three Conditions of Fraud in Light of the Type of Entity Being Audited

The three conditions of fraud need to be considered in light of the size, complexity and ownership attributes of the entity. For example, a larger entity might have controls that constrain improper conduct by management including:

- Existence of an audit committee
- Use of an internal audit function
- Existence and enforcement of a formal code of conduct

Conversely, a smaller, usually closely held entity will not have any of the same constraints placed on the management of a larger entity, as noted above. Rarely is an audit committee or internal audit function in use. Moreover, a formal code of conduct is not only non-existent, but also may be discouraged for stifling the entrepreneurial environment. Instead of having formal controls, a smaller entity might have other attributes such as developing a culture that emphasizes integrity and ethical behavior. In such situations, the auditor should be careful not to be fooled into a sense of security.

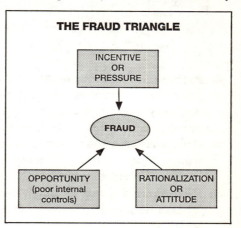

STUDY QUESTION

10. Under the fraud triangle, in general, there are three conditions usually present when a fraud occurs. *True or False?*

Fraud and Small Businesses

According to the 2002 Report to the Nation, Occupational Fraud and Abuse (Association of Certified Fraud Examiners),[1] in a sample of frauds examined, 32% of the frauds involved privately held companies, with the median loss being $127,000. 39% of the frauds involved companies with fewer than 100 employees.

What these statistics confirm is that fraud is not an act reserved for larger, publicly held companies. Instead, every day small, closely held businesses are victims of fraud. In most cases, the fraud involves theft, not necessarily fraudulent financial reporting.

Why does fraud affect smaller businesses?

Smaller businesses have certain characteristics that make them more susceptible to fraud than their larger counterparts. Examples of such characteristics include several factors:

- **Poor segregation of duties:** Most small businesses do not have the resources to justify hiring adequate accounting personnel to ensure a strong segregation of duties. In particular, many businesses have a weak segregation of duties between the recording and custody of assets. Many small businesses do not have formal job descriptions or duties for each employee. Instead, employees tend to be cross-trained to perform several functions horizontally within the organization.

> **EXAMPLE**
>
> The employee who makes the deposits may record them, perform the bank reconciliation and maintain the accounts receivable aging.

- **Poor control over the custody and access to assets:** Many small businesses do not maintain strong physical control over their assets. Thus, inventory can be stolen, light machinery (even motor vehicles) may be pilfered, without the owner knowing it.
- **Disinterested management/owner:** For many smaller companies, top management may be the owner or shareholder of the entity. Many small business owners do not take a serious role in setting a proper "tone at the top", emphasizing the importance of strong internal controls. In fact, it is not unusual for small business owners to challenge any attempt to strengthen internal control on the grounds that it may stifle the entrepreneurial process- that is, their small business is the antithesis of the rigid, and larger publicly held corporations.
- **Informal approval process:** Most small businesses do not have formal established procedures for approving transactions. The processing of invoices, recording of sales and receivables, and ordering of goods and materials may be performed casually, maybe even orally, with little documentation and formal approval for those transactions.

DEALING WITH THE REALITIES OF SAS NO. 99

Who is Going to Pay for SAS No. 99?

The most important question for all auditors is whether they can pass on the additional cost for complying with SAS No. 99, since it could significantly increase audit time, particularly in the planning stage. For auditors of publicly held entities, the auditors should be able to pass along the additional cost to the client, of implementing SAS No. 99.

SEC companies are fully aware that the cost of their audits is going up. New requirements made by Sarbanes-Oxley Act along with the negative financial press against auditors, puts the audit committees and boards of directors of SEC companies on notice. Expect your audit fees to go up.

Walking on Eggshells with Clients

Auditors of all entities have the responsibility of explaining to clients their and the auditor's responsibilities related to fraud. The more sophisticated the client, the easier it will be to make that client understand the fraud requirements. Auditors of most non-public entities have a different and more difficult challenge. Clients may push back when asked to pay more for their audits to comply with SAS No. 99 and other accounting and auditing pronouncements, for a number of reasons:

- There is a disconnect between non-public and public entities. Owners and management of non-public entities believe they are insulated from the events affecting SEC companies. That is, the events that impacted Enron and WorldCom affect only SEC companies, and do not trickle down to non-public entities.
- Management and owners of non-public entities are typically less sophisticated financially than their counterparts at SEC companies. Thus, they are less likely to understand their present and new responsibilities for fraud.
- Non-public entities have been conditioned to consider an audit as a commodity, rather than a value-added service. Therefore, the cost of the audit is usually the driving condition as to whether an auditor is hired.
- Many of the changes being made, including those related to SAS No. 99 are of little importance to management and owners of non-public entities. Most smaller businesses do not take fraud and its prevention seriously.

What Can an Auditor of a Non-Public Entity do to Implement SAS No. 99 Without Absorbing the Cost of Doing So?

Assuming an auditor is going to find resistance in increasing auditing fees, the auditor needs to consider how he or she audits. This author has been an advocate for reducing audit time using various techniques. Based on his discussions with other firms, it is clear that most firms over-audit, wasting time on procedures in low risk areas. Recommendations to reduce audit time include:

- Increase use of analytical procedures in lieu of tests of account balances. Use analytical procedures to test accounts such as:
  - Interest expense as percent average debt
  - Payroll tax expense as percent of payroll
  - Variable selling expenses as percent of sales

TOP AUDITING ISSUES FOR 2005 CPE COURSE

- Focus your audit in those areas where there is a high degree of inherent risk. Examples of such higher risk areas include:
  - Cash
  - Inventories
  - Accounts receivable
  - Trade payables
  - Revenue
- Reduce time spent in the areas of accruals and prepaid items.
- Consider using OCBOA (income tax basis) financial statements to reduce audit time. Income tax basis accrual statements are very effective for profitable, closely held businesses. Such statements eliminate the need to audit certain items such as:
  - Allowance for bad debts
  - Related party accruals
  - Deferred income taxes
  - Goodwill impairment
  - Long-lived asset impairment
- Use more experienced personnel in audit areas that are complex.

> **OBSERVATION**
>
> Many CPA firms use OCBOA statements for compilations and reviews, but rarely for audits. Yet, it is with audits that auditors reduce the most amount of time using OCBOA. Consider the fact that with OCBOA, certain elements required by GAAP, such as an allowance for bad debts, are not required. If such items are not required, the auditor does not have to audit those items. Therefore, every element not required not only is eliminated from GAAP requirements (e.g., disclosure), but also the requirement to audit the item is eliminated.

Increasing Audit Fees

If the auditor must increase fees to reflect the additional time to adopt SAS No. 99, it is critical that the auditor communicate to the client, in advance, the reason for the increase. The communication should be made before the engagement begins rather than subsequently billing the client for the additional work without conveying the reasons for the increase. Also, the auditor who discusses the new fraud requirements with a client has the challenge of bridging the "expectation gap" between what the auditor's responsibility is for fraud, and what the client perceives that responsibility to be.

Expectation Gap

Client perception	Reality of auditor's responsibility
Auditor is responsible for finding all fraud.	Auditor is required to assess fraud risk in planning the audit.
Auditor is an "all knowing sleuth;" the "Sherlock Holmes" of auditors.	Auditor is not responsible for finding fraud. The odds of auditor finding fraud are less than winning the lottery or the Red Sox winning the World Series.
Auditor is a guarantor of the financial statement accuracy.	Auditor is not a guarantor of the financial statements.
Auditor is responsible for the accuracy of the financial statements.	Management is responsible for the presentation of the financial statements.

In explaining to a client the increased effort to assess fraud, the auditor needs to be careful that he or she does not oversell the responsibility. Because the client already has a higher-than-reality expectation about the auditor's responsibility for fraud, the client might anticipate that the expectation will be increased even higher. Some ideas on how to communicate to the client the new standard requirements include:

- Discuss client expectations for fraud including their responsibility and that of the auditor.
- Explain the benefits of the auditor implementing SAS No. 99 including the fact that the auditor will be able to assist the company in better planning to mitigate the risks of fraud.
- Identify some statistics about fraud; that is, that misappropriation of assets (theft) affects all companies, even smaller, non-public entities.
- Make sure that both the engagement letter and management representation letter include language about management's responsibility for fraud.
- Worst case, blame the changes on the trickle-down effect of Enron, WorldCom, and other SEC companies.

THE AFTERMATH OF SARBANES-OXLEY

Overview of Sarbanes-Oxley

In August 2002, Congress passed new legislation that has had a monumental impact on the accounting profession and federal securities laws. The Sarbanes-Oxley Act of 2002 (Sarbanes-Oxley) was a joint effort of both Houses of Congress and resulted in changes that affect not only accountants, but also lawyers, corporate officers and board members. In essence, Sarbanes does the following:

- Places new restrictions on SEC auditors, including providing a list of prohibited activities that an SEC auditor cannot perform for his or her SEC audit client, other restrictions including a mandatory audit partner rotation.

- Introduces a new Public Company Accounting Oversight Board (PCAOB) to oversee the audits of SEC companies.
- Places the authority for establishing GAAP and GAAS with the new PCAOB.
- Requires CEOs and CFOs to certify the fair presentation of their company's quarterly and annual financial statements.
- Enhances required disclosures of off-balance sheet and certain related party transactions.
- Places further responsibility on audit committees and the corporate governance process.
- Establishes new requirements for attorneys to report material violations of securities law by their corporate clients.
- Creates criminal penalties of up to 25 years for certain types of securities fraud.

Many accountants believe that Sarbanes affects only auditors of SEC companies. Yet, the entire profession is and will continue to be impacted by Sarbanes and its trickle-down effect to even the smallest closely held business. Specifically, more than 20 states have modified or are in the process of modifying their accountancy acts to incorporate many of the Sarbanes changes in them. Unfortunately, the changes are not being limited to auditors of SEC companies.

Instead, they are applying the changes to all auditors, those of SEC and non-SEC companies, alike. Additionally, certain governmental agencies are applying the Sarbanes provision of mandatory partner rotation. Some are even expanding beyond Sarbanes by requiring mandatory audit firm rotation, a requirement that the final Sarbanes did not include. The author believes it is vital that all accountants and auditors understand what Sarbanes does and what their local state legislatures are considering for adopting certain provisions of Sarbanes.

The new Public Company Accounting Oversight Board (PCAOB)

The Act establishes a new oversight board called the Public Company Accounting Oversight Board (the Board) to oversee the audit process of SEC companies. The purpose of the Board is to replace the self-regulatory process that has existed in the accounting profession. Prior to the Act's passage, auditing standards for all companies were centralized in the Auditing Standards Board (AICPA), while GAAP rules were issued by the FASB and the AICPA's Executive Committee (AcSEC).

With the new Board, the self-regulation process will change, as may the profession's ability to continue to promulgate auditing and accounting standards. Specifics about this Board follow:
- The Board is not an agent of the United States government. Its powers are subject to oversight by the SEC with Board rules requiring SEC approval.

MODULE 1 — CHAPTER 1 — Auditing: Selected Developments **15**

- The Board is funded through required fees that must be paid from SEC issuer (based on market capitalization) and all registered accounting firms.
- The Board's responsibilities are to:
  - Register public accounting firms that prepare audit reports for issuers (e.g., auditors of SEC companies)
  - Establish or adopt auditing, quality control, ethics, independence and other Standards relating to auditors of SEC companies.
  - Conduct inspections of registered public accounting firms, as well as perform investigations and disciplinary proceedings concerning registered public accounting firms, including, if necessary, imposing sanctions against those firms.
  - Enforce compliance with the Act, the Board's rules, professional standards, and securities laws related to the preparation of audit reports by registered accounting firms and associated persons.
  - Perform other duties or functions as the Board of the SEC commissioner determine are necessary.
- The Board has five (5) full-time members appointed by the SEC in consultation with the Secretary of the Treasury and the Chairman of the Federal Reserve.
  - Members are selected from among prominent individuals of integrity and reputation who have demonstrated commitment to investors and the public, understand the responsibilities and nature of financial disclosures, and understand the obligations of accountants in the issuance of audit reports.
  - A maximum of two (2) members must be or have been CPAs. If one of the two CPAs is the chairperson, he or she must not have practiced in a public accounting format within five years from his or her appointment to the Board.
  - A Board member may not serve for more than two, five-year terms, regardless of whether those terms are consecutive.
- Board members may not receive any payments from a public accounting firm except those that are fixed continuing payments (e.g., retirement plan payments).
  - Board members may not engage in any other professional or business activity during his or her term.
  - The five member terms shall be scattered so that no term expires at the same time as another term. Each member's term shall expire in annual increments.
- The Board is required to conduct inspections of each registered public accounting firm:
  - The inspection must be done annually for firms that provide more than 100 annual audit reports on issuers,
  - The inspection must be done every three years for firms that issue 100 or fewer annual reports.

TOP AUDITING ISSUES FOR 2005 CPE COURSE

- The Board may refer an investigation to the SEC, Federal regulator, Attorney General of the state or United States, or other authorities.
- Annually, the Board must submit a report, including audited financial statements to the SEC with a copy to the Senate's Committee on Banking, Housing, and Urban Affairs, and the Financial Services Committee of the House.

Changes Affecting SEC Auditors

The Act adds significant responsibilities and restrictions to auditors of SEC companies (referred to as registered accounting firms):

- **Registration with the Board:** In order for auditors of SEC companies to prepare, issue, or participate in the preparation or issuance of an audit report on an issuer, that firm must register with the Board and provide information such as:
- **Registration fees:** Registered firms must pay registration fees to the Board in an amount that is sufficient to cover the costs of processing and reviewing applications and annual reports.
- **New standards that registered firms must adopt:** Registered accounting firms must adopt new standards in their quality control system and reporting standards:
  - *A seven-year workpaper retention policy:* The firm must maintain audit workpapers and other information related to any audit report, in sufficient detail to support the conclusions reached in the audit report.
  - *A concurring or second partner review:* On each audit, the firm must provide a concurring or second partner review and approval of each audit report. The second review must be performed by a qualified person associated with the firm, other than the person in charge of the audit, or by an independent reviewer.
  - *Report on internal control:* In each audit report, the auditor must disclose the scope of auditor's testing of the internal control structure and the procedures of the issuer and present it as part of the audit report or in a separate report.
  - *Quality control standards for registered accounting firms:* Firms must establish new quality control standards.
  - *Mandatory partner rotation rules:* A firm may not perform audit services that the lead or review partner has performed audit services for the issuer client for five (5) consecutive fiscal years.
  - *Auditors must report directly to the audit committee:* Engagement letter
  - *Partner compensation limitations:* An accountant is not independent of an audit client if, at any point during the audit and professional engagement period, any audit partner earns or receives compensation based on the audit partner procuring engagements with the audit cli-

ent to provide any products or services other than the audit, review or attest services. Small firms with ten or fewer partners and five or fewer audit clients are exempt from the partner compensation limitations.

Conflicts of Interest and Auditor Independence Rules

- **One-year cooling off period:** A firm is precluded from auditing an issuer if the issuer's CEO, controller, CFO, CAO, or any person serving in an equivalent position for the issuer, was employed by the firm and participated in any capacity in the audit of that issuer during the one-year period preceding the date of the initiation of the audit. The cooling-off provision applies only to those officers that served on the audit in the preceding year. If, instead, the officer served elsewhere in the firm, such as in the tax or consulting department, the preclusion would not apply.
- **Prohibited activities by accounting firms:** A registered public accounting firm may not perform for an issuer any of the following non-audit services contemporaneously with the audit:
  - Bookkeeping or other services related to the accounting records or financial statements of the audit client
  - Financial information systems design and implementation
  - Appraisal or valuation services, fairness opinions, or contribution-in-kind reports
  - Actuarial services
  - Internal audit outsourcing services
  - Management functions or human resources
  - Broker or dealer, investment adviser, or investment banking services
  - Legal services unrelated to the audit
  - Expert services[2]
  - Any other service that the Board determines, by regulation, is impermissible.

> **OBSERVATION**
>
> A firm may perform any non-audit service (including tax services) not on the above list for an audit client only if the activity is approved in advance by the audit committee of the issuer. Such approval must be disclosed in the issuer's reports. Note further that the Board has the authority to exempt any firm, on a case-by-case basis, from a prohibited transaction noted on the above list.

Changes Affecting Boards and Audit Committees

The Act makes significant changes to the responsibilities of corporate boards and audit committees including effecting better communication between the audit committee and the auditor and making the committee directly responsible for the selection of the audit firm. Further, the Act attempts to improve the competence of the audit committee by ensuring that its members are financially savvy:

- **Audit committee make up:** Each member of the audit committee must also be a member of the board of directors. And may not accept any consulting, advisory, or other compensatory fee from the issuer, or be an affiliated person of the issuer or any subsidiary thereof.
- **Audit committee responsibility for the auditor:** The audit committee of an issuer is *directly responsible* for the appointment, compensation, and oversight of the work of any registered public accounting firm employed by the issuer, (including the resolution of any disagreements between management and the auditor regarding financial reporting) for the purpose of preparing and issuing an audit report.
  - All auditing services and non-audit services (other than those services prohibited) must be preapproved by the audit committee of the issuer.
  - De minimis exception: Preapproval by the committee is waived with respect to non-audit services if certain conditions are met.
  - The registered accounting firm must report directly to the audit committee.
- **Handling complaints:** The audit committee must establish procedures for handling the receipt, retention, and treatment of complaints received by the issuer regarding accounting, internal control, or auditing matters, and, the confidential, anonymous submission by employees of concerns regarding questionable accounting and auditing matters.
- **Audit committee financial expert:** The issuer *must disclose in its reports* whether at least one member of the audit committee is a *"financial expert"* who understands GAAP, has experience in the preparation or auditing of financial statements, and experience with internal controls, and understands audit committee functions.

Changes Affecting Corporate Officers

The Act places responsibility on corporate officers for the fair presentation of financial statements by requiring them to sign off on financial statements issued. Additionally, the Act severely restricts the ability of corporate officers to reap financial benefits such as bonuses when financial statements are misstated. Specific requirements of the Act related to corporate officers include:

- **CFO/CEO Certification:** The principal executive officer or officers and the principal financial officer or officers, or persons performing similar functions, must certify in the annual or quarterly report filed with the SEC that the report does not contain any untrue statement of a material fact or omit a material fact, and the financial statements, and other financial information included in the report, fairly present, in all material respects, and that the officers are responsible for establishing and maintaining internal controls, among other certifications.

MODULE 1 — CHAPTER 1 — Auditing: Selected Developments

- **Officer forfeiture of bonuses and profits:** If an issuer's financial statements are restated due to a material noncompliance as a result of misconduct with any financial reporting requirement under the securities law, the CEO and CFO must reimburse the issuer for any bonus or other incentive-based or equity-based compensation received by that person from the issuer during the 12-month period following the first public issuance or filing with the SEC (whichever comes first) of the financial document that includes the financial reporting requirement, and any profits realized from the sale of securities of the issuer during that 12-month period.
- **Prohibited trading provision:** The Act prohibits any director or executive officer of the issuer directly or indirectly, to purchase, sell, or acquire or transfer any equity security of the issuer during any blackout period if such director or officer acquires the equity security in connection with his or her service or employment as a director or executive officer.
- **Prohibited personal loans:** The Act prohibits any issuer directly or indirectly (including through an affiliate) from extending or maintaining credit, arranging for the extension of credit, or renewing credit, in the form of a personal loan to or for any executive officer or director, or the equivalent thereof, of the issuer.
  - Loans in effect at the date of enactment are not subject to the prohibition provided there are no material modifications to any term of the loan or renewal of the loan on or after the enactment date.
  - Loans not prohibited include home improvement and manufactured home loans, an extension of credit under an open-end credit plan, credit cards, and certain extensions of credit by a broker or dealer to an employee of that broker or dealer to buy, trade, or carry securities.

New Corporate Disclosures

The Act enhances the required disclosures that an issuer must include in each financial report:

- **Reflection of material correcting adjustments:** Each financial report that contains financial statements prepared in accordance with GAAP must reflect all material correcting adjustments that have been identified by the accounting firm in accordance with GAAP and SEC rules.
- **Off-balance sheet transactions:** An issuer's financial statements must disclose all material off-balance sheet transactions, arrangements, obligations (including contingent obligations) and other relationships with unconsolidated entities or other persons, that may have a material, current or future effect on the financial condition, changes in financial condition, results of operations, liquidity, capital expenditures, capital resources, or significant components of revenues or expenses.
- **Real time disclosure of financial information:** Each issuer shall disclose to the public on a rapid and current basis such additional information concerning material changes in the financial condition or operations in

plain English, which may include trend and qualitative information and graphic presentations.

- **Disclosure of non-audit service fees approved by the audit committee:** Each issuer must disclose approval by an audit committee of a non-audit service to be performed by the auditor of the issuer. The disclosure should be made in the periodic reports under four captions: audit fees, audit-related fees, tax fees, and all other fees.
- **Code of ethics:** The issuer must disclose in its periodic reports whether or not the issuer has adopted a code of ethics for senior financial officers, applicable to its principal financial officer and comptroller or principal accounting officer, or persons performing similar functions. An additional disclosure is required if there is a change to, or a waiver from, a company's code of ethics for its senior financial officers.

New Penalties and Criminal Fraud Provisions

The Act dramatically increases the penalties for violations of securities laws including enhanced criminal penalties as follows.

Violation	Punishment
Securities fraud in violation of the SEC Act of 1934 and other SEC violations	25 years imprisonment and up to $25 million fine
Destruction, alteration, or falsification of records in Federal investigations and bankruptcy, or commits securities, mail or wire fraud	Up to 20 years imprisonment
Destruction of corporate records	Up to 10 years imprisonment
Knowingly or willfully violating certain SEC rules	Up to 10 years imprisonment
False certification by CFO or CEO	$1-5 million fine plus 10-20 years imprisonment
Retaliation against whistleblowers	Up to 10 years imprisonment
Failure to maintain audit and review workpapers for a period of five years from the end of the fiscal period in which the audit or review was concluded.	Fined and imprisoned up to 10 years.
Statute of limitations for discovering fraud	Extended from two to five years

Rules for Investment Bankers and Analysts

The Act calls for stricter rules to be drafted on analysts and investment bankers to mitigate some of the conflicts of interest that exist on Wall Street. Such rules shall include:

- Limiting the supervision and compensatory evaluation of analysts to officers and employees who are not engaged in investment banking
- Restricting the prepublication clearance or approval of research reports by individuals who work in investment banking or those not directly responsible for research, exclusive of legal or compliance staff
- Requiring that each analyst disclose in public appearances, and each

MODULE 1 — CHAPTER 1 — Auditing: Selected Developments **21**

broker-dealer disclose in each research report, any conflicts of interest that he or she knows or should know exist.

Other Provisions of the Act

The Act provides various incidental provisions, some of which are noted as follows:

- **Whistleblower Protection:** The Act provides protection to whistleblowers by creating a new civil action for employees of public companies who believe they have been discharged due to their disclosing violations of federal securities laws.
- **Improper influence on conduct of audits:** The Act makes it unlawful for any officer, director of the issuer, or any other person acting under their direction, to take any action to fraudulently influence, coerce, manipulate, or mislead any accountant in the performance of an audit of the issuer's financial statements in order to make the financial statements misleading.
- **Rules of professional responsibility for attorneys:** Attorneys are required to report evidence of a material violation of securities law or breach of fiduciary duty or similar violation by the company or any agent thereof. The report should be made to the chief legal counsel or the CEO of the company.
- **Debts not discharged in bankruptcy:** Title 11 of the Bankruptcy Code is amended to provide that an individual who files for bankruptcy will not be discharged from any debt that is as a result of a violation of any federal or state securities laws, regulations or any common law fraud, related to the purchase or sale of any security, judgment, order, decree, or any settlement agreements, including any damages, penalties, fines, attorneys fees related thereto.

STUDY QUESTIONS

> **11.** The new Oversight Board has five full-time members. *True or False?*
>
> **12.** The Sarbanes-Oxley Act provides for a four-year workpaper retention policy. *True or False?*
>
> **13.** Under the Sarbanes-Oxley Act, a mandatory CPA firm rotation is required every three years. *True or False?*
>
> **14.** The Sarbanes-Oxley Act has a five-year cooling off period for firm employees that are employed by the audit client of the firm. *True or False?*
>
> **15.** Loans not prohibited to officers and executives under the Act include credit cards. *True or False?*

The Trickle-Down Effect of Sarbanes-Oxley

As expected, the repercussions of the Act are just starting to be felt by the accounting profession. Accountants and auditors at all levels will be impacted within the next few years for several reasons:

- There is a major increase in the number of GAAP and GAAS statements being issued that apply to all entities, public and nonpublic, alike.
- Many states are adopting portions of the Sarbanes-Oxley Act in their accountancy acts and having those provisions apply to all auditors, including those that audit nonpublic entities.
- With the increase in audit and accounting rules, auditors are required to perform more audit work the time for which may be difficult to pass on to clients in fixed-fee engagements.

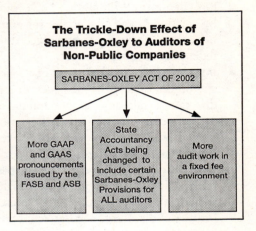

At the state level, more than twenty states have introduced or are about to introduce legislation bills that will adopt significant portions of the Sarbanes-Oxley Act into their state accountancy acts. Although the Sarbanes-Oxley Act affects SEC auditors only, many states are applying its provisions across the board to all auditors, including those who audit nonpublic entities.

2003/2004 Developments: Sarbanes-Oxley

In 2003 and 2004, the SEC and the Public Company Accounting Oversight Board (PCAOB) have issued final or proposed rules as required under Sarbanes. The SEC and PCAOB have focused on the implementation of the following three sections of the Act:

- Section 404: Internal Control Reporting
- Sections 302 and 906: Certification of Disclosures in Companies' Quarterly and Annual Reports
- Section 301: Requirements for Audit Committees

The *AICPA Audit Risk Alert- 2003/2004* discusses each of these changes that are noted in the following pages.

Section 404: Internal Control Reporting

Section 404 of the Act requires companies to include in their annual reports a report on the company's internal control over financial reporting. The auditor must also attest to, and report on, the assessment made by management of the issuer. In May 2003, the SEC adopted final rules related to the requirements of Section 404.

The Section 404 compliance requirement represents a significant challenge for public companies as they must:

- Assess their control environment, systems capabilities, and accounting principles and practices.
- Identify and document significant controls.
- Test and evaluate those controls.
- Correct deficiencies.
- Prepare an internal control report.

Under the final rules, the internal control report must:

- State the responsibility of management for establishing and maintaining an adequate internal control structure and procedures for financial reporting.
- Contain management's assessment of the effectiveness of the company's internal control over financial reporting as of the end of the company's most recent fiscal year.
- Include a statement identifying the framework used to evaluate the effectiveness of the company's internal control over financial reporting.
- Include a statement that the registered public accounting firm that audited the company's financial statements included in the annual report has issued an attestation report on management's assessment of the company's internal control over financial reporting.

Further, there is a requirement that management evaluate any change in the company's internal control that occurred during a fiscal quarter that has a material effect, or is likely to have a material effect, on the company's internal control.

Auditor's Responsibility Under Section 404

Auditors of public companies must issue a report on management's assessment of the company's internal control.

Can a Company's Auditor Perform Work Under Section 404?

Usually, no. Sarbanes requires the auditor to be independent to perform an audit of internal controls over financial reporting. Under the SEC rules on auditor independence, an auditor impairs his or her independence if the auditor audits his or her own work, including working on the design or implementation of an audit client's internal control system.

Consequently, an auditor of a public entity is prohibited from assisting the client in the design and implementation work required to comply with Section 404.

Further, the auditors cannot perform the evaluation of the effectiveness of internal controls, which, instead, must be done by management. The auditor's responsibility is to report on management's assessment of the company's internal control.

> **OBSERVATION**
>
> A significant business opportunity exists for regional and local CPA firms who do not audit public companies. Because public company auditors cannot assist their clients with compliance with Section 404, those regional or local firms can specialize in Section 404 compliance work by assisting public companies in designing and implementing a system of internal control needed to comply with Section 404.

Sections 302 and 906: Certification of Disclosures in Companies' Quarterly and Annual Reports

In August 2002 and May 2003, the SEC issued final rules related to the Certification of Disclosure in Companies' Quarterly and Annual Reports. Section 302 of the Act requires that the CEO and CFO of each company prepare a statement to accompany the audit report to certify the appropriateness of the financial statements and disclosures contained in the report, and that those financial statements and disclosures fairly present, in all material respects, the operations and financial condition of the issuer.

In October 2003, the SEC announced that the certification does not apply to reports of employee benefit plans and reports on Form 8-K. The Section 906 certification is collected by the SEC and given to the Department of Justice. Among other items, the certification states that the report complies with the SEC Act of 1934.

Section 301: Public Company Audit Committees

Section 301 of the Act relates to the audit committee requirements including those related to member independence, responsibility for the auditor, whistle blower rules, and other responsibilities required of the audit committee.

In April 2003, the SEC adopted final rules for Section 301 compliance. As part of those final rules, the national securities exchanges and associations are prohibited from listing any security of an issuer that has not complied with the audit committee requirements in Section 301 of the Act.

Results of the GAO's Mandated Study on Consolidation and Competition in the Accounting Profession

Section 701 of the Act required the GAO to conduct a study regarding the consolidation of public accounting firms since 1989, including the present and future impact of the consolidation, and the solutions to any problems discovered. In July 2003, the GAO issued its final report entitled, *Public Accounting Firms: Mandated Study on Consolidation and Competition* (herein referred to as the Report or the GAO Report). The Report's analyses and conclusions are summarized below:

- The "Big 4" currently audit more than 78% of all U.S. public companies and 99% of public company annual sales.
- Internationally, the "Big 4" dominate the market for audit services.
- The GAO found no empirical evidence that consolidation of accounting firms has impacted competition in the audit services market, the quality of audits, audit fees or the capital markets
- There has been an impact of consolidation on the limited number of auditor alternatives for larger national and multinational companies that require firms with extensive staff resources, industry-specific and technical expertise, geographic coverage, and international reputation.
- Most public companies believe they have limited choices if they were to switch auditors:
  - 88% of large multinationals said they would not consider using a non-"Big 4" audit firm.
  - 94% of public companies said that they had three or fewer alternatives were they to switch audit firms.
  - 100% of audit chairpersons surveyed said they had three or fewer alternatives if they were to switch audit firms.
  - 42% of companies surveyed said they did not have enough options for audit and attest services.
  - 76% said they would not be willing to expand choices if it meant letting market forces operate without government intervention.
  - 80% of respondents said that industry specialization or expertise would be of great or very great importance to them if they had to choose a new auditor.
  - 91% said they would not consider a non-"Big 4" firm because of lack of technical skills or knowledge of their industry.
- Sarbanes-Oxley has further limited the competition among audit firms. The new independence rules, which limit the non-audit services firms can provide to their audit clients, limits the choices available for audit firms. In specialized industries, most companies have only two choices in selecting an audit firm.

> **EXAMPLE**
>
> Assume a company uses one "Big 4" firm for its audit and attest services and another "Big 4" firm for its outsourced internal audit function. If it wishes to switch auditors, it cannot use one of those two "Big 4" firms. Consequently, it only has the two remaining "Big 4" firms to consider as its replacement auditor. Assume further that one of the remaining "Big 4" firms is not interested in bidding on the new business because the industry does not fall within its target markets. That would leave only one remaining "Big 4" firm to be the replacement firm and no alternative viable choices.

TOP AUDITING ISSUES FOR 2005 CPE COURSE

- Smaller riskier public companies are being impacted by both Sarbanes and the consolidation of the national firms:
  - As the "Big 4" have increased their focus on larger public companies, smaller companies and those that are not profitable are losing access to the "Big 4" as they shed some of their clients that represent unacceptable risks to their firms.
  - There are fewer audit firms willing to audit smaller, higher-risk, and less-profitable SEC companies in the wake of the Sarbanes-Oxley.
  - Because of the higher risk of being audited, the cost of capital for smaller public entities is expected to continue to increase.
- There are concerns about the impact of further consolidation and lack of viable alternatives in certain industries.
- Because of the barriers to entry, market forces are not likely to result in the expansion of the current "Big 4". Smaller accounting firms face significant barriers to entry into the audit market for large multinational public companies for several reasons including:
  - Smaller firms generally lack the staff, technical expertise, and global reach to audit large and complex national and multinational public companies.
  - The "Big 4" had almost three times as many partners and over five times as many staff as the average for the next three largest firms.
  - Even through merger of the next tier of non-"Big 4" firms, any new firm would still lack the resources needed to compete, to any significant degree, with the "Big 4" for larger clients.

> **OBSERVATION**
>
> Under a best-case scenario, the GAO projected that a merger of the five largest non-"Big 4" firms would result in a firm with a 11.2% market share, compared with an 8.6% market share for the five first, if they were not consolidated. Thus, there would be only a 2.6% increase in market share by consolidating those five firms.

  - The capital markets are familiar with the "Big 4" and are hesitant to recommend that companies use firms with whom they are not familiar.

> **OBSERVATION**
>
> Many investment bankers and institutional investors often stated that they preferred that public companies use a "Big 4" firm for their audits.

  - 83% of non-"Big 4" firms surveyed indicated that the litigation risks and insurance costs associated with auditing a large public company made growth into the large public company market less attractive than other growth opportunities.

> **OBSERVATION**
>
> Many non-"Big 4" firms also noted that changes in accounting principles and standards, the complexity of audits, and the price of talent and training to be factors that placed an upward influence on costs that would make growth into the large public company market less attractive.

- Raising the amount of capital to build the infrastructure necessary to audit large multinational companies is difficult, in part because the partnership structure of accounting firms limits these firms' ability to raise outside capital.
- Certain state laws make it difficult for firms to expand nationally. For example, firms face the burden and additional expense of obtaining state licenses for staff across the country.

■ The GAO provided no recommendations as what, if anything, can be done to address the lack of competition issue among the "Big 4."

Largest U.S. Accounting Firms (Global Operations) 2002

"Big 4"	Actual market share (percent)*	Revenue ($$ per thousands)	Partners	Professional staff (non-partner)
Price Waterhouse Coopers	18.98%	$13,782	7,020	97,109
Deloitte & Touche	14.94%	$12,500	6,714	73,810
KPMG	14.38%	$10,720	6,600	69,100
Ernst & Young	19.73%	$10,124	6,131	60,713

Next tier				
BDO Seidman	3.13%	$2,395	2,182	16,078
Grant Thornton	4.21%	$1,840	2,256	14,019
McGladrey & Pullen	.82%	$1,829	2,245	12,775

Source: Tables 4 and 5 published in the GAO Report.
*Market share is based on the log of total company assets.

Largest U.S. Accounting Firms (US Operations) 2002

"Big 4"	Revenue ($$ per millions)	Audit and attest revenue ($$ in millions)	Partners	Professional staff (non-partner)
Deloitte & Touche	$5,900	$2,124	2,618	22,453
Ernst & Young	$4,515	$2,664	2,118	17,196
Price Waterhouse Coopers	$4,256	$2,596	2,027	18,801
KPMG	$3,200	$2,016	1,535	12,502

Next 5 firms: non "Big 4:"	Revenue ($$ per milliions)	Audit and attest revenue ($$ in millions)	Partners	Professional staff (non-partner)
Grant Thornton	$400	$200	312	2,380
BDO Seidman	$353	$145	281	1,510
BKD	$211	$93	193	1,165
Crowe, Chizek and Co.	$205	$45	101	1,037
McGladrey & Pullen	$203	$187	475	2,369
Total: next 5 non "Big 4" firms	$1,372	$670	1,362	8,461

Source: Table 1 of the GAO Report, as modified by the author.

The Aftermath of Arthur Andersen: Who Audits the Former Andersen Clients?

In 2001, Arthur Andersen LLP (Andersen) was the fourth-largest public accounting firm in the United States, with global net revenues of more than $9 billion. On March 7, 2002, Andersen was indicted by a federal grand jury and charged with obstructing justice for destroying evidence relevant to investigations into the 2001 financial collapse of Enron.

At the time of its demise, Andersen performed audit and attest services for approximately 2,400 public companies in the United States, including many of the largest public companies in the world. In addition, Andersen served private companies and provided additional professional services such as tax and consulting services.

The GAO report published information on who absorbed the Andersen clients after that firm's demise:

- Of the former Andersen clients, only 13% switched to non-"Big 4" firms.
- The switch of Andersen clients to the "Big 4" firms was more pronounced within specialized industries that had little choice of firms that had expertise within their specific industry.
- In the post Andersen environment, many of the "Big 4" firms have more than a 25% market share in selected industries.

First Hired by Former Andersen Clients: As of December 31, 2002

Accounting firm	Number of former Andersen clients	% of total Andersen clients	Average assets (millions)
"Big 4"	938	87%	$2,508
Grant Thornton	45	4%	$644
BDO Seidman	23	2%	$54
Other	79	7%	$193
Total:	1,085	100%	$2,210

Source: Table 10 of GAO Report

Concentration of Industries Among the "Big 4" (Firms with 25% or more of the Industry)

Industry	Deloitte & Touche	Ernst & Young	KPMG	Price Waterhouse Coopers
Oil and gas extraction				X
General building contractors		X		
Paper and allied products	X			
Food stores	X			X
Apparel and accessory stores	X			
Health services		X	X	
Hotels and lodging	X	X		
Communications		X		X

Source: Table 14 of the GAO Report

> **OBSERVATION**
>
> Based on the above table, it would appear that firms with 25% or more industry market share would dominate the particular industry. Consequently, it is assumed that companies in those industries would have few choices of audit firms and limited options in switching audit firms.

Notes

[1] Report to the Nation—Association of Certified Fraud Examiners (2002)

[2] In the Act, the list included nine non-audit services with expert services being part of legal services. In its final rule, the SEC segregated the "expert services" into a tenth category.

MODULE 1 — CHAPTER 2

SAS No. 101: Auditing Fair Value Measurements and Disclosures

LEARNING OBJECTIVES

At the completion of this chapter, you should be able to:

- Understand the requirements of SAS No. 101 as it relates to an auditor's responsibility for auditing fair value measurements and disclosures.
- Identify selected GAAP statements in which fair value measurement is used.
- Determine how an auditor should use the work of a specialist in evaluating fair value measurements.

INTRODUCTION

The use of fair value measurements in accounting has expanded over the past decade. In fact, the FASB Board has a project on its agenda to establish greater clarification on the use of fair value measures within the accounting model.

If the accounting model expands to include greater use of fair value measurements, auditors, in turn, must address the auditing requirements to deal with use of fair value. Under present GAAP, fair value measurements are used in numerous GAAP statements, examples of which include:

- FASB No. 107, *Disclosures about Fair Value of Financial Instruments*
- FASB No. 142, *Goodwill and Other Intangible Assets*
- FASB No. 144, *Accounting for the Impairment or Disposal of Long-Lived Assets*
- FASB Interpretation 46 of ARB No. 51, *Consolidation of Variable Interest Entities—An Interpretation of ARB No. 51*
- FASB No. 150, *Accounting for Certain Financial Instruments with Characteristics of Both Liabilities and Equity*

Fair value measurements of assets, liabilities, and components of equity may arise from both the initial recording of transactions and later changes in value. Changes in fair value measurements that occur over time may be treated in different ways under GAAP. For example, GAAP may require that some fair value changes be reflected in net income and that other fair value changes be reflected in other comprehensive income and equity. The table below details some of these treatments.

Changes in Fair Value

Presented in the Income Statement	Presented in Stockholders' Equity
Unrealized gains or losses on trading securities	Unrealized gains or losses on securities available for sale
Certain derivative transactions	Foreign exchange gains or losses

While SAS No. 101 provides guidance on auditing fair value measurements and disclosures, evidence obtained from other audit procedures also may provide evidence relevant to the measurement and disclosure of fair values.

> **EXAMPLE**
>
> Inspection procedures to verify the existence of an asset measured at fair value also may provide relevant evidence about its valuation, such as the physical condition of the asset.

REQUIREMENTS OF SAS NO. 101

SAS No. 101 requires that the auditor should obtain sufficient competent audit evidence to provide reasonable assurance that fair value measurements and disclosures are in conformity with GAAP. GAAP requires that certain items be measured at fair value.

Financial Accounting Standards Board (FASB) Statement of Financial Accounting Concepts No. 7, *Using Cash Flow Information and Present Value in Accounting Measurements,* defines the fair value of an asset (or liability) as:

> the amount at which that asset (or liability) could be bought (or incurred) or sold (or settled) in a current transaction between willing parties, that is, other than in a forced or liquidation sale.[1]

In general, GAAP suggests that the first approach to determining fair value is to use observable market prices to make the determination. In the absence of observable market prices, GAAP requires fair value to be based on the best information available in the circumstances. Ultimately, absent any observable or other means to arrive at fair value, discounted cash flows, using the expected cash flows method in Concept Statement No. 7 should be used.

Management is ultimately responsible for making the fair value measurements and disclosures included in the financial statements. In fulfilling that responsibility, management should:

- Develop an accounting and financial reporting process for determining the fair value measurements and disclosures.
- Select appropriate valuation methods, as well as identify and adequately support any significant assumptions used.
- Prepare the valuation.
- Make sure that the presentation and disclosure of the fair value measurements are in accordance with GAAP.

SAS No. 101 states that fair value measurements for which observable market prices are not available are inherently imprecise because those fair value measurements may be based on assumptions about future conditions, transactions, or events whose outcome is uncertain and will therefore be subject to change over time.

The auditor's consideration of such assumptions is based on information available to him or her at the time of the audit. The auditor is *not responsible* for predicting future conditions, transactions, or events that, had they been known at the time of the audit, may have had a significant effect on management's actions or management's assumptions underlying the fair value measurements and disclosures.[2]

Assumptions used in fair value measurements are similar in nature to those required when developing other accounting estimates. If observable market prices are not available, GAAP requires that valuation methods reflect assumptions that marketplace participants would generally use in estimating fair value, whenever that information is available without undue cost and effort. If information about market assumptions is not available, an entity may use its own assumptions as long as there is no contrary data indicating that marketplace participants would use different assumptions.

TOP AUDITING ISSUES FOR 2005 CPE COURSE

> **OBSERVATION**
>
> SAS No. 101 states that assumptions used in fair value measurements are generally not relevant for accounting estimates made under measurement bases other than fair value. SAS No. 57, *Auditing Accounting Estimates,* offers guidance on auditing accounting estimates in general. SAS No. 101 also addresses considerations similar to those in SAS No. 57, as well as others, in the specific context of fair value measurements and disclosures in accordance with GAAP.

SAS No. 101 does not address specific types of assets, liabilities, equity components, transactions, or industry-specific practices. GAAP requires or permits a variety of fair value measurements and disclosures in financial statements. GAAP also varies in the level of guidance that it provides on measuring fair values and disclosures.

The measurement of fair value may be relatively simple for certain assets or liabilities, such as investments that are bought and sold in active markets that provide readily available and reliable information on the prices at which actual exchanges occur. For those items, the existence of published price quotations in an active market is the best evidence of fair value.

> **OBSERVATION**
>
> The measurement of fair value for other assets or liabilities may be more complex. Certain assets may not have observable market prices or may possess characteristics which make it necessary for management to estimate their fair value based on the best information available in the circumstances (for example, a complex derivative financial instrument). The estimation of fair value may be achieved through the use of a valuation method, such as a model premised on discounting of estimated future cash flows.

STUDY QUESTIONS

1. SAS No. 101 states that fair value measurements for which observable market prices are not available are inherently imprecise because those fair value measurements may be based on assumptions about future conditions, transactions, or events whose outcome is uncertain and will therefore be subject to change over time. *True or False?*

2. The auditor is ultimately responsible for making the fair value measurements and disclosures included in the financial statements. *True or False?*

Relevant Controls and Assessment of Risks

The auditor should obtain an understanding of the entity's process for determining fair value measurements and disclosures and of the relevant controls in enough detail to develop an effective audit approach.

> **OBSERVATION**
>
> Management is ultimately responsible for establishing an accounting and financial reporting process for determining fair value measurements. In some cases, the measurement of fair value, and therefore the process set up by management to determine fair value, may be simple and reliable. For example, management may be able to refer to published price quotations in an active market to determine fair value for marketable securities held by the entity. In some cases, however, fair value measurements are inherently more complex to apply and involve uncertainty about the occurrence of future events or their outcome. Therefore, assumptions that may involve the use of judgment need to be made as part of the measurement process.

SAS No. 55, *Consideration of Internal Control in a Financial Statement Audit,* as amended, requires the auditor to obtain an understanding of each of the five components of internal control sufficiently to plan the audit. In connection with SAS No. 101, the auditor should obtain such an understanding regarding the determination of the entity's fair value measurements and disclosures, in order to plan the nature, timing, and extent of the audit procedures.

In obtaining an understanding of the entity's process for determining fair value measurements and disclosures, the auditor should consider various factors, including:

- The types of controls in existence over the process used to determine fair value measurements. These may include, for example, controls over data, as well as the segregation of duties between those committing the entity to the underlying transactions and those responsible for undertaking the valuations.
- The expertise and experience of persons involved in determining the fair value measurements.
- The use of information technology in the valuation process.
- Information about the accounts or transactions requiring fair value measurements or disclosures, such as whether the accounts arise from the recording of routine and recurring transactions or whether they arise from non-routine or unusual transactions.
- The extent to which service organizations are involved where their use might impact the fair value measurements or the data that supports the measurements. When an entity uses a service organization, the auditor considers the requirements of SAS No. 70, *Service Organizations (AICPA, Professional Standards,* vol. 1, AU sec. 324), as amended.
- The use of specialists, if any, in determining fair value measurements and disclosures.
- The extent to which management assumptions are used in determining fair value.

TOP AUDITING ISSUES FOR 2005 CPE COURSE

- Documentation that supports management's assumptions.
- The process used to develop and apply management assumptions, including whether management used available market information to develop the assumptions.
- The process used to monitor changes in management's assumptions.
- The integrity of change controls and security procedures for valuation models and relevant information systems, including approval processes.
- The controls over the consistency, timeliness, and reliability of the data used in valuation models.

The auditor uses his or her understanding of the entity's process, including its complexity and controls, when assessing the risk of material misstatement. Based on that risk assessment, the auditor determines the nature, timing, and extent of the audit procedures. The risk of material misstatement may increase as the accounting and financial reporting requirements for fair value measurements become more complex.

SAS No. 55 addresses the inherent limitations of internal controls. Fair value determinations often involve subjective judgments by management, which may affect the nature of controls that are able to be implemented, including the possibility of management override of controls. The auditor considers the inherent limitations of internal controls in such circumstances when assessing control risk.

STUDY QUESTION

> **3.** In obtaining an understanding of the entity's process for determining fair value measurements and disclosures, the auditor should considers various factors that include the types of controls in existence over the process used to determine fair value measurements, including, for example, controls over data and the segregation of duties between those committing the entity to the underlying transactions and those responsible for undertaking the valuations. ***True or False?***

EVALUATING CONFORMITY OF FAIR VALUE MEASUREMENTS AND DISCLOSURES WITH GAAP

The auditor should evaluate whether the fair value measurements and disclosures in the financial statements are in conformity with GAAP. The auditor's understanding of the requirements of GAAP and knowledge of the business and industry, together with the results of other audit procedures, are used to evaluate the accounting for assets or liabilities requiring fair value measurements, the disclosures about the basis for the fair value measurements, and significant uncertainties related thereto.

The evaluation of the entity's fair value measurements and audit evidence depends, in part, on the auditor's knowledge of the nature of the business. This is particularly true where the asset or liability or the valuation method is highly complex.

MODULE 1 — CHAPTER 2 — SAS No. 101

> **EXAMPLE**
>
> Derivative financial instruments may be highly complex, with a risk that differing assumptions used in determining fair values will result in different conclusions.

The measurement of the fair value of certain items, such as "in process research and development" or intangible assets acquired in a business combination, may involve special considerations that are affected by the nature of the entity and its operations.

> **OBSERVATION**
>
> The auditor's knowledge of the business, along with the results of other audit procedures, may help identify assets for which management should assess the need to recognize an impairment loss under applicable GAAP.

The auditor should evaluate management's intent to carry out specific courses of action where that intent is relevant to the use of fair value measurements, the related requirements involving presentation and disclosures, and how changes in fair values are reported in financial statements. The auditor also should evaluate management's ability to carry out those courses of action.

Management often documents plans and intentions relevant to specific assets or liabilities and GAAP may require it to do so. While the extent of evidence to be obtained about management's intent and ability is a matter of professional judgment, the auditor's procedures ordinarily include inquiries of management, with appropriate corroboration of responses. These include:

- Considering management's past history of carrying out its stated intentions with respect to assets or liabilities.
- Reviewing written plans and other documentation, including, where applicable, budgets, minutes, and other such items.
- Considering management's stated reasons for choosing a particular course of action.
- Considering management's ability to carry out a particular course of action, given the entity's economic circumstances, including the implications of its contractual commitments.

When there are no observable market prices and the entity estimates fair value using a valuation method, the auditor should evaluate whether the entity's method of measurement is appropriate in the circumstances. Such an evaluation requires the use of professional judgment, as well as obtaining an understanding of management's rationale for selecting a particular method by discussing with management its reasons for selecting the valuation method. The auditor considers whether:

TOP AUDITING ISSUES FOR 2005 CPE COURSE

- Management has sufficiently evaluated and appropriately applied the criteria, if any, provided by GAAP to support the selected method.
- The valuation method is appropriate in the circumstances, given the nature of the item being valued.
- The valuation method is appropriate in relation to the business, industry, and environment in which the entity operates.

> **OBSERVATION**
>
> Management may have determined that different valuation methods result in a range of significantly different fair value measurements. In such cases, the auditor evaluates how the entity has investigated the reasons for the differences in establishing its fair value measurements.

The auditor should evaluate whether the entity's method for determining fair value measurements is applied consistently and if so, whether the consistency is appropriate, considering possible changes in the environment, circumstances affecting the entity, or changes in accounting principles.

If management has changed the method for determining fair value, the auditor considers whether management can adequately demonstrate that the method to which it has changed provides a more appropriate basis of measurement or whether the change is supported by a change in the GAAP requirements or a change in circumstances. [3]

> **EXAMPLE**
>
> The introduction of an active market for an equity security may indicate that the use of the discounted cash flows method to estimate the fair value of the security is no longer appropriate.

STUDY QUESTIONS

4. SAS No. 101 requires that the auditor should obtain sufficient competent audit evidence to provide reasonable assurance that fair value measurements and disclosures are in conformity with GAAP. *True or False?*

5. SAS No. 101 does not require an auditor to evaluate whether the disclosures about fair values made by the entity are in conformity with GAAP. *True or False?*

6. In SAS No. 101, when there are no observable market prices and the entity estimates fair value using a valuation method, the auditor should evaluate whether the entity's method of measurement is appropriate in the circumstances. *True or False?*

ENGAGING A SPECIALIST

The auditor should consider whether to engage a specialist and use his or her work as evidential matter in performing substantive tests and evaluations of material financial statement assertions. The auditor may have the necessary skill and knowledge to plan and perform audit procedures related to fair values or may decide to use the work of a specialist. If the use of such a specialist is planned, the auditor should consider the guidance in SAS No. 73, *Using the Work of a Specialist.*

When planning to use the work of a specialist in auditing fair value measurements, the auditor considers whether the specialist's understanding of the definition of fair value and the method that the specialist will use to determine fair value are consistent with those of management and with GAAP.

> **EXAMPLE**
>
> The method used by a specialist for estimating the fair value of real estate or of a complex derivative may not be consistent with the measurement principles specified in GAAP. Accordingly, the auditor considers such matters, often through discussions with the specialist or by reading the report of the specialist.

SAS No. 73 provides that the reasonableness of assumptions, the appropriateness of methods used, and the application of methods are the responsibility of the specialist. The auditor, however, should obtain an understanding of the assumptions and methods used. If the auditor believes the findings are unreasonable, he or she applies additional procedures as required in SAS No. 73.

STUDY QUESTION

> **7.** With respect to SAS No. 101, the auditor should consider whether to engage a specialist and use the work of that specialist as evidential matter in performing substantive tests to evaluate material financial statement assertions. ***True or False?***

TESTING THE ENTITY'S FAIR VALUE MEASUREMENTS AND DISCLOSURES

Based on the auditor's assessment of the risk of material misstatement, the auditor should test the entity's fair value measurements and disclosures. Because of the wide range of possible fair value measurements, from relatively simple to extremely complex, and the varying levels of risk of material misstatement associated with the process for determining fair values, planned audit procedures can vary significantly in nature, timing, and extent.

TOP AUDITING ISSUES FOR 2005 CPE COURSE

> **EXAMPLE**
>
> Substantive tests of the fair value measurements may involve:
> - Testing management's significant assumptions, the valuation model, and the underlying data.
> - Developing independent fair value estimates for corroborative purposes.
> - Reviewing subsequent events and transactions.

Some fair value measurements are inherently more complex than others. This complexity arises either because of the nature of the item being measured at fair value or because of the valuation method used to determine fair value.

> **EXAMPLE**
>
> In the absence of quoted prices in an active market, an estimate of a security's fair value may be based on valuation methods such as the discounted cash flow method or the transactions method. Complex fair value measurements normally are characterized by greater uncertainty regarding the reliability of the measurement process. This greater uncertainty may be a result of:
> - The length of the forecast period
> - The number of significant and complex assumptions associated with the process
> - A higher degree of subjectivity associated with the assumptions and factors used in the process
> - A higher degree of uncertainty associated with the future occurrence or outcome of events underlying the assumptions used
> - Lack of objective data when highly subjective factors are used

The auditor uses both the understanding of management's process for determining fair value measurements and his or her assessment of the risk of material misstatement to determine the nature, timing, and extent of the audit procedures. There are a number of factors to consider in the development of audit procedures.

Some fair value measurements, such as a valuation by an independent appraiser, may be made at a date that does not coincide with the date at which the entity is required to report such information in its financial statements. In such cases the auditor obtains evidence that management has taken into account the effect of events, transactions, and changes in circumstances occurring between the date of the fair value measurement and the reporting date.

Collateral often is assigned for certain types of investments in debt instruments that either are required to be measured at fair value or are evaluated for possible impairment. If the collateral is an important factor in measuring the fair value of the investment or evaluating its carrying amount, the auditor obtains sufficient competent audit evidence regarding the existence, value, rights, and access to or transferability of such collateral, including consideration of whether all appropriate liens have been filed. The auditor also should consider whether appropriate disclosures about the collateral have been made.

In some situations, additional procedures, such as the inspection of an asset by the auditor, may be necessary to obtain sufficient competent audit evidence about the appropriateness of a fair value measurement.

> **EXAMPLE**
>
> Inspection of the asset may be necessary to obtain information about the current physical condition of the asset relevant to its fair value, or inspection of a security may reveal a restriction on its marketability that may affect its value.

TESTING MANAGEMENT'S SIGNIFICANT ASSUMPTIONS, THE VALUATION MODEL, AND THE UNDERLYING DATA

The auditor's understanding of the reliability of the process used by management to determine fair value is an important element in support of the resulting measurements and therefore affects the nature, timing, and extent of audit procedures.

When testing the entity's fair value measurements and disclosures, the auditor evaluates whether:

- Management's assumptions are reasonable and reflect, or are not inconsistent with, market information.
- The fair value measurement was determined using an appropriate model, if applicable.
- Management used relevant information that was reasonably available at the time.

Estimation methods and assumptions, as well as the auditor's comparison of fair value measurements from prior periods (if any) to those obtained in the current period, may provide evidence of the reliability of management's processes. However, the auditor also considers whether variances from the prior-period fair value measurements result from changes in market or economic circumstances.

Where applicable, the auditor should evaluate whether the significant assumptions used by management in measuring fair value, taken individually and as a whole, provide a reasonable basis for the fair value measurements and disclosures in the entity's financial statements.

Assumptions are integral components of more complex valuation methods, such as those that employ a combination of estimates of expected future cash flows

TOP AUDITING ISSUES FOR 2005 CPE COURSE

together with estimates of the values of assets or liabilities in the future, discounted to the present. Auditors pay particular attention to the significant assumptions underlying a valuation method. They evaluate whether such assumptions are reasonable and reflect (or are not inconsistent with) market information. Specific assumptions will vary with the characteristics of the item being valued and the valuation approach used (such as cost, market, or income). For example, where the discounted cash flows method (a method under the income approach) is used, there will be assumptions about the level of cash flows, the period of time used in the analysis, and the discount rate.

Assumptions ordinarily are supported by differing types of evidence from internal and external sources that provide objective support for the assumptions used. The auditor evaluates the source and reliability of evidence supporting management's assumptions, including consideration of the assumptions in light of historical and market information.

> **OBSERVATION**
>
> Audit procedures dealing with management's assumptions are performed in the context of auditing the entity's financial statements. The objective of the audit procedures is therefore not intended to obtain sufficient competent audit evidence to provide an opinion on the assumptions themselves. Rather, the auditor performs procedures to evaluate whether the assumptions provide a reasonable basis for measuring fair values in the context of an audit of the financial statements taken as a whole.

Identifying those assumptions that appear to be significant to the fair value measurement requires the exercise of judgment by management. The auditor focuses attention on the significant assumptions that management has identified. Generally, significant assumptions cover matters that materially affect the fair value measurement and may include those that are:

- Sensitive to variation or uncertainty in amount or nature. For example, assumptions about short-term interest rates may be less susceptible to significant variation than assumptions about long-term interest rates.
- Susceptible to misapplication or bias.

The auditor considers the sensitivity of the valuation to changes in significant assumptions, including market conditions that may affect the value. Where applicable, the auditor encourages management to use techniques such as sensitivity analysis to help identify particularly sensitive assumptions. If management has not identified particularly sensitive assumptions, the auditor considers whether to employ techniques to identify those assumptions.

The evaluation of whether the assumptions provide a reasonable basis for the fair value measurements relates to the whole set of assumptions as well as to each assumption individually. Assumptions are frequently interdependent and therefore need to be internally consistent. A particular assumption that may appear reasonable when taken in isolation may not be reasonable when used in conjunction with other assumptions. The auditor considers whether management has identified the significant assumptions and factors influencing the measurement of fair value. To be reasonable, the assumptions on which the fair value measurements are based (for example, the discount rate used in calculating the present value of future cash flows), both individually and taken as a whole, need to be realistic and consistent with:

- The general economic environment, the economic environment of the specific industry, and the entity's economic circumstances.
- Existing market information.
- The plans of the entity, including what management expects will be the outcome of specific objectives and strategies.
- Assumptions made in prior periods, if appropriate.
- Past experience of or previous conditions experienced by the entity, to the extent currently applicable.
- Other matters relating to the financial statements, such as assumptions used by management for accounting estimates in financial statement accounts other than those relating to fair value measurements and disclosures.
- The risk associated with cash flows, if applicable, including the potential variability in the amount and timing of the cash flows and the related effect on the discount rate.

Where assumptions are reflective of management's intent and ability to carry out specific courses of action, the auditor considers whether they are consistent with the entity's plans and past experience. If management relies on historical financial information in the development of assumptions, the auditor considers the extent to which such reliance is justified.

However, historical information might not be representative of future conditions or events, for example, if management intends to engage in new activities or circumstances change. For items valued by the entity using a valuation model, the auditor does not function as an appraiser and is not expected to substitute his or her judgment for that of the entity's management. Rather, the auditor reviews the model and evaluates whether the assumptions used are reasonable and if the model is appropriate, considering the entity's circumstances.

> **EXAMPLE**
>
> It may be inappropriate to use discounted cash flows for valuing an equity investment in a start-up enterprise if there are no current revenues on which to base the forecast of future earnings or cash flows.

The auditor should test the data used to develop the fair value measurements and disclosures and evaluate whether the fair value measurements have been properly determined from the data and from management's assumptions. Specifically, the auditor evaluates whether the data on which the fair value measurements are

TOP AUDITING ISSUES FOR 2005 CPE COURSE

based, including the data used in the work of a specialist, is accurate, complete, and relevant. The auditor also evaluates whether fair value measurements have been properly determined using the data and management's assumptions.

The auditor's tests also may include procedures such as verifying the source of the data, mathematical recomputation of inputs, and reviewing information for internal consistency, including whether such information is consistent with management's intent and ability to carry out specific courses of action.

STUDY QUESTION

> **8.** In testing management's significant assumptions, the valuation model, and the underlying data, the auditor's understanding of the reliability of the process used by management to determine fair value is an important element in support of the resulting amounts and therefore affects the nature, timing, and extent of audit procedures. *True or False?*

DEVELOPING INDEPENDENT FAIR VALUE ESTIMATES FOR CORROBORATIVE PURPOSES

The auditor may make an independent estimate of fair value, for example, by using an auditor-developed model, to corroborate the entity's fair value measurement (See SAS No. 56, *Analytical Procedures* [AICPA, *Professional Standards,* vol. 1. AU sec 329]).

When developing an independent estimate using management's assumptions, the auditor evaluates those assumptions. However, rather than using management's assumptions, the auditor may develop his or her own assumptions to make a comparison with management's fair value measurements.

In this situation, the auditor nevertheless understands management's assumptions. The auditor uses that understanding to ensure that his or her independent estimate takes into consideration all significant variables and to evaluate any significant difference from management's estimate. The auditor also should test the data used to develop the fair value measurements and disclosures.

REVIEWING SUBSEQUENT EVENTS AND TRANSACTIONS

Events and transactions that occur after the balance-sheet date but before completion of fieldwork (for example, sale of an investment shortly after the balance-sheet date), may provide audit evidence regarding management's fair value measurements as of the balance-sheet date. [4]

Some subsequent events or transactions may reflect changes in circumstances occurring after the balance-sheet date and thus do not constitute competent evidence of the fair value measurement at the balance-sheet date (for example, the prices of actively traded marketable securities that change after the balance-sheet date). When using a subsequent event or transaction to substantiate a fair value measurement, the auditor considers only those events or transactions that reflect circumstances existing at the balance-sheet date.

DISCLOSURES ABOUT FAIR VALUES

The auditor should evaluate whether the disclosures about fair values made by the entity are in conformity with GAAP (See SAS No. 32, *Adequacy of Disclosure in Financial Statements* [AICPA, *Professional Standards,* vol. 1, AU sec. 431]). Disclosure of fair value information is an important aspect of financial statements. Often, fair value disclosure is required because of the relevance to users of information in the evaluation about an entity's performance and financial position. In addition to the fair value information required under GAAP, some entities voluntarily disclose additional fair value information in the notes to the financial statements.

When auditing fair value measurements and related disclosures included in the notes to the financial statements, whether required by GAAP or disclosed voluntarily, the auditor ordinarily performs essentially the same types of audit procedures as those employed in auditing a fair value measurement recognized in the financial statements. The auditor obtains sufficient competent audit evidence that the valuation principles are appropriate under GAAP, are being consistently applied, and that the method of estimation and significant assumptions used are adequately disclosed in accordance with GAAP. The auditor evaluates whether the entity has made adequate disclosures about fair value information. If an item contains a high degree of measurement uncertainty, the auditor assesses whether the disclosures are sufficient to inform users of such uncertainty (See Statement of Position 94-6, *Disclosure of Certain Significant Risks and Uncertainties).*

When disclosure of fair value information under GAAP is omitted because it is not practicable to determine fair value with sufficient reliability, the auditor evaluates the adequacy of disclosures required in these circumstances. If the entity has not appropriately disclosed fair value information required by GAAP, the auditor evaluates whether the financial statements are materially misstated.

EVALUATING THE RESULTS OF AUDIT PROCEDURES

The auditor should evaluate the sufficiency and competence of the audit evidence obtained from auditing fair value measurements and disclosures, as well as the consistency of that evidence with other audit evidence obtained and evaluated during the audit.

The auditor's evaluation of whether the fair value measurements and disclosures in the financial statements are in conformity with GAAP is performed in the context of the financial statements taken as a whole.

MANAGEMENT REPRESENTATION

SAS No. 85, *Management Representations,* requires that the independent auditor obtain written representations from management as a part of an audit of financial statements performed in accordance with generally accepted auditing standards. It also provides guidance concerning the representations to be obtained.

TOP AUDITING ISSUES FOR 2005 CPE COURSE

The auditor ordinarily should obtain written representations from management regarding the reasonableness of significant assumptions, including whether they appropriately reflect management's intent and ability to carry out specific courses of action on behalf of the entity, where relevant to the use of fair value measurements or disclosures. Depending on the nature, materiality, and complexity of fair values, management representations about fair value measurements and disclosures contained in the financial statements also may include representations about:

- The appropriateness of the measurement methods and related assumptions used by management in determining fair value and the consistency in application of the methods.
- The completeness and adequacy of disclosures related to fair values.
- Whether subsequent events require adjustment to the fair value measurements and disclosures included in the financial statements.

COMMUNICATION WITH AUDIT COMMITTEE

SAS No. 61, *Communication With Audit Committees,* requires auditors to determine that certain matters related to the conduct of an audit are communicated to audit committees. Certain accounting estimates are particularly sensitive because of their significance to the financial statements and because of the possibility that future events affecting them may differ markedly from management's current judgments.

The auditor should determine that the audit committee is informed about the process used by management in formulating particularly sensitive accounting estimates, including fair value estimates, and about the basis for the auditor's conclusions regarding the reasonableness of those estimates.

> **EXAMPLE**
>
> The auditor considers communicating the nature of significant assumptions used in fair value measurements, the degree of subjectivity involved in the development of the assumptions, and the relative materiality of the items being measured at fair value to the financial statements as a whole. The auditor considers the guidance contained in SAS No. 61 when determining the nature and form of communication.

STUDY QUESTIONS

9. SAS No. 85, Management Representations, requires that the independent auditor obtain written representations from management as a part of an audit of financial statements performed in accordance with generally accepted auditing standards and provides guidance concerning the representations to be obtained. *True or False?*

MODULE 1 — CHAPTER 3 — Fraud Detection   **45**

> **10.** SAS No. 61, Communication With Audit Committees, recommends, but does not require, auditors to determine that certain matters related to the conduct of an audit are communicated to audit committees. *True or False?*

Notes

[1] Accepted accounting principles (GAAP) contain various definitions of fair value. However, all of the definitions reflect the concepts in the definition that appears in Financial Accounting Standards Board (FASB) Statement of Financial Accounting Concepts No. 7, *Using Cash Flow Information and Present Value in Accounting Measurements.*

For example, Governmental Accounting Standards Board Statement of Governmental Accounting Standards No. 31. *Accounting and Financial Reporting for Certain Investments and for External Investment Pools,* defines fair value as "the amount at which an investment could be exchanged in a current transaction between willing parties, other than in a forced or liquidation sale."

[2] For purposes of this Statement, "management's assumptions" include assumptions developed by management under the guidance of the board of directors and assumptions developed by any specialist engaged or employed by management.

[3] Paragraph 16 of Accounting Principles Board Opinion No. 20, *Accounting Changes,* states that the presumption that an entity should not change an accounting principle may be overcome only if the entity justifies the use of an alternative acceptable accounting principle on the basis that it is preferable.

[4] The auditor's consideration of a subsequent event or transaction is a substantive test and thus differs from the review of subsequent events performed pursuant to SAS No. 1, *Codification of Auditing Standards and Procedures* (AICPA, *Professional Standards,* vol. 1, AU sec. 560, "Subsequent Events").

MODULE 1 — CHAPTER 3

Fraud Detection: Understanding and Applying SAS No. 99

LEARNING OBJECTIVES

> At the completion of this chapter, you should understand:
>
> - Definition and characteristics of fraud
> - Importance of exercising professional skepticism
> - Requiring the engagement personnel to discuss the risks of or potential for fraud
> - Evidential procedures that help identify the risks of fraud
> - Identifying risks that may result in a material misappropriation due to fraud
> - Responding to the results of the assessment
> - Evaluating audit evidence

INTRODUCTION

This chapter provides a detailed overview of a major new auditing standard, SAS No. 99. Given that users and regulators have placed an added emphasis on fraud detection, knowledge of this standard is crucial to auditors.

CHARACTERISTICS OF FRAUD

Background of SAS No.99

SAS No. 99, *Consideration of Fraud in a Financial Statement Audit,* was issued in December 2002. The AICPA put this out before the Enron and other Financial Reporting Scandals broke. The issuance of SAS was very timely but was not a result of the scandals. The publication date coincided with the highly publicized cases of financial reporting fraud in such companies as Enron and World Com, which had cast an unfavorable reflection on independent auditors. However, though the issuance date was timely, the SAS was in the works prior to these events.

The American Institute of Certified Public Accountants (AICPA) decided to launch an anti-fraud program "... designed to rebuild investor confidence in our capital markets and re-establish audited financial statements as a clear picture window into corporate America" (AICPA, The CPA Letter, Vol. 82 No. 9 (Nov. 2002, p. 1)). It supercedes SAS No. 82, which bore the same title.

SAS No. 82 was part of a group of pronouncements issued in 1997 to address the "expectations gap," i.e., the gap between what users of financial statements thought auditors did to detect fraud and irregularities, and what auditors actually did. SAS No. 82 was the first SAS that focused solely on financial statement fraud, in fact it was the first SAS to have used the term "fraud." SAS No. 82 did not change the degree of the auditor's responsibility to detect fraud per-se; i.e., the auditor was responsible to plan and perform the audit to "obtain reasonable assurance about whether the financial statements are free of material misstatement, whether caused by error or fraud." (SAS No. 82, Consideration of Fraud in a Financial Statement Audit, AICPA, Feb. 1997 (before being superceded by SAS No. 99)).

However, as was true before its issuance, "The auditor has no responsibility to plan and perform the audit to obtain reasonable assurance those misstatements, whether caused by errors or fraud, that are not material to the financial statements are detected." (SAS No. 82, *Consideration of Fraud in a Financial Statement Audit*). SAS 82 did provide for new procedures and tests. Specifically, the auditor was required to assess the risk of material misstatement due to possible fraud.

To aid the auditor in this assessment, the SAS identified three categories of risks factors for the occurrence of fraudulent financial reporting (SAS No. 82, *Consideration of Fraud in a Financial Statement Audit,*):

- Management's characteristics and influence over the control environment
- Industry conditions
- Operating characteristics and financial stability

Two categories of risk factors for the misappropriation of assets were given:
- Susceptibility of assets to misappropriation
- A lack of controls

The SAS also provided guidance to auditors who found that illegal acts might exist. The auditor should take these three steps (SAS No. 82, *Consideration of Fraud in a Financial Statement Audit*):
- Inquire of management at one level above those who may have committed the illegal act(s).
- Consult with the client's legal counsel or other knowledgeable specialist.
- Consider accumulating additional evidence to determine if an illegal act was committed.

Although it was believed that SAS No. 82 would improve the likelihood of identifying fraudulent financial reporting, the SAS did not require the auditor to detect fraud as evidenced by the following observation about SAS No. 82: "Is the auditor responsible for detecting any kind of fraud that may have occurred?" Absolutely not. The auditor's responsibility relates to the detection of material misstatements caused by fraud and is not directed to the detection of fraudulent activity per se." (Mancino, Jane, "The Auditor and Fraud," Journal of Accountancy, April 1997, p. 32). An examination of the overview of SAS No. 99 reveals a considerable increase in emphasis on fraud detection.

OVERVIEW OF SAS NO.99

Scope of SAS No. 99

The statement establishes standards and provides guidance in the context of an audit of financial statements conducted in accordance with generally accepted auditing standards (GAAS). It is not intended to be applied to special investigations aimed at detecting suspected fraud. Such "forensic audits" would typically contain procedures beyond that in a financial statement audit. The statement is effective for audits of financial statements beginning on or after December 15, 2002. However, early compliance is permissible. SAS No. 99 contains:
- A more comprehensive description and definition of fraud than its predecessor
- A cautionary discussion of the importance of exercising professional skepticism
- A requirement that the audit team consider how and where fraud might exist
- A requirement that the auditor gather information necessary to identify risks of material misstatement due to fraud
- A requirement that the auditor use the information gathered to so identify the risks of material misstatement due to fraud

- Assessing the identified risks
- Responding to the results of the assessment
- Evaluating audit evidence
- Communicating about fraud to management, the audit committee, and others
- Documenting the auditor's consideration of fraud

Integration of the SAS

The requirements and guidance of SAS No. 99 are to be integrated into an overall audit process. This should be done in a logical manner consistent with other SASs. Included are SAS No. 22, *Planning and Supervision,* SAS No. 47, *Audit Risk and Materiality in Conducting an Audit,* and SAS No. 55, *Consideration of Internal Control in a Financial Statement Audit* (See AICPA, *Professional Standards,* Vol. 1, AU sec. 311, 312, and 319, respectively). It is noted that the sequence of the requirements and guidance provided by the SAS may be implemented differently among audit engagements. This is so because an audit constitutes a continuous process of gathering and analyzing evidence.

Management's Responsibility

It is noted that although SAS #99 focuses on fraud detection, management carries the responsibility to "design and implement programs and controls to prevent, deter, and detect fraud" (Op. Cit., footnote # 7, para. 4). The statement provides guidance for the responsibility of management in this regard:

> Management, along with those who have responsibility for oversight of the financial reporting process (such as the audit committee, board of trustees, board of directors, or the owner in owner-managed entities), should set the proper tone: create and maintain a culture of honesty and high ethical standards; and establish appropriate controls to prevent, deter, and detect fraud. When management and those responsible for the oversight of the financial reporting process fulfill those responsibilities, the opportunities to commit fraud can be reduced significantly.

Definition and Characteristics of Fraud

Knowledge of the definition and characteristics of fraud enables the practitioner to distinguish among different types of fraud, recognize conditions that may indicate fraud, and understand how fraud may be concealed. SAS No. 99 continues to regard the auditor's interest in fraud as that specifically relating to "acts that result in a material misstatement of the financial statements." Further, the definition of fraud for auditing purposes continues to be ". . .an intentional act that results in a material misstatement in financial statements that are the subject of an audit." (Ibid) As in SAS #82, a distinction is made between fraudulent financial reporting and misappropriation of assets:

- **Fraudulent financial reporting:** intentional misstatements or omissions in financial statements that are designed to deceive users. The result is that financial statements are not fairly presented in conformity with GAAP.
- **Misappropriation:** the effect is to cause the financial statements to not be fairly presented in conformity with GAAP.

Examples of fraudulent financial reporting include:

- Manipulation, falsification, or alteration of accounting records or documents that support financial statements.
- Misrepresentation or intentional failure to disclose in the financial statements events, transactions, or other significant information.

The SAS notes that a grand plan or conspiracy need not be present in order for fraudulent financial reporting to exist. Instead it may be manifested in an aggressive interpretation of complex accounting rules, or as a temporary misstatement of financial statements where the intent is to correct the misstatements at a later time. Examples of misappropriation of assets include:

- Embezzling receipts
- Stealing assets
- Causing an entity to pay for goods or services not received

Environment in Which Fraud Occurs

The SAS asserts that three conditions are generally present when fraud occurs:

- Management/employees either have an incentive or are under pressure.
- There exists the opportunity for fraud, e.g., the absence of controls, controls that are not effective, or management override.
- The ability of the people involved to rationalize the fraudulent act. Such ability to rationalize might be due to defects in attitude, character, or ethical values.

The SAS notes, however, that even otherwise honest individuals may, if under sufficient pressure, commit fraud.

Perpetuating Fraud

Management's ability to override accounting controls and to "... directly or indirectly manipulate accounting records and present fraudulent financial information," (Ibid, para. 8) gives them a unique ability to engage in fraud.

Concealing Fraud

The SAS notes that fraud may be concealed in a number of ways:

50   TOP AUDITING ISSUES FOR 2005 CPE COURSE

- Withholding evidence or misrepresenting information in response to inquiries or by falsifying documents; e.g., concealing the theft of cash by forging signatures or by falsifying electronic approvals on disbursement authorizations.
- The collusion among management, employees, or third parties.   Collusion may result in the auditor making false inferences about audit evidence; e.g., anomalies revealed by analytical procedures may be explained away by two or more individuals in a misleading fashion.

Conditions Indicating the Possibility of Fraud
The SAS notes these examples of conditions that may indicate the presence of fraud (though other circumstances may be the cause):
- An important contract missing
- A subsidiary ledger that does not reconcile to the control account
- Results of an analytical procedure that is not consistent with expectations

Although the auditor does have a responsibility to plan and perform the audit so as to obtain "reasonable assurance"[1] about whether the financial statements are free of material misstatements, absolute assurance is not possible. Therefore, material misstatements due to fraud may not be detected even in a properly planned and performed audit. The SAS asserts that "... a material misstatement may not be detected because of the nature of the audit evidence."[2] In addition, a material misstatement may not be detected because the auditor may rely on audit evidence that appears valid, but is not.

STUDY QUESTIONS

---

1. An example of fraudulent financial reporting is:
   a. Employee theft of inventory
   b. Intentional failure to disclose a pending lawsuit
   c. Incorrectly estimating the useful life of a patent

2. Which of the following *does not* constitute a misappropriation of assets?
   a. Alteration of the date of a sales invoice so that the sale could be recorded in an earlier period
   b. Theft of inventory
   c. Deliberate double payment of purchase invoice to supplier who is related to the employee

---

IMPORTANCE OF EXERCISING PROFESSIONAL SKEPTICISM

SAS No. 1, *Codification of Auditing Standards,* requires the auditor to exercise professional skepticism. The SAS defines professional skepticism as "... an attitude that includes a questioning mind and a critical assessment of audit evidence." (Op. Cit., footnote # 7). Setting aside any pre-conceived notion about management's honesty and integrity, the auditor should "... conduct the engagement with a mindset that recognizes the possibility that a material misstatement due to fraud could be present ..." (Ibid).

The auditor should have a continuous questioning of whether the evidence suggests the occurrence of a material fraudulent event. A belief that management is honest should not lead the auditor to accept less than persuasive evidence.

STUDY QUESTIONS

3. The auditor is required to exercise professional skepticism:
  a. Only in auditing for possible misappropriation of assets
  b. So that all material transactions are examined critically
  c. Because it is required by an SAS

4. Which of the following is indicative of a mindset of professional skepticism?
  a. An expectation that fraudulent misstatements are likely to occur in all entities
  b. Recognition that "clean" financial statements in prior years do not necessarily mean that current year's financial statements are free of material misstatements
  c. An expectation that all management's assertions must be challenged for their veracity

RISKS OF OR POTENTIAL FOR FRAUD

The SAS requires members of the audit team to discuss the potential for fraud. The SAS discusses specific evidential procedures designed to detect fraud (discussed below). The discussion with the audit team should occur prior to, or in conjunction with the performance of these evidential procedures. The discussion should include:

- Brainstorming among the audit members. The in-charge auditor should be present. Such idea exchanges should include where the financial statements are vulnerable to fraud, how management might be able to perpetuate and conceal fraud, and how assets of the entity could be misappropriated.
- Emphasizing the importance of maintaining an attitude of professional skepticism regarding the potential for fraud.

Required Items to Discuss Among the Audit Team

Certain external and internal factors may increase the likelihood of fraud. Those factors may:

- Create incentives or pressures for management to commit fraud.
- Provide an opportunity for the committing of fraud.
- Indicate a culture or environment enabling management to rationalize committing fraud.

In discussing these factors, it is important for audit team members to have a questioning mind set that enables them to set "... aside any prior beliefs the audit team members may have that management is honest and has integrity." (Ibid, para. 15). Items included in the discussion among the audit team should include:

- The risk of management override of internal controls
- The audit team's response to an indication that the entity possesses susceptibility to material misstatement due to fraud

The audit team should not "... dismiss information or other conditions that indicate a material misstatement due to fraud may have occurred," but rather should possess a "... questioning mind ..." and should exercise "... professional skepticism in gathering and evaluating evidence throughout the audit ..." Such an attitude of professional skepticism should result in the audit team to be alert for the presence of factors that indicate possible fraud, and should "... lead audit team members to thoroughly probe the issues, acquire additional evidence as necessary, and consult with other team members and if appropriate, experts in the field." (Ibid, para. 16.)

Composition and Timing of the Audit Team Discussions

The SAS notes that the discussion ordinarily should involve key members of the audit team, and communication among the audit team should continue throughout the audit. Multiple locations of the audit team would require multiple discussions. It may be useful to include specialists in the discussion.

STUDY QUESTION

> **5.** Having audit teams discuss the potential for fraud is:
>   **a.** Optional, but strongly encouraged
>   **b.** Required
>   **c.** Recommended if the auditor's initial assessment of the likelihood of fraud is high
>   **d.** Especially helpful in auditing smaller companies

IDENTIFY THE RISKS OF FRAUD

The auditor must make inquiries to help identify the risks of fraud and determine the role of analytical procedures and other information in identifying the risks of fraud. The auditor should obtain knowledge about the entity's business and the industry as discussed in SAS No. 22 (AU Sec. 311.06-311.08). Specifically, the following procedures should be performed (Ibid, para. 19):

MODULE 1 — CHAPTER 3 — Fraud Detection **53**

- Inquire of management and others in the entity about their views regarding the risks of fraud, and how those risks are addressed.
- Consider any unusual or unexpected relationships identified from the performance of analytical procedures used in planning the audit.
- Consider whether fraud risk factors exist.
- Consider other information deemed helpful in identifying fraud risk.

Inquiries of Management About the Risks of Fraud

In addition to obtaining written representation from management regarding fraud (as required by SAS No. 85, *Management Representations* (AICPA), *Professional Standards,* vol. 1, AU sec. 333), the auditor should inquire of management (Op. Cit., footnote # 7, para. 20.):

- Whether management has knowledge of any actual or suspected fraud
- Whether management is aware of allegations of any actual or suspected fraud
- Their understanding about the risks of fraud, including any specific fraud risk identified, or likely fraud risks existing in accounting balances or transactions
- About any controls the entity has implemented to mitigate specific fraud risks, or that aid in preventing, deterring, and detecting fraud
- Where operating and business segments are located, and whether particular operating locations or business segments are more likely to have higher risks of fraud
- Whether and how management communicates to its employee's management views on business practices and ethical behavior

Inquiries of the Audit Committee and the Internal Auditors: Others in the Entity

Other inquires that should be made, including inquiries to the audit committee about their views on the risks of fraud and any knowledge the committee may have of actual or suspected fraud, as well as inquiries to internal auditors about:

- Their views about the risks of fraud
- Procedures performed during the year to identify or detect fraud
- Management's response to any findings from those procedures
- Whether the internal auditors have knowledge of actual or suspected fraud

Professional judgment should be exercised in respect to making inquiries of other employees, including:

- Personnel with whom the auditor interacts in the course of the audit
- Operating personnel
- Employees who initiate, record, or process complex or unusual transactions

- In-house legal counsel

Importance of Inquiries; Evaluating Responses

The SAS states that inquiries are important because fraud is often detected through such inquiries. Inquiries of non-management personnel may provide different perspectives and may corroborate management's responses, or alternatively might provide examples of management override.

In evaluating inquiries of management, the auditor should be aware that management is best situated to perpetuate fraud. If responses are not corroborated by others, the auditor should gather additional evidence in order to resolve the inconsistencies.

The Role of Analytical Procedures in Identifying the Risks of Fraud

Analytical procedures are required to be performed when planning the audit. The SAS notes that when ratios, trends, and recorded amounts yield unusual or unexpected results, the auditor should consider those results in identifying the risks of fraud. Specific analytical procedures should be applied to revenue; e.g., comparing sales volume with production capacity, or doing a trend analysis of revenues and sales returns by month.

However, the SAS notes that while analytical procedures may be helpful in identifying the risks of fraud, the fact that the data is usually highly aggregated may result in "only a broad initial indication about whether a material misstatement of the financial statements may exist" (Ibid, para. 28-30).

The Consideration of Fraud Risk Factors

The appendix to the SAS provides several examples of "fraud risk factors," i.e., "… events or conditions that indicate incentives/pressures to perpetrate fraud, opportunities to carry out the fraud, or attitudes/rationalizations to justify a fraudulent action." (Ibid, para. 33.). The auditor must use professional judgment in both determining whether a risk factor is present, and if so, whether such risk factor should be considered in identifying and assessing the risk of material misstatements due to fraud.

Examples of Fraud Risk Factors of Fraudulent Financial Reporting

Incentives or pressures to commit fraud may result when (Appendix to SAS No. 99, *Fraud Risk Factors*, AICPA, Dec. 2002):
- Economic, industry, or entity operating conditions threaten financial stability or profitability;
- Requirements or expectations of third parties put excessive pressure on management;
- Management or the board of directors' personal financial wealth is threatened by the entity's financial performance; or

- Management or operating personnel feel excessive pressure to meet financial targets imposed by the board of directors or management.

Opportunities to commit fraud may exist when:
- The nature of the industry or the entity's operations provides opportunities to engage in fraudulent financial reporting;
- Management is not effectively monitored by the board of directors;
- The organizational structure is complex or unstable; or
- Internal control components are deficient.

Attitudes or rationalizations by board members, management, or employees allowing them to engage in and/or justify fraud could include:
- Management's lack of ethical standards
- The selection or participation in the selection of accounting principles/accounting estimates by nonfinancial management.
- Aggressive or unrealistic forecasts by management
- A relationship between the auditor and management that is strained by, e.g., frequent disputes regarding accounting issues

Examples of Fraud Risk Factors From Misappropriation of Assets

Incentives/pressures to misappropriate assets may result when:
- Personal financial obligations may create pressure on management.
- Adverse relationships between the entity and employees (e.g., employee layoffs) may motivate employees to misappropriate assets.

Opportunities to misappropriate assets may exist when:
- Circumstances within the entity increase the likelihood of misappropriation (e.g., large amounts of cash on hand)
- Internal controls are inadequate (e.g., lack of segregation of duties).

Attitudes or rationalizations of employees allowing them to engage in and/or justify misappropriation of assets may include:
- Lack of interest in monitoring or reducing the risk of asset misappropriation
- Overriding internal control or not correcting deficiencies of internal control
- Behavior indicative of displeasure with the company
- Symptomatic changes in behavior of lifestyle

Other Information That May Identify Risks of Fraud

In addition to helpful information that may be provided by the brainstorming among the audit team, information from these sources may be helpful (Op. Cit., footnote # 7, para. 34):
- Procedures relating to the acceptance and continuance of clients as related in SQCS No. 2, System of Quality Control for a CPA Firm's Accounting and Auditing Practice (AICPA), Professional Standards, vol. 2, QC sec. 20.14-16, as amended
- Reviews of interim financial statements

56 TOP AUDITING ISSUES FOR 2005 CPE COURSE

- The identification of accounts that contain inherent risks

STUDY QUESTIONS

6. Inquiries of management regarding fraud:
    a. Are conducted after inquiries to the audit committee are conducted
    b. Are made regarding management's opinion as to the likelihood of fraud
    c. Are limited to their knowledge of actual or suspected fraud
    d. Include asking if management is aware of allegations of fraud

7. Which of the following need not be contacted in order to help identify the risks of fraud?
    a. Internal auditors
    b. Suppliers to the entity
    c. In-house legal counsel
    d. The audit committee of the entity

8. A feature of the data that auditors draw from to apply analytical procedures is that the data is:
    a. Usually not in quantitative form
    b. Used primarily to conduct compliance tests of controls
    c. Often highly aggregated, thus making it difficult to draw specific conclusions

9. Reviews of interim financial statements:
    a. May help in identifying the risks of fraud
    b. Should be conducted before making inquiries of management regarding the risks of fraud
    c. Are helpful in identifying the risks of misappropriation of assets
    d. Are especially helpful in identifying the risks of fraud resulting from deficient internal control components

MATERIAL MISAPPROPRIATION DUE TO FRAUD

Identifying Risks That May Result In
A Material Misappropriation Due to Fraud

The auditor needs to consider various criteria and types of transactions that may increase the risks of fraud. To do so, he or she must learn the four attributes of risks of fraud.

Using the Information Obtained to Identify Fraud Risks

When the auditor gathers information to help identify the risk of material misstatement due to fraud, the three conditions present when such fraud occurs (i.e., incentives/pressures; opportunities; and attitudes/rationalizations) should be considered. However, the auditor cannot assume that the lack of these three

MODULE 1 — CHAPTER 3 — Fraud Detection **57**

conditions means that fraud is not present (Op. Cit., footnote # 7, para. 35).

The identification of fraud risks may vary according to such criteria as the size of the business, the complexity of the business, ownership attributes of the business, and the physical location of operating units or business segments. The SAS notes that in larger corporations the audit committee and the internal control function may be more important, while in smaller entities, the culture of management (e.g., emphasizing integrity and ethical behavior) may act to discourage fraud.

The SAS points out that certain accounts, classes of transactions and assertions that involve a high degree of management judgment and subjectivity may be more likely to result in fraudulent misrepresentation because they can be manipulated by management; e.g., assets stemming from investment activities are high risk assets because the subjectivity and management judgment required to estimate fair value of the assets.

The auditor must use professional judgment in considering four attributes of risk:

- **The type of risk:** Whether the risk is of fraudulent financial reporting or of misappropriation of assets
- **Significance of the risk:** Whether it could lead to material misstatements of the financial statements
- **Likelihood of the risk:** The chance that it will lead to a material misstatement of the financial statements
- **Pervasiveness of the risk:** Whether the potential risk would pervade the entire financial statements or a specific account, transaction, or assertion

In identifying fraud risks, "... the auditor should ordinarily presume that there is a risk of material misstatement due to fraud relating to revenue recognition." (Ibid, para. 41)   The SAS also requires the auditor to address the risk of management override. This is required even if no specific risks of fraud are identified.

STUDY QUESTIONS

---

10. In smaller companies, the culture of management may discourage fraud. *True or False?*

11. Which of the following would be characterized as high-risk assets?
   a. Plant and equipment
   b. Notes receivable
   c. Prepaid insurance
   d. Equity ownership in a supplier

RESPONDING TO THE RESULTS OF THE ASSESSMENT

The auditor is required by SAS No. 55 to possess an understanding of the five components of internal control that is sufficient to plan the audit,

TOP AUDITING ISSUES FOR 2005 CPE COURSE

and to use that knowledge to consider risk factors, design tests of controls (compliance tests), and design tests of accounts and transactions (substantive tests).Examples of programs and controls that the auditor may examine include:

- Specific controls (e.g., controls to address theft)
- Broader controls and programs (e.g., company code of ethics)

The auditor needs to consider whether such controls could either reduce or increase the risks of fraud. Then, after evaluating the entity's controls and programs, the auditor should assess the risks of fraud by taking into account such evaluation. This risk would form part of "... the auditor's response to the identified risks of material misstatement due to fraud" (Ibid, para. 45).

Responding to the Results of the Assessment

The SAS again notes that the auditor should keep an attitude of professional skepticism in response to the risks of fraud. Applying professional skepticism might involve:

- Designing additional audit procedures to obtain higher quality evidence
- Getting additional corroborative evidence of management's assertions, e.g., third party confirmations

The auditors' response to the assertion is influenced by the nature and significance of the risks identified and the entity's processes and controls. There are three ways in which the auditor might respond to risks of material misstatements:

- A response that has an overall effect on how the audit is conducted
- A response that would involve the nature, timing, and extent of audit procedures (e.g., increasing the sample of sales transactions around the fiscal year-end in response to an increased perceived risk in misrepresentation of revenue)
- Specific responses to address the risk of management override

If the auditor concludes that designing such additional audit procedures would not be practical, withdrawal from the engagement may be appropriate.

Overall Responses to the Risk of Material Misstatement

The manner in which the audit is performed is affected by the auditor's judgment of the risks of fraud in these three ways:

- In the assignment of personnel and in the supervision of personnel (e.g., those with specialized skills or those more experienced personnel may be assigned)
- In the selection of accounting principles. "The auditor should consider whether "their collective application indicates a bias that may create such a material misstatement of the financial statements"
- In the predictability of auditing procedures

MODULE 1 — CHAPTER 3 — Fraud Detection **59**

Responses Involving the Nature, Timing, and Extent of Procedures to be Performed to Address the Identified Risks

The SAS notes that while the types of audit procedures to be applied in response to identified risks of fraud, "...it is unlikely that audit risk can be reduced to an appropriately low level by performing only tests of controls." (Ibid, para. 51)

The nature, timing, and extent of auditing procedures may be changed in the following ways:

- **Nature of the auditing procedures:** More reliable evidence or additional corroborative evidence may be obtained. Physical observation or inspection of assets may become more important.
- **Timing of substantive tests:** Depending on the circumstances, the auditor may decide to do more year-end tests. Alternately, the auditor might decide to apply tests earlier in the fiscal year.
- **Extent of the procedures:** This should reflect the assessment of risk due to fraud, e.g., sample sizes might be increased, or more detailed analytical procedures performed. The SAS notes that computer-assisted techniques may enable more extensive testing of electronic transactions, e.g., to sort transactions with specific characteristics.

The SAS lists six examples of the modifications in audit tests discussed above:

- Unannounced or surprise procedures, e.g., a surprise cash count
- Having the entity count inventory close to the balance sheet date
- In addition to written confirmations from third parties, making oral inquiries of such
- Performing more disaggregated substantive analytical procedures
- Interviewing personnel in identified areas of high risks of fraud
- Discussing the risks of fraud with the other independent auditors involved in the audit

Additional Examples of Responses to Identified Risks of Misstatements Stemming From Fraud

The SAS discusses three additional examples of responses to identified risks of fraud:

- **Revenue recognition:** Ordinarily the auditor would develop audit procedures tailored to the entity, and based on the auditor's understanding of the entity and its environment. This is so because accounting principles and practices can vary by industry. However, the auditor may also want to:
  - Perform more disaggregated substantive analytical procedures.
  - Confirm with customers certain relevant contract terms as well as the absence of side agreements.

60 TOP AUDITING ISSUES FOR 2005 CPE COURSE

- Inquire of sales and marketing personnel and in-house legal counsel regarding any unusual terms or conditions associated with year-end sales.
- Be physically present at one or more locations at the end of the fiscal period to observe goods being shipped.
- Test controls over electronically initiated transactions.

- **Inventory quantities:** If there is a fraud risk with respect to inventories, the SAS suggests that examining inventory records may help to indicate locations or items that may require specific procedures such as observation of inventory taking on an unannounced basis, counting inventory at all locations on the same date, or counting inventory at or near the close of the fiscal year. Additional procedures during the observation of inventory may also need to be performed, e.g., using the work of a specialist or additional testing of quantities and quality. Various analytical tests on inventory may also need to be performed (Ibid).

- **Management estimates:** The SAS states that this risk may affect many accounts and assertions (e.g., asset valuations) as well as significant changes in assumptions relating to recurring estimates. It is noted that a potential bias exists in such estimates even though management may be competent and using relevant and reliable data. The SAS notes that specialists can be engaged to develop independent estimates, and retrospective reviews of similar estimates by management may also be helpful (Ibid).

Examples of Responses to Identified Risks of Fraud from Misappropriation

The SAS notes that the auditor's response to a risk of material misstatement due to fraud would usually be directed toward account balances, and the scope of the work should be aimed at the identified misappropriation risk. Such work might involve obtaining an understanding of the internal controls relating to the asset, physical inspection of such asset, or the use of substantive analytical procedures.

Responses to Further Address the Risk of Management Override

Given that management is uniquely positioned to perpetuate fraud, the SAS requires the auditor to examine journal entries and other adjustments. The SAS notes that fraud is often perpetuated by recording inappropriate journal entries or by making adjustment to the financial statements that are not evidenced by journal entries. In connection with this audit procedure, the auditor should:

- Obtain an understanding of the entity's financial reporting process
- Identify and select journal entries for testing
- Determine the timing of the testing
- Inquire of individuals involved in financial reporting about inappropriate or unusual activity with regard to journal entries

The SAS notes that the auditor's understanding of the entity may help in identifying typical adjustments to the financial statements, e.g., who can initiate entries, needed approval, and the manner in which adjustments are made. The auditor should examine entity controls over the formulation of journal entries to determine suitability.

In exercising professional judgment when deciding on the nature, timing, and extent of the testing of journal entries, the auditor should consider:

- His or her assessment of the risks of fraud
- The effectiveness of controls over journal entries (but even effective controls does not eliminate the need for testing)
- The entity's financial reporting process and the nature of the evidence. The SAS notes that journal entries may exist in either paper or electronic form. Further, to audit electronically generated journal entries may require the use of a specialist
- The characteristics of fraudulent entries, such as one of the following:
  - Made to unrelated, unusual, or seldom-used accounts
  - Made by individuals who usually do not make entries
  - Recorded at the end of the period or as post-closing entries and that have inadequate explanation
  - Made without account numbers
  - Contain round numbers or a consistent ending number
- The nature and complexity of the accounts. Although inappropriate entries may be made to any accounts, the SAS notes that certain accounts may be more susceptible to inappropriate entries, such as:
  - Those accounts containing complicated or unusual transactions
  - Those with significant estimates and period-ending adjustment
  - Those accounts that have been error prone in the past
  - Those which have not been timely reconciled
  - Those accounts with inter-company transactions
  - Those accounts which are otherwise associated with an identified fraud risk
- Entries processed outside the normal course of business. Nonstandard entries (e.g., those to record nonrecurring transactions) might not have the same level of control as those standard entries (e.g., monthly sales entries).

In addition to focusing on period-end journal entries, the auditor should consider testing journal entries made throughout the period to be audited.

Reviewing Accounting Estimates for Biases
That Could Lead to Fraud

The SAS notes that even if differences between individual estimates made by management and estimates supported by audit evidence appear reasonable, the auditor should consider whether the totality of the estimates indicates management bias. The auditor should also perform a retrospective review

TOP AUDITING ISSUES FOR 2005 CPE COURSE

of prior year's accounting estimates. The estimates tested should include "... highly sensitive assumptions ..." as well as estimates "... significantly affected by judgments made by management." However, the purpose of the review is not to call into question the auditor's professional judgment made in the prior year. If a possible bias is discovered, the auditor must determine whether there is a risk of fraud; e.g., adjustments recorded at management's instructions to achieve an earnings target (Ibid, para. 65).

Evaluating the Business Rationale for Significant Unusual Transactions

Unusual transactions or those outside the normal course of the entity's business should be examined for a business purpose because the lack of such a purpose may indicate fraud. To understand the business purpose, the auditor should consider whether:

- The form of the transaction is overly complex.
- Management emphasizes the accounting treatment more than the underlying economics of the transactions.
- Transactions involving unconsolidated related parties (e.g., special purpose entities) have been properly reviewed and approved by the board of directors.
- Transactions involve previously unidentified related parties or parties lacking the financial strength to undertake the transaction without assistance from the entity.

STUDY QUESTIONS

12. One reason for the auditor to examine the entity's system of internal controls is to determine whether the controls increase or decrease the risks of fraud. *True or False?*

13. A company's code of ethics constitutes an example of:
- **a.** Broad programs and controls
- **b.** Specific programs and controls
- **c.** A control affecting the pervasiveness of the risk

14. An auditor ordinarily would not respond to a perceived high risk of material misstatement by obtaining third party confirmations of management's assertions. *True or False?*

15. The predictability of auditing procedures performed:
- **a.** Should be independent of the assessment of the risks of fraud
- **b.** May be varied by the auditor in response to an identified high risk of fraud
- **c.** Should be established irrevocably at the outset of the audit
- **d.** Is governed by the auditor's assessment of internal controls

MODULE 1 — CHAPTER 3 — Fraud Detection

16. Which of the following is not a recommended response to identified risks of fraud?

a. Changing the timing of substantive tests
b. Changing the extent of auditing procedures
c. Changing the conclusions drawn from statistical samples
d. Changing the types of auditing procedures performed

17. Because accounting principles and practices over revenue recognition vary among industries, auditing procedures are often tailored to the entity. *True or False?*

18. An increase in fraud risks with respect to inventory might cause the auditor to do all but which of the following?

a. Engage the services of a specialist.
b. Perform additional analytical tests.
c. Observe inventory on an unannounced basis.
d. Suspend compliance testing.

19. One reason that the auditor should select journal entries for testing is to respond to the risk of management override. *True or False?*

20. If the results of compliance testing indicate effective controls over the initiation and recording of journal entries, substantive testing of the entries would be unnecessary. *True or False?*

21. In determining the extent of testing of journal entries, the auditor should not test a larger sample of accounts that were error prone in the past, rather she should conduct a random sample of the entire universe of journal entries. *True or False?*

22. The purpose of a retrospective review of the prior year's accounting estimates is to test the accuracy of the auditor's professional judgment made in the prior year. *True or False?*

23. Which of the following would not lead the auditor to exercise professional skepticism over the business purpose of a transaction?

a. The transaction is with a large customer.
b. The transaction is with an unconsolidated related party.
c. The transaction is extremely complex.
d. Parties to the transactions appear to lack the financial strength to engage in the transaction without assistance from the entity.

EVALUATING AUDIT EVIDENCE

The auditor needs to be aware of circumstances that could change the judgment of the risks of fraud and to consider the usefulness of certain analytical tests in evaluating fraud risks. He or she also must learn how to respond to, communicate, and document, evidence of possible fraud.

Assessing Fraud Risks Throughout the Audit

The SAS notes that the assessment of the risks of fraud should be ongoing throughout the audit. However, the following events or circumstances may change the judgment of the risks of fraud (Ibid, para. 68):

- Discrepancies in the accounting records, including:
  - Transactions improperly or untimely recorded
  - Unsupported or unauthorized balances or transactions
  - Last-minute adjustments significantly affecting financial results
  - Evidence that the "limited access" concept of internal control is not present
  - Tips or complaints to the auditor about alleged fraud
- Conflicting or missing evidential matter, including:
  - Missing documents
  - Altered documents
  - Unavailability of original documents expected to exist
  - Significant unexplained items on reconciliations
  - Inconsistent, vague, or implausible responses from management or employees to inquiries or analytical procedure anomalies
  - Unusual discrepancies between records and confirmations
  - Significant inventory or other assets missing
  - Electronic evidence that, according to the entity's record retention policy should be present, but which is not
  - Inability to produce evidence of key systems development and program change testing and implementation activities for current-year system changes and deployments
- Problematic or unusual relationships between the auditor and the client, including:
  - Denial of access to records
  - Undue time pressures imposed by management to resolve issues
  - Unusual delays in producing requested information
  - Unwillingness to facilitate auditor access to electronic files for "auditing through the computer"
  - Denial of access to IT facilities
  - Unwillingness to make financial statement disclosures more complete and transparent

Evaluating Whether Analytical Procedures Indicate a Fraud Risk Previously Unrecognized

The SAS notes that the auditor should perform analytical procedures relating to revenue recognition. While determining which particular trends indicate a risks of fraud requires professional judgment, unusual relationships are especially relevant (e.g., large amounts of income reported in the last week of the reporting period from unusual transactions, or income inconsistent

MODULE 1 — CHAPTER 3 — Fraud Detection   **65**

with trends in cash flow from operations). Certain relationships are helpful to examine because management is less likely to be able to manipulate them. Examples include:

- Comparing net income to cash flow (difficult to manipulate cash)
- Changes in inventory, accounts payable, sales, or cost of sales from the prior period (an employee engaged in theft may not have access to all those accounts)
- Comparing the entity's profitability compared to industry trends
- Comparing bad debt write-offs to comparable industry data (could indicate a theft of cash receipts)
- Comparing sales volume as evidences by accounting records with production statistics (could indicate a misstatement of sales)
- Whether responses to anomalies identified by analytical tests have been vague or implausible, or indicate inconsistencies

Evaluating the Risks of Fraud Around the End of Fieldwork

The SAS notes that toward the end of the fieldwork, the auditor needs to evaluate whether the various auditing procedures used (including analytical procedures discussed above), have changed the assessment of the risks of fraud.

If such auditing procedures indicate a higher risk of fraud than previously estimated, this evaluation may lead to new or additional audit procedures. To ensure that adequate communication exists among the audit team, the auditor may want to conduct another team meeting regarding the assessment of the risks of fraud.

Responding to Misstatements That May Indicate Fraud

If audit tests uncover misstatements that may indicate fraud, the effect may or may not be material to the financial statements. In conjunction with determining the materiality of the misstatement, the auditor should:

- Attempt to obtain additional evidence that would ascertain the materiality of the misstatement.
- Consider its implications with respect to other aspects of the audit (e.g., its impact on the nature, timing, and extent of audit tests and effectiveness of the internal control system).
- Discuss the matter with an appropriate level of management, as well as with the audit committee.
- Where deemed appropriate, recommend that the client consult their attorneys. The auditor should, if the auditor believes that the fraud is (Ibid, para. 76-77):
  - *Not material to the financial statements:* Nevertheless, evaluate the implications, especially with respect to the organizational level of the individual's committing fraud (the higher the organizational level, the more likely that the fraud indicates a pervasive problem)

- *Material (or could be material) to the financial statements:* The auditor should consider withdrawing from the audit engagement, and communicating the reasons to the audit committee or others having commensurate authority. This decision may depend on the implications about the integrity of management as well as the cooperation of management or the board of directors. The auditor may wish to consult with legal counsel in considering this decision.

Communicating the Possible Fraud

The SAS states that management should be informed of even minor thefts by low-level employees, while fraud involving senior management must be reported to the audit committee. The SAS also notes that the auditor "... should reach an understanding with the audit committee regarding the nature and extent of communications with the committee about misappropriations perpetuated by lower-level employees" (Ibid, para. 79).

Risks that have continuing control implications may be evidence of reportable conditions relating to internal control that should be communicated to the board of directors as well as senior management. Other risks of fraud may also need to be communicated.

Although the auditor generally is not expected to report fraud to other parties (usually confidentiality requirements would prevent disclosure unless disclosed in the annual report), in these circumstances the auditor may be required to disclose to parties outside the entity:

- To comply with various legal and regulatory requirement (e.g., required reports on the termination of the engagement)
- To a successor auditor who makes inquiries (after receiving permission from the client)
- In response to a subpoena
- To funding or other agencies to meet government prescribed requirements for entities receiving governmental financial assistance

Documenting the Auditor's Consideration of Fraud

The following items should be documented:

- The audit team's discussion of its plan to assess the likelihood of fraud. Included should be the date/time of discussion, participating members, and subject matter
- The procedures performed to obtain information necessary to evaluate and assess the risk of fraud
- Identified specific fraud risks and the auditor's response to such
- Reasons supporting the auditor's conclusions any fraud risk stemming from improper revenue recognition
- The reasons the auditor did not find improper revenue recognition

MODULE 1 — CHAPTER 3 — Fraud Detection   **67**

- Results of procedures performed to address the risk of management override
- Any other conditions and analytical relationships causing the auditor to make further responses to address fraud risk
- The nature of the communications about fraud made to management, the audit committee, and others

Amendments Made to SAS No. 1,
Codification of Auditing Standards and Procedures

The original SAS No. 1 contained a brief discussion of fraud and the impact of collusion on the auditor's ability to detect fraud. The amendment contains an enlarged discussion of the characteristics of fraud, noting that such characteristics include (SAS No. 1, Codification of Auditing Standards and Procedures, para. 1.12 (as amended by SAS No. 99)):

- Concealment through collusion among management, employees, or third parties
- Withheld, misrepresented, or falsified documentation
- The ability of management to override or instruct others to override what otherwise appears to be effective controls

The enlarged discussion of collusion and other manipulations by management is as follows (Ibid):

> Collusion may cause the auditor who has properly performed the audit to conclude that evidence provided is persuasive when it is, in fact, false. In addition, an audit conducted in accordance generally accepted auditing standards rarely involves authentification of documentation, nor are auditors trained as or expected to be experts in such authentication. Furthermore, an auditor may not discover the existence of a modification of documentation through a side agreement that management or a third party has not disclosed. Finally, management has the ability to directly or indirectly manipulate accounting records and present fraudulent financial information by overriding controls in unpredictable ways.

Amendments Made to SAS No. 85, *Professional Standards*

SAS No. 85 requires the auditor to make inquiries of management regarding fraud and its risk. Added to management representation requirements is a statement acknowledging management's responsibility "... for the design and implementation of programs and controls to prevent and detect fraud." (SAS No.85, Management Representations, vol. 1, AU sec 333.06 (as amended by SAS No. 99).) Also added is a requirement for management to disclose "Knowledge of any allegations of fraud or suspected fraud affecting the entity received in communications from employees, former employees, analysts, regulators, short sellers, or others" (Ibid).

TOP AUDITING ISSUES FOR 2005 CPE COURSE

STUDY QUESTIONS

24. Discovering an event such as last-minute accounting adjustments would confirm, but not change, the auditor's initial assessment of the risks of fraud. *True or False?*

25. A useful analytical procedure in determining the risks of fraud is to compare net income to cash flow. *True or False?*

26. Which of the following is the most appropriate step to take if the auditor uncovers fraud that is not material to the financial statements?

    a. Withdraw from the engagement.
    b. Attempt to determine the pervasiveness of the problem.
    c. Initiate immediate communication with the audit committee of the board of directors.

27. The predecessor auditor must in all instances communicate evidence of fraud to successor auditors. *True or False?*

28. Documenting the auditor's consideration of fraud is not required, and in fact is inadvisable from a legal liability standpoint. *True or False?*

Notes

[1] The concept of "reasonable assurance" is defined and discussed in SAS No. 1, *Codification of Auditing Standards and Procedures,* AICPA, *Professional Standards,* Vol. 1, AU Sec. 230.10-.13.

[2] Op. Cit., footnote # 7., para. 12. Note: the author believes that this "mea culpa" of sorts will not ultimately stand up when the Public Company Accounting Oversight Board (PCAOB) begins setting generally accepted auditing standards (GAAS).

MODULE 2 — CHAPTER 4

Compilation and Review: Important and Evolving Issues

LEARNING OBJECTIVES

At the completion of this chapter you should be able to:

- View the ways in which market forces are changing the compilation and review process.
- Determine how the creation of a management-use only financial statement option affects compilation reports for your clients.
- Understand the differences between preparing and presenting financial statements and their effect on responsibilities under the SSARSs.
- Adapt the sample letters and forms for use in your practice.

- Distinguish among the four exemptions from the SSARSs.
- Mitigate the risk arising in practice from controllership engagements.

INTRODUCTION

This chapter focuses on recent developments affecting compilation and review engagements, including SSARS No. 8 and newly issued interpretations of SSARS No. 1. It also incorporates some of the matters discussed in the AICPA's Compilation and Review Alerts, which are nonauthoritative practice aids designed to help accountants plan their compilation and review engagements. The alerts clarify certain existing standards and assist accountants in implementing the SSARSs and related interpretations.

The chapter distinguishes among the four exemptions from SSARSs for engagements. Finally, it offers information about new opportunities for expanding compilation and review practices and details what actually transpires in compilation and review engagements.

CONTROVERSY ON THE COMPILATION FRONT

Market forces require that CPA firms practice more efficiently in delivering compilation and review services to their clients. Like the direction that auditing has taken, compilation and review engagements are now perceived as a commodity to be purchased from the lowest bidder. The result is that finding a way to perform these engagements faster and cheaper, while not compromising on the quality of work performed, is the challenge of the CPA firm today.

Most of the controversy surrounds compilation engagements as consolidators, such as American Express, have reduced the prices charged for compilation engagements. Moreover, these same consolidators have forced another issue within several State Licensing Boards and in the courts—that is, whether nonlicensed CPA firms can issue compilation reports. This issue has been boiling in the courts and has now culminated with a decision in the Florida Courts and a response by the AICPA Council that is discussed further below.

In response to these market pressures, the AICPA Accounting and Review Services Committee (ARSC) and the AICPA Council have focused on resolving two important issues surrounding the future application of the compilation engagement:

- Whether there should be alternatives to the traditional compilation engagement including revision to the definition of submission
- Whether non-CPA firms should be able to issue compilation reports

ALTERNATIVES TO THE TRADITIONAL COMPILATION ENGAGEMENT: THE DEBATE OVER ASSEMBLY, PLAIN PAPER, AND OTHER ALTERNATIVES

Since the turn of this century an intense debate has developed over the future reporting threshold for compilation engagements, and whether a new lower level of service should be introduced. The following is a discussion of the issues at hand.

Understanding When to Compile Financial Statements

In 1979, the AICPA issued SSARS No. 1. It continues to be the framework for compilation and review engagements. A CPA must comply with SSARS No. 1 (e.g., issue either a compilation or review report on financial statements) if certain criteria are met.

The general rule says that an accountant must at least compile financial statements and attach a compilation report if he or she has submitted the financial statements. The definition of *submission* has evolved little since 1979 and is based on the actions of the CPA rather than the ultimate use of the financial statements. For example, regardless of whether financial statements are to be used by a third party or retained for internal use, the reporting requirements are the same.

Since 1979, a series of interpretations exempted certain activities from the applications of SSARS No. 1. However, the general consensus among commentators continues to be that the existing exemptions are outdated and fall well short of the changes needed to keep current with technological changes and the demands of the marketplace. Required was either a revision of the definition of submission or additional exemptions to SSARS No. 1. Consistent criticisms presented to the ARSC continued to focus around the general theme that the definition of submission is application driven instead of use driven—whether one is required to compile financial statements is based on the actions of the CPA rather than whether the financial statements are intended for management-use only or use by a third party.

Consider the following general comments typically made by practitioners and published by the ARSC:

- Many clients want "shortcut" financial statements for use during interim periods and are not willing to pay for a formal set of GAAP or OCBOA financial statements if those statements are intended for management-use only.
- Much client software does not have the mechanisms that permit the CPA to issue a compilation report from the client's office. The result is that the CPA must return to the office to reformat and formalize the financial statements, which is more costly to the client.
- All compilation engagements are subject to peer review. There is still the perception that additional work must be done to comply with peer review.

MODULE 2 — CHAPTER 4 — Compilation and Review Issues

> **EXAMPLE**
>
> Some programs still do not allow for a footer for *See Accountant's Compilation Report,* which is required by SSARS No. 1. Further, the client's financial statement format may not be in accordance with GAAP or OCBOA, yet GAAP or OCBOA statements are required under SSARS No. 1.

ARSC Timeline

From 1995 to 1999, the Accounting and Review Services Committee (ARSC) of the AICPA considered several options that are noted on the following timeline.

1995 to 1997: First Stop—Assembly Statement Considered. The debate over alternative levels of service started in September 1995, when the *Accounting and Review Services Committee* (ARSC) issued an exposure draft of a proposed SSARS (originally earmarked as SSARS No. 8), entitled Assembly of Financial Statements for Internal-Use Only. The purpose of this statement was to introduce a new, lower level of service called an assembly, which would have been positioned below a compilation engagement.

Essentially, the proposed statement would have permitted CPAs to prepare financial statements for internal use by the client without having to comply with the compilation and review standards found in SSARS No. 1. Meaning, the reporting and disclosure rules as well as compliance with GAAP would not have applied. It would have also restricted the assembly report to internal use by the client and would have confirmed this restriction in a required written engagement letter.

A record-breaking 500 letters of comments were received in response to the proposed statement, many of which were polarized on the issue, making this proposed statement difficult to pass.

1997 to 1998: Second Stop—Plain-Paper Engagement Considered. In August 1997, the ARSC held a public hearing in Rosemont, Illinois, to consider the future of the assembly statement and to consider a second option, a plain-paper engagement. In addition, the ARSC considered other solutions to simplifying the reporting process including implementing an exemption from SSARSs for certain activities.

With respect to plain-paper financial statements, the ARSC addressed certain specific issues such as: Should CPAs be permitted to issue plain-paper financial statements, that is, statements that a CPA does not report on that may be circulated to clients and others? Such statements would have to be issued without the CPA's identity being disclosed.

At the August 1997 hearing, nineteen speakers participated, all with diversified views of the issues at hand. The majority opposed a plain-paper engagement.

In October 1997, the ARSC met to discuss the views received from the August 1997 public hearing to determine the next course of action. Decisions made at the October 1997 meeting included official withdraw of the assembly statement from the docket, as well as elimination of the plain-paper financial statement engagement from further consideration. Other options for providing more flexibility in conducting compilation engagements were also considered.

1998 to 1999: Third Stop—Other Alternatives to Assembly and Plain-Paper. On April 20, 1998, the ARSC met to consider other options to simplify the reporting process, such as modifying SSARS No. 1 to exempt certain activities from the compilation requirements.

The ARSC voted to issue three new exposure drafts that would provide relief from the definition of submission for certain activities, exempted financial statements included in a business valuation from the application of the SSARSs, and closed a loophole in which a CPA, who is part of management, would be precluded from issuing compiled financial statements. To date only the exposure draft on business valuations is under serious consideration, as further discussed next.

STUDY QUESTION

> **1.** The ARSC developed modifications to SSARS No. 1 to simplify the reporting process for businesses. *True or False?*

SSARS NO. 8, *AMENDMENT TO STATEMENT ON STANDARDS FOR ACCOUNTING AND REVIEW SERVICES NO. 1, COMPILATION AND REVIEW OF FINANCIAL STATEMENTS*

On December 31, 1999, the ARSC concluded its simplification campaign by issuing an exposure draft entitled *Amendment to Statement on Standards for Accounting and Review Services 1, Compilation and Review of Financial Statements.* This proposed statement had a comment deadline of June 9, 2000, resulting in approximately 80 letters of comment. In general, the letters of comment were in favor of the proposed statement.

In August 2000, the ARSC voted to issue the exposure draft, with some modifications, as final statement, SSARS No. 8. SSARS No. 8 is effective for financial statements submitted after December 31, 2000.

In October 2000 the ARSC also issued *Practical Guidance for Implementing SSARS 8,* a nonauthoritative practice aid that is designed to assist CPAs with implementing SSARS No. 8.

What Does SSARS No. 8 Do?

The new statement makes two fundamental changes to SSARS No. 1:
- It changes the definition of *submission* presently used in SSARS No. 1.

MODULE 2 — CHAPTER 4 — Compilation and Review Issues   **73**

- It introduces new, management-use only financial statements as an option when compiled financial statements are not expected to be issued to any third parties. The management-use only financial statements consist of a compilation engagement without a report.

Change in the Definition of *Submission*

Presently, SSARS No. 1 has a general standard in deciding whether an accountant must compile financial statements.

Existing General Rule

The following compilation requirement applied under the SSARS No. 1 general standard:

> An accountant must at least compile financial statements and issue a compilation report if he or she has *submitted financial statements.* If he or she has not submitted financial statements, a compilation report is not required.

The general rule of submission is important to understanding because its impact extends well beyond the mere inconvenience of having to attach a compilation report to a set of financial statements. If an accountant submits financial statements, he or she is brought under the requirements of SSARS No. 1, including having to comply with the performance requirements of SSARS No. 1 (e.g., have a level of knowledge about the industry, general understanding of the entity's transactions, etc.).

Further, once an engagement is covered by SSARS No. 1, it is subject to peer review, and there is the risk of litigation in the event there is fraud or a going concern problem. Thus, the definition of submission is critical because if one avoids it, he or she is outside the realm of SSARS No. 1 and all the additional requirements that come with it.

Existing Pre-2001 Definition of *Submission*

Submission is presently defined under SSARS No. 1 as presenting to a client or others *financial statements* that the accountant has either:
- Generated, manually or through use of computer software
- Modified by materially changing account classification, amounts, or disclosures directly on client-prepared financial statements

The definition focuses on the accountant's involvement with a client's financial statements, and *not* with its trial balance. Therefore, the preparation of a trial balance and not a financial statement is not covered by the definition of submission and does not bring the accountant under compliance requirements for the SSARS No. 1 compilation rules.

Since its inception, the definition of *submission* has been ambiguous and outdated. The definition has included two terms that have been difficult for practitioners to understand and apply in practice: *generate* and *modified … directly.*

TOP AUDITING ISSUES FOR 2005 CPE COURSE

What is the definition of *generate* in a computer environment? Is the person who prints out the statements or the one who views the financial statements on the computer terminal the one who generates them?

The following was published in the AICPA's *Compilation and Review Alert* a few years ago and illustrates the challenge that has existed in applying this definition in practice.

> **EXAMPLE**
>
> An accountant enters adjustments directly into the client's general ledger using the client's computer, prints out the adjusted financial statements, and takes the statements with him or her without giving the financial statements to the client.
>
> The client does have the ability to access the adjusted financial statements by viewing them on the computer monitor or by printing them after the accountant leaves.

Generating the Financial Statements

The conclusion in the *Compilation and Review Alert* is that, by creating the financial statements in the client's computer, the accountant has, in effect, *generated* them. Despite the fact that the accountant did not present the statements directly to the client, he or she has made the statements available to the client. In effect, the client can easily print out statements at any time without the assistance of the accountant. This example demonstrates the confusion over the existing definition of *submission* because the term *generate* is ambiguous.

The second section of the existing definition is just as confusing:

> Modified by *materially* changing account classifications, amounts, or disclosures *directly* on client-prepared financial statements.

Consider the following questions as they relate to the second part of the definition:

- What is the threshold of *materially?* If the accountant makes one or two adjusting entries, has he or she materially modified the financial statements?
- What is meant by *directly?* What if modifications are done "indirectly" through use of the client's bookkeeper—has the accountant submitted financial statements?

Another example published by the *Compilation and Review Alert* illustrates the continued confusion with this part of the definition.

> **EXAMPLE**
>
> On a separate sheet of paper, an accountant prepares adjusting entries for the client. The client posts the entries to the financial statements and sends adjusted statements to the accountant for review.

Conclusion of the *Compilation and Review Alert*

The accountant has not submitted financial statements because the client, not the accountant, *directly modified* the client-prepared financial statements by posting the adjusting entries. The accountant indirectly modified the financial statements. Thus, under the existing rules, the accountant is exempt from the requirements of SSARS No. 1 and is not required to compile the financial statements.

Clearly, in this example, the accountant's involvement in the preparation of the financial statements is the same regardless of whether he or she recorded the adjusting entries directly or indirectly into the client's computer system. Yet, the existing SSARS No. 1 definition provides a different conclusion depending on whether the accountant directly or indirectly modifies the financial statements.

SSARS No. 8. Post-2000 Definition of *Submission*

SSARS No. 8 changed the existing definition of submission effective for financial statements submitted after December 31, 2000. Paragraph No. 4 of SSARS No. 8 provides the following new definition of *submission:*

> *Presenting* to a client or third parties financial statements that the accountant has *prepared* either manually or through the use of computer software.

The new definition of *submission* eliminates the concepts of *generate, modify ... directly,* and removes the *materiality* threshold altogether from the definition. Instead, it focuses on whether the accountant *prepared* the financial statements. The result is that the newer definition may clear up much of the confusion surrounding the degree of the accountant's involvement in the financial statements to come under the definition of submission under SSARS No. 1 (as modified by SSARS No. 8). The definition of *submission* has two elements that must be met:

- First, the CPA must *prepare* the financial statements, either manually or through the use of computer software.
- Second, the CPA must *present* the financial statements to the client or third party.

If both of these two elements are not satisfied, the submission threshold is not met and SSARS No. 1 is not applicable to the engagement.

The Meaning of *Prepare*

SSARS No. 8 does not define *prepare,* and the ARSC has no intention of providing formal guidance on this definition in the near future. Therefore, as the newer statement is applied, judgment will be required in determining whether a CPA has, in fact, prepared financial statements.

The definition of *prepare* as used in everyday English, according to *The American Heritage Dictionary*, is:

To put together or make by combining various elements or ingredients; manufacture; compound.

The definition suggests that the person who prepares something is actively involved in the process of putting together elements similar to being the creator of a product. Also, in preparing a product, a preparer is the primary individual involved in the process of developing the product, not just assisting in the process.

Applying this logic to the preparation of financial statements in the context of the new SSARS No. 8 definition, in order to prepare financial statements, the CPA must be the primary developer of the financial statements. That is, the CPA must be the principal person who places the data into a financial statement format. Merely making a few adjusting entries to a trial balance and reviewing the client's computer-generated financial statements may not be enough to place the CPA above the preparer threshold.

Although not authoritative, the AICPA's *Practical Guidance for Implementing SSARS 8* (The Guide) supports these conclusions and further states that the CPA should consider the difference between performing bookkeeping services (e.g., adjustments, corrections, and accruals), and the actual preparation of financial statements. The Guide states:

To *prepare* financial statements, you must use your *knowledge, education, and experience* to create financial statements that would not have existed otherwise.

The Guide provides two examples modified here to help bring clarity to this situation.

EXAMPLE

A client's bookkeeper prepares financial statements that are "pretty good" to begin with and the accountant merely "tweaks a couple of things."

Conclusion: The accountant probably has not prepared financial statements.

EXAMPLE

The client gives the accountant an unadjusted trial balance and the accountant makes all the adjustments necessary to convert the information into financial statements, including assigning general ledger accounts to individual financial statement lines.

Conclusion: The accountant probably has prepared financial statements. The key is whether the accountant has used his or her knowledge, education, and experience to create financial statements that would not have existed otherwise. In this case, the statements would not have existed if the accountant had not created them.

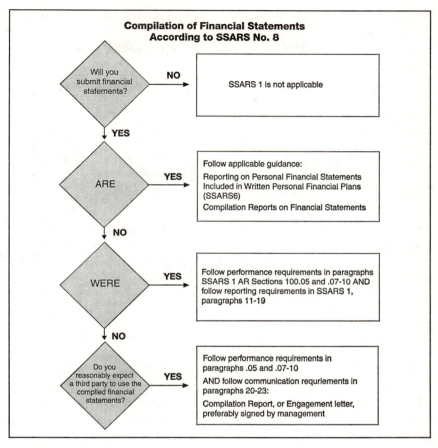

Meaning of *Present:*
SSARS No. 8 Does Not Define the Term *Presenting*

Several years ago, the AICPA published a scenario in the *Compilation and Review Alert* that dealt with the question of whether financial statements had been presented to the client merely by giving the client the ability to print out his or her own financial statements through use of the diskette. The conclusion reached in that scenario was that by giving the client the ability to access the financial statements on the diskette, it was treated the same as if the CPA had directly given the client a paper copy of the financial statements. The same logic applies when financial statements are delivered by any nonpaper medium (e.g. diskette, or electronically), the financial statements have been presented to the client.

Moreover, there is no requirement to supplement financial statements delivered by diskette or electronically with a hard copy on paper. Clearly, delivering financial statements in a paper form is considered presenting financial statements. The following is a summary of the modes of communication that generally satisfy the definition of *presenting*, such as one of the following:

TOP AUDITING ISSUES FOR 2005 CPE COURSE

- Handing or mailing a set of paper financial statements to the client or third party
- Giving the financial statements to the client or third party on a diskette or CD-ROM
- Sending the financial statements to the client or third party electronically

> **EXAMPLE**
>
> The CPA mails the client a diskette that has the financial statement on it in a Word® or PDF® format. The client or third party prints out the financial statements from the diskette. The financial statements have been presented to the client or third party.

Appendix A-1 contains a chart that presents scenarios adapted from those included in the SSARS No. 8 Guide to illustrate how these rules apply. The scenarios are not authoritative but should clarify the parameters that should be followed in applying SSARS No. 8.

STUDY QUESTIONS

> **2.** SSARS No. 8 changes the definition of submission presently used in SSARS No. 1. *True or False?*
>
> **3.** The definition of submission has three elements. *True or False?*
>
> **4.** To prepare financial statements, the accountant must use expertise to create financial statements that would not have existed. *True or False?*
>
> **5.** For management-use financial statements, the modes of communication that generally satisfy the definition of present include giving a client a trial balance. *True or False?*

FINANCIAL STATEMENTS GENERATED USING GENERAL LEDGER SOFTWARE

The previous scenarios illustrate the confusion that can exist in determining whether financial statements have been both prepared and presented to a client or third party.

Most accounting software packages have a financial statement feature embedded in the general ledger software component. As the CPA makes adjusting entries to the general ledger or trial balance, the financial statements for that period of time are also updated. In order to create financial statements, the CPA or client chooses selection criteria such as the range of dates for the financial statements, the basis of accounting (cash versus accrual), and financial statement format (comparative, use of percentages, etc.). This scenario is commonplace for CPAs who update their clients' databases using programs such as QuickBooks® and One-Write Plus®.

Issues for Accountants Using General Ledger Software

Two major questions need to be answered in connection with the accountant's involvement with financial statements in this situation:

- Is the CPA who merely updates a trial balance or general ledger also considered the preparer of financial statements because the financial statements are also updated?
- If the CPA presents an updated general ledger to the client that also has the financial statements embedded in the software, has the CPA also presented the financial statements to the client?

The following examples apply the prepare-and-present criteria to determine whether SSARS No. 8 applies.

EXAMPLE

A CPA updates a client's database (general ledger) by making a series of adjusting and correcting entries to the general ledger. Assume that the financial statements are already linked to the general ledger so that financial statements can be printed with the click of an icon. Has the CPA prepared financial statements because the financial statements are updated as the general ledger is updated?

Conclusion: No. According to the ARSC *Practice Guidance for Implementing SSARS 8,* in order to prepare financial statements, the CPA must use his or her knowledge, education, and experience to create the financial statements. Moreover, there are no financial statements because the CPA has taken no action to create them. For example, with QuickBooks®, the CPA must select certain criteria such as dates, the basis of accounting, format, etc. to create financial statements from the general ledger database.

EXAMPLE

The financial statements are printed out and delivered to the client in a paper form.

Conclusion: If the financial statements are printed out by the CPA and delivered to the client, they have been presented even if the CPA did not prepare the financial statements.

EXAMPLE

The entire client database file (including the embedded financial statements) is delivered to the client on a diskette. In order to create financial statements from the database, the client must choose certain selection criteria such as dates, format and basis of accounting.

80   TOP AUDITING ISSUES FOR 2005 CPE COURSE

> **Conclusion:** If the entire database (including the embedded financial statements) is presented to the client on a diskette, only the database has been presented, not the financial statements. The reason is because within the database there is only the potential to create financial statements. In order to create financial statements, the client would have to select certain criteria (e.g., dates, basis of accounting, etc.) from the database once the client receives the database from the CPA. Therefore, the CPA has presented to the client a database that has the potential to create financial statements, but not financial statements themselves. This is the case regardless of whether the database is delivered on a diskette or via modem.

EXAMPLE

The entire client database file (including the embedded financial statements) is delivered to the client electronically via modem. In order to create financial statements from the database, the client must choose certain selection criteria such as dates, format, and basis of accounting.

Conclusion: As in the previous example, the database, not the financial statements, has been presented, regardless of whether the database (and embedded financial statements) is presented in the form of a diskette or electronically via modem.

STUDY QUESTION

> **6.** Under SSARS No. 8, if a CPA prints out financial statements he or she did not prepare and then delivers them to the client, they have not been presented. *True or False?*

Presenting Financial Statements for a Specific Period in a Microsoft Word® or Excel® File

In this case, the CPA is presenting a specific set of financial statements for a particular period of time. The financial statements have already been created by the CPA, with the client not required to choose any selection criteria in order to create financial statements from the file. The client only has to print out the financial statements. Thus, the CPA has presented financial statements to the client in the form of either a diskette or electronic file, which is treated the same as if presented in a paper form. See Appendix A-2 for a sample engagement letter with protective language for when a CPA performs bookkeeping services and delivers a file to the client electronically with embedded financial statements.

The SSARS No. 8 Loophole: The CPA Who Prepares But Does Not Present Financial Statements

The definitions of *prepare* and *present* in the previous four examples include a loophole that exists whereby a CPA can prepare financial statements and deliver them to a client, while still avoiding any reporting requirements related to the financial statements in the hands of the client under SSARS No. 1.

> **EXAMPLE**
>
> Harold Johansen, CPA, is hired by Abraham Bernstein of Bernstein Concrete Corporation to perform monthly bookkeeping work. Each month Bernstein sends the general ledger file to the Johansen electronically. He adjusts the general ledger and prepares financial statements by linking the general ledger accounts to the financial statement lines and by revising account classifications (e.g., current versus long-term on the balance sheet, expense classifications on the income statement).
>
> Once Johansen has adjusted the general ledger and prepared the financial statements, he sends the entire file to Bernstein electronically. From the adjusted file, Bernstein creates financial statements for the month by selecting that month's financial statement date range, the basis of accounting, and the format, then prints out the financial statements. Bernstein sends the financial statements to third parties without any report from CPA Johansen.
>
> **Conclusion:** This is the classic example of a loophole under SSARS No. 8. The CPA has *prepared* the financial statements and has *presented the general ledger file* to the client that includes the potential for the client to create financial statements for the same timeframe for which the CPA prepared the financial statements. But because the client must select financial statement criteria (including the dates, etc.), Johansen has *not presented financial statements* to the client. Thus, Johansen has prepared, but not presented, the financial statements to Bernstein. The definition of submission of financial statements has not been satisfied and Johansen has no reporting responsibility even though a third party may receive those same statements that CPA Johansen prepared.

> **OBSERVATION**
>
> Obviously the intent here is not to encourage a CPA to use this loophole, which could result in a third party receiving financial statements prepared by a CPA with no accompanying report. Yet, SSARS No. 8 provides no remedy for this situation. The fact is, technology has created a scenario for which there may be no easy solution. A CPA should be extremely cautious to ensure that a client does not receive financial statements with no report when the CPA has prepared the statements.

In any circumstance in which a CPA sends a general ledger to a client on diskette/CD-ROM or electronically, the CPA may wish to include protective language in the engagement letter and any transmittal letter. The language should refer to the fact that the CPA has not *submitted* financial statements. Presumably, the CPA would perform bookkeeping services for the first eleven months of the year and then prepare financial statements for the year ended December 31, 20XX, using a new engagement letter.

> **NOTE**
>
> The sample engagement letter should include the wording that *the CPA has not submitted financial statements in accordance with SSARS No. 8.* By stating that he or she has not *submitted* financial statements, the CPA is stating that he or she has not both prepared and presented financial statements. The CPA could prepare but not present financial statements, and still be protected using the submitted threshold language. Further, in both letters, the CPA references bookkeeping services and the adjusted general ledger, but makes no suggestion that he or she has prepared or presented financial statements.

Summary of SSARS No. 8 Changes to the Definition of *Submission*

In summary, SSARS No. 8 changes the definition of *submission* in SSARS No. 1. In deciding whether a CPA has submitted financial statements, a CPA should assess each scenario in terms of whether he or she has satisfied the two criteria required under the submission definition. Has he or she *prepared and presented* financial statements to the client or third parties? In looking at each of the criteria, the following guidelines from *ARSC Practical Guidance for Implementing SSARS 8* may be helpful to consider:

- Preparing financial statements:
    - Preparing financial statements involves use of the CPA's knowledge, education, and experience to create financial statements that would not have existed otherwise. Preparing involves much more than merely updating or "cleaning up" already linked financial statements through making adjusting entries to a trial balance.
    - If a CPA does not perform the function of linking the general ledger accounts or assign account classifications to the financial statement lines, he or she probably has not prepared financial statements.
    - There is no materiality threshold in determining whether financial statements have been prepared. If the CPA uses his or her knowledge, education, and experience to create a portion of financial statements (including the accompanying footnotes) that would not have existed otherwise, the CPA has prepared the financial statements.

MODULE 2 — CHAPTER 4 — Compilation and Review Issues **83**

- Presenting financial statements:
  - Financial statements, and not a trial balance or general ledger, must be presented to the client or third party in order for there to be a submission under SSARS No. 1.
  - Delivering financial statements by different modes, such as paper, diskette or electronically, to a client is considered presenting financial statements.
  - If a client database (general ledger) file is delivered to a client that has financial statements embedded, the financial statements have not been presented to the client if the client is required to choose certain selection criteria (e.g., dates, format, basis of accounting, etc.) to create financial statements.

Part 2 of SSARS No. 8: Introduction of the Management-Use Only Financial Statement

The second significant change in SSARS No. 8 is that it introduces management-use only financial statements as an alternative to the traditional compilation report engagement. The new statement permits a CPA who compiles financial statements to issue management-use only financial statements if the financial statements are not expected to be used by a third party (e.g., they are management-use only).

This section summarizes requirements for the issuance of management-use only financial statements. Section 4 of the chapter describes the rules for issuing management-use only financial statements.

SSARS No. 8 amends SSARS No. 1 by providing communication and performance requirements for unaudited financial statements submitted to a client that are not expected to be used by a third party (e.g., management-use only financial statements).

> **EXAMPLE**
>
> A CPA is hired to perform a management-use only financial statement engagement for each of the first eleven months of the fiscal year, and then to prepared a twelve-month compilation for issuance to third parties.

General Rule in SSARS No. 1

A CPA should not submit unaudited financial statements of a nonpublic entity to his or her client or a third party unless, as a minimum, he or she complies with the provisions of SSARS No. 1 (as amended by SSARS No. 8) applicable to a compilation engagement.

If a CPA submits financial statements to a client (presents and prepares), the options available depend on the expected ultimate use of the financial statements:

- If the CPA is engaged to report on compiled financial statements or submits financial statements to the client that are, or reasonably might be, expected to be used by a third party, a compilation report must be issued.

- If the CPA submits financial statements to a client that are not reasonably expected to be used by a third party, the CPA can choose to issue a compilation report in accordance with SSARS No. 1, or not issue a compilation report and instead follow the rules for issuing management -use only financial statements.

STUDY QUESTION

> **7.** A significant change in SSARS No. 8 is that it introduces management-use only financial statements as an alternative to a traditional compilation report engagement. *True or False?*

Special Rules for the Engagement Letter for Management-use Only Financial Statements

Unlike a traditional compilation engagement, a management-use only financial statement engagement requires that an engagement letter be obtained to document the understanding between the parties. Although a letter is required, it does not have to be signed by management. If not signed, it is essentially a transmittal letter from the CPA to management, resulting in no evidence that management agreed to or even received the letter. The Guide deals with several important issues in connection with the letter.

- **Issue 1: Can the Letter Cover Multiple Periods?** The Guide states that the letter can cover more than one period, but should be updated *at least annually* to ensure that changes in the client relationship over time have been properly documented.

> **EXAMPLE**
>
> A CPA wishes to prepare management-use only financial statements for a client for each of the twelve months in the fiscal year. Because the CPA expects to continue with this service into the following year, she decides to issue one management-use only engagement letter that covers the financial statements for each month for the next 24 months.
>
> **Conclusion:** Although the engagement letter can cover more than one period, the AICPA Guide recommends that the letter be updated at least annually. Therefore, it is advisable that the CPA issue one engagement letter covering twelve months and then issue another letter covering the next twelve months.

- **Issue 2: Can the Letter Cover Multiple Services?** It is acceptable to add additional services to the engagement letter such as tax, payroll, and bookkeeping services. However, it is not advisable to include both management-use only and traditional compilation engagements in the *same* letter. If the client needs compiled financial statements for third-

MODULE 2 — CHAPTER 4 — Compilation and Review Issues   **85**

party use, the CPA should issue a separate engagement letter to cover that engagement, thereby ensuring that there is no misunderstanding about the two kinds of engagements.

> **EXAMPLE**
>
> A CPA is hired to perform a management-use only financial statement engagement for each of the first eleven months of the fiscal year, and then to prepared a twelve-month compilation for issuance to third parties.
>
> **Conclusion:** The CPA should obtain two engagement letters. The first letter would cover each of the eleven management-use only financial statements. The second letter would be issued to cover the twelve-month compilation for third-party use. It is advisable not to include both engagements in the same engagement letter.

- **Issue 3: If the Engagement Letter Is Not Signed by Management, How Should the CPA Document That the Letter Was Sent to the Client?** Although management is not required to sign the engagement letter in a management-use only engagement, it is clearly advisable for management to do so to avoid any misunderstandings. Assuming management is not signing the letter, the CPA may wish to send the letter by *certified mail, by facsimile, or via e-mail* to provide proof of receipt. In fact, it is more prudent to send the letter by facsimile or as an e-mail attachment, rather than by certified mail.

The reasons are twofold. First, sending anything by certified mail may be misconstrued by the client as being legal in nature. Second, a document sent by facsimile or as an e-mail attachment provides a better paper trail and stronger evidence since the CPA can prove that the engagement letter was received by the client. With certified mail, the CPA can only prove that a document was received by the client but cannot prove which document was received.

> **EXAMPLE**
>
> A CPA is hired to prepare management-use only financial statements for a client. The CPA decides to send an engagement letter without requiring the client's signature, sending it certified mail, receipt requested.
>
> Two years later, the CPA is sued by a third party who relied on the financial statements. The CPA asserts that the client was fully aware that the financial statements were restricted from issuance to third parties as evidenced in the engagement letter. The client asserts that he never signed or saw an engagement letter.
>
> The CPA pulls out the certified mail receipt that shows that a package was received by the client on a certain date. The client asserts that the certified mail must have included some tax letter or something else not important.

Conclusion: The CPA has a real problem in proving that the package received by the client included the engagement letter. All the CPA can prove is that a package was received by the client on a certain date, the contents of which cannot be proved. Without evidence of the letter being received, the CPA may have difficulty proving that the client knew about the restriction of use by third parties, thereby curtailing the CPA's claim against the client. Had the CPA sent a copy of the letter via e-mail or facsimile, he would have had evidence that the specific engagement letter was received by the client.

The moral of this example is, if an accountant decides not to obtain a client's signature on a management-use only engagement letter, he or she should make sure to send a copy of the letter by facsimile or e-mail or another mode of communication by which the accountant can prove the client received that specific letter.

Sample Engagement Letters: Internal Use Financial Statements

Engagement letters are tailored for both options: when management signs the engagement letter and when it does not.

> **OBSERVATION**
>
> If an engagement letter is sent without obtaining a client's signature, the CPA should send it either before or at the same time the financial statements are submitted. Most likely, this letter would accompany the financial statements as a transmittal letter with the option of including additional information such as comments on the tax returns.

> **OBSERVATION**
>
> It is rare for management-use only financial statements to have supplementary information. Typically, the CPA develops management-use only financial statements from the client's general ledger program. The statements are printed out in the format offered by the client's program, which does not usually include a separate schedule of operating expenses or other supplementary information. Instead, all operating expenses will probably be presented directly on the income statement.

Advantages of the Management-use Only Financial Statement and Its Proper Use

Management-use only financial statements are useful only for certain clients. To consider issuing these statements, the CPA should consider several key factors:

- **The third-party need for financial information:** Do the client's third parties require financial statements to be issued on a regular basis?

MODULE 2 — CHAPTER 4 — Compilation and Review Issues **87**

- **Cost vs. benefits associated with the statements:** Are there significant savings to be derived from issuing management-use only financial statements versus conducting a traditional compilation engagement?

> **OBSERVATION**
>
> The CPA might also wish to consider whether he or she can make the engagement more profitable by converting to management-use only financial statements and retaining the existing fee. That is, charge the same amount for the engagement and reduce the time required to complete it. By converting to management-use only financial statements, the CPA may be able to shift a marginally profitable engagement into a more profitable one.

- **The integrity of management:** Can the accountant rely on management's representation to restrict the use of the financial statements to management only?
- **Risk management consideration:** Is the accountant willing to accept the additional risk associated with a management-use only engagement whereby an unauthorized third party receives and relies on the financial statements?

STUDY QUESTION

> **8.** Two factors considered in creating management-use only financial statements include:
> - **a.** Whether the engagement is less profitable and the lower risk of management-use only statements is justified.
> - **b.** Whether the client's third parties require regularly issued financial statements and issuing management-use only financial statements offers cost savings.
> - **c.** Whether such an engagement is a one-time only contract and whether the number of third parties using the statements will increase over time.

Applying Management-use Only Financial Statements in Nontraditional Business Situations: Personal Financial Statements, Eldercare Services, Not-for-Profit or Governmental Entities, and Trusts or Estates

SSARS No. 8 stipulates that management-use only financial statements may be issued provided they are not expected to be used by third parties. Differentiating third parties and eligible members of management in a business setting is not difficult compared with other situations, such as not-for-profit entities or Eldercare.

In such situations, the CPA may be precluded from using management-use only financial statements solely because the statements must be distributed to third parties by law or contract. The AICPA Guide includes a table for assessing the options available for such an engagement.

Options for Management-use Only Reporting for Specialized Engagements

Engagement	Is a Management-use Only Compilation Allowed?	Comments
Personal financial statements	Yes, provided the financial statements are restricted to management use only.	In connection with personal financial statements, only the individual whose financial statements are presented would be considered management. The individual's advisors, such as the attorney, financial planner, or banker, would be considered third parties.
Eldercare services	Yes, provided the financial statements are restricted to management use only.	The person(s) responsible for achieving the objectives of the individual and having the authority to establish policies and make decisions would be considered management. Management may consist of the person for whom Eldercare services are performed, or that person's family member(s) who are responsible for the affairs of the elderly person. The individual's advisors, such as the attorney, financial planner, or banker would probably be considered third parties unless one of them is responsible for the affairs of the elderly person.
Not-for-profit organizations	Yes, provided the financial statements are restricted to management use only. However, if the organization's financial statements are subject to public examination, then management-use only financial statements would not be appropriate. Management cannot legally agree to restrict the financial statements to management's use only.	Like for-profit organizations, management would consist of those individuals who are generally knowledgeable and understand the nature of the procedures applied and the basis of accounting and assumptions used in the preparation of the financial statements. Generally, the not-for-profit organization's board of directors would not be considered eligible to receive management-use only financial statements.
Trusts and estates	Yes, provided the financial statements are restricted to management use only.	Generally, the trustee or executor, but not the beneficiaries, would be considered eligible management.
Governmental entities	No. Financial information of governmental entities is subject to public examination. Management cannot legally agree to restrict the financial statements to management's use.	Management-use financial statements cannot be used for governmental entities.

Source: AICPA's Practical Guide for Implementing SSARS 8, *modified and expanded by Steve Fustolo.*

Saving Time on the Management-Use Only Financial Statements

To assess the overall impact of preparing management-use only financial statements, practitioners may question whether the statements provide significant benefit to a CPA in terms of time savings. Management-use only financial statements have a limited benefit when monthly or quarterly financial statements will be issued and the statements may have GAAP departures. In this case, the CPA could obtain an engagement letter covering each of the twelve months to be compiled during the year and issue management-use only financial statements each month at the client's office.

> **EXAMPLE**
>
> The client of a CPA engages the CPA to visit his office each month, adjust the trial balance, make correcting entries, and issue financial statements out of Quickbooks®.
>
> The client uses the monthly financial statements for internal use only during each of the first eleven months of the year. At year-end, the CPA prepares twelve-month compiled financial statements that are distributed by the client to a few suppliers.
>
> **Conclusion:** For each of the eleven months during the year, the CPA could issue management-use only financial statements. Then, at the end of the year, the CPA could issue one compilation report for distribution to the suppliers.

Logistically, the CPA could obtain one management-use only engagement letter covering the eleven months and signed by the client. Then, the CPA could visit the client's office each month, correct the trial balance, and, before leaving, print out financial statements for the client. Those statements would not have to be accompanied by a compilation report according to SSARS No. 8. The only item left would be the *Restricted for Management Use Only* legend on each page. This legend could be obtained either by adding a footer to the Quick Books® financial statements or, by using a stamp that the CPA could take to the client's office.

The overall benefit of this management-use only engagement is that the CPA can complete the entire engagement at the client's office without having to return to his or her office to prepare compiled financial statements. Further, with management-use statements, the CPA does not have to worry about compliance with GAAP.

> **EXAMPLE**
>
> If the client does not customarily record an allowance for bad debts or depreciation, the CPA does not have to be concerned that there are GAAP departures because management-use-only financial statements, by definition, can have material GAAP or OCBOA departures as long as language is included in the engagement letter noting that GAAP or OCBOA departures exist.

TOP AUDITING ISSUES FOR 2005 CPE COURSE

A second scenario when the management-use only statements may benefit a CPA is where the CPA's practice is primarily a tax practice, and compiled financial statements (without footnotes and the statement of cash flows) are issued and sent to the client along with the business tax returns. In this situation, the CPA could issue management-use only financial statements that accompany the tax return.

An engagement letter not requiring the client's signature could be sent that is converted into a transmittal letter that covers not only the management-use only engagement, but other matters such as tax planning and tax return filing instructions.

EXAMPLE

Freddie Johnson, CPA, has a very active tax practice. When Freddie sends out corporate or partnership tax returns, he typically also prints out a balance sheet, income statement, and operating expense schedule, and issues a compilation report with no footnotes and cash flows statement.

The financial statements are sent out with the tax return. Freddie doesn't believe in issuing engagement letters for his compilation engagements because his clients hire him principally to prepare the tax returns, not the financial statements.

Unfortunately, Freddie has to go through peer review because he issues compilation reports. He would welcome the opportunity to be exempt from peer review.

Conclusion: Freddie could be a good candidate for the management-use only financial statements. Instead of sending out compiled financial statements, he would prepare management-use only financial statements and send them to the client along with the corporate or partnership tax returns. An engagement letter would be sent as a transmittal letter accompanying the tax return and the management-use only financial statements, and would not be signed by the client.

An engagement letter could include both instructions for filing returns and fulfill Freddie's management-use only financial statement engagement. See Appendix A-3 for a sample of an engagement letter with language for these situations.

OBSERVATION

If an engagement letter is sent without obtaining a client's signature, the CPA should send it either before or at the same time the financial statements are submitted. Most likely, this letter would accompany the financial statements as a transmittal letter with additional information included in it, including perhaps comments on the tax returns, etc. If the letter does accompany the tax return and/or financial statements, the language in the letter must be changed to the past tense, as noted in bold in the sample.

RULES FOR ISSUING MANAGEMENT-USE ONLY FINANCIAL STATEMENTS

SSARS No. 8 Rules

SSARS No. 8 requires that the following rules be followed in order for a CPA to issue management-use only financial statements.

Rule 1: A management-use only financial statement engagement is a compilation engagement without a report.

Rule 2: Because there is no compilation report, the CPA must document a written understanding with the client using an engagement letter, preferably signed by management, regarding the services to be performed and limitations on the use of the financial statements.

The statement recommends, but does not require, that the engagement letter be signed by management. If not signed, the letter is similar to a transmittal letter. Therefore, the CPA can use two types of engagement letters, samples of which can be found in Appendix A-4 and A-5:

- Traditional engagement letter signed by management, documenting an understanding regarding the services to be performed and the limitations on the use of those financial statements
- Engagement letter not signed by management, similar to a transmittal letter (sent either before the financial statements are issued or the letter accompanies the financial statements as a transmittal letter)

> **OBSERVATION**
>
> Because a report is not issued in a management-use only engagement, many of the items that are customarily found in the traditional compilation report are instead presented in the engagement letter.

The ARSC received several letters of comment from AICPA members who believed that there should be a requirement, rather than an option, that the engagement letter be signed. Several members were concerned about the potential litigation that could result from not having a signed letter from a client confirming management's acceptance of the engagement. In fact, ARSC member, Richard Jones, qualified his assent by stating that he believed that the engagement letter should be signed by both the client and the CPA. The ARSC decided to recommend, rather than require, that the letter be signed by management so as to provide more flexibility in the use of the management-use only engagement. The ARSC's concern was that if the engagement letter had to be signed, many CPAs would consider that requirement to be too laborious to warrant using the management-use only statement.

TOP AUDITING ISSUES FOR 2005 CPE COURSE

> **EXAMPLE**
>
> In a traditional compilation engagement, a CPA is required to establish an understanding of the engagement to be performed, but it does not have to be in writing. SSARS No. 8 applies a stricter standard to management-use only financial statements by requiring that an understanding be established in writing with the use of an engagement letter, regardless of whether it's signed by management.

Rule 3: Each page of the management-use only financial statements must include a restriction, such as one of the following samples:

Restricted for Management's Use Only

Solely for the Information and Use by the Management of XYZ Corporation and is not intended to be and should not be used by any other party

The AICPA's *Practical Guide for Implementing SSARS 8* (The Guide) states that other more descriptive legends may be used. Examples noted in the Guide include:

These financial statements are for use by management only and should not be relied upon by others. These statements may contain material departures from generally accepted accounting principles and the effects of those departures, if any, are not disclosed.

Restricted for Management-Use Only—Not for External Distribution.

The legend may be placed by any means, including using a financial statement footer in the software program. Most financial statement software packages, including QuickBooks® and One-Write Plus®, have the ability to place a footer on each page of the financial statements. Absent that option, the CPA could use a rubber stamp or simply write the legend manually on each page of the financial statements.

> **OBSERVATION**
>
> Several ARSC members wanted to make this legend optional rather than required. However the ARSC's legal counsel was concerned that third parties who inadvertently received the management-use only financial statements might not understand the scope of the engagement unless the management-use only legend was visible. Further, because most software packages now provide for a footer to be placed on each page of the financial statements, adding a legend to the financial statements is usually not difficult. Consequently, the ARSC decided to make the legend a requirement for management-use only financial statements.

MODULE 2 — CHAPTER 4 — Compilation and Review Issues

Rule 4: The issuance of management-use only financial statements is still a compilation engagement and must adhere to the performance requirements of SSARS No. 1. The performance requirements for a compilation engagement found in SSARS No. 1 are applicable to management-use only financial statements:

The performance requirements state that the CPA must:

- Establish an understanding with the entity about the services to be performed, preferably in writing. With respect to traditional compilation engagements, SSARS No. 1 states that the understanding should preferably be in writing. However, if a management-use only financial statement engagement is performed, the understanding *must be in writing,* preferably signed by the client.
- Possess a level of knowledge of the accounting principles and practices of the industry in which the entity operates. For example, the CPA should:
  - Understand accounting principles that are unique to the industry.
  - Possess a general understanding of the nature of the entity's business transactions, the form of the accounting records, the stated qualifications of accounting personnel, the accounting basis used, and the form and content of the financial statements.
  - Obtain additional or revised information if he or she becomes aware that information supplied by the client is incorrect.
  - Read the financial statements and consider whether they are free from obvious material errors. Errors include arithmetical or clerical mistakes, and the mistakes in the application of accounting principles, including inadequate disclosure.

> **OBSERVATION**
>
> Part of the debate among ARSC members was whether the management-use only financial statement engagement should be kept within the SSARSs or brought outside of them as a fourth level of service. As another option, the ARSC considered providing an exemption from SSARS No. 1 rather than as management-use only financial statements. The ARSC ultimately voted to approve the management-use only statements as a form of a compilation engagement so that the engagement would be covered under SSARS No 1, subject to the performance requirements of SSARS No. 1. By keeping the management-use financial statements within SSARS No. 1, CPA's would be required to maintain a certain level of work in conducting the engagement.

Rule 5: Material departures from GAAP or OCBOA are acceptable provided the engagement letter notes that there may be departures. The financial statements do not have to be prepared in accordance with GAAP or OCBOA.

TOP AUDITING ISSUES FOR 2005 CPE COURSE

The engagement letter should state that there are GAAP or OCBOA departures, but the letter need not identify the specific departures. Sample language to include in the engagement letter is:

Material departures from generally accepted accounting principles (GAAP) or other comprehensive basis of accounting (OCBOA) may exist and the effects of those departures, if any, on the financial statements may not be disclosed.

> **OBSERVATION**
>
> The sample engagement letter presented in Appendix D of SSARS No. 8 states, *"The CPA may wish to identify known departures"* from GAAP. However, there is no requirement to do so. Advisedly, the CPA should never list known departures and, instead, should merely include the standard language noted above that covers all GAAP departures. To identify certain known departures places the CPA in a position of being accused of not listing other GAAP departures, whether known or not.

Although the CPA is not required to identify GAAP departures in the engagement letter for management-use only financial statements, a similar option is not available when the CPA has GAAP departures and issues a compilation report on financial statements to be issued to third parties. Appendix A of SSARS No. 8 states that a generic statement in the compilation report that states that *"material departures from GAAP or OCBOA may exist and the effects may not be disclosed"* is not appropriate when a compilation report is issued and would be tantamount to expressing an adverse opinion on the financial statements taken as a whole.

Instead, if the financial statements are accompanied by a report, each known departure that would have a material effect on the financial statements must be either corrected or identified, along with the effect of the departure on the financial statements, if the effect is known. There is no limit on the number of departures that can exist. Following are common types of GAAP departures:

- Missing an allowance for bad debts
- Not netting prepaid interest and notes payable for presentation purposes
- Not recording the unrealized gain or loss on securities
- Presenting lines of credit as long-term on the balance sheet
- Not recording depreciation expense during an interim period
- Recording section 263A costs as part of the book inventory
- Not recording deferred income taxes

GAAP titles are not required. Any title that management understands is acceptable even if it is not a GAAP title.

MODULE 2 — CHAPTER 4 — Compilation and Review Issues

> **EXAMPLE**
>
> A CPA prepares a client's financial statements using QuickBooks®. The financial statement titles used by QuickBooks® are "Balance Sheet" and "Profit and Loss."
>
> **Conclusion:** Although Profit and Loss is not a typical GAAP title for an income statement, GAAP titles are not required for management-use only financial statements provided the client is familiar with the titles used.

How do GAAP departures interrelate with the requirement to have financial statements free from error? In management-use only financial statements, GAAP departures are acceptable provided there is a general reference to such departures in the engagement letter. There is no requirement to identify (list) specific GAAP departures.

Yet, SSARS No. 1 also states that the CPA is required to obtain additional or revised information if he or she becomes aware that information supplied by the client is incorrect. If management-use only financial statements have GAAP departures, the CPA is therefore aware that information supplied by the client is incorrect.

How do these two sections interrelate? Although not stated in SSARS No. 1, the CPA must consider the GAAP departures in the context of whether management is aware of such departures and the limitations such departures may place on the financial statements. That is, if the financial statements will be issued for management-use only, the fact that there are material errors may not be important because management is fully aware that such departures exist. The result is that the requirement that the CPA obtain additional information about such departures is generally moot where financial statements will be used for management-use only and management is aware of such departures.

A CPA can issue a single management-use only financial statement such as an income statement or balance sheet. Just as a CPA can issue a compilation report on a single statement such as an income statement or balance sheet, the same option is available for a management-use only financial statement. The engagement letter should cover only the single statement.

Rule 6: Disclosures are permitted but not required. Like regular compilations, disclosures are permitted, but not required. Generally, CPAs will prepare management-use only financial statements without notes because management does not need a full set of financial statements.

If disclosures are not included, the engagement letter should include the following language:

In addition, substantially all disclosures required by GAAP (or OCBOA, if applicable) may be omitted.

96 TOP AUDITING ISSUES FOR 2005 CPE COURSE

If both the statement of cash flows and substantially all disclosures are omitted, the engagement letter should include the following language:

> In addition, substantially all disclosures and the statement of cash flows required by GAAP (or OCBOA, if applicable) may be omitted.

If a statement of comprehensive income is required but not presented, the language changes as follows:

> In addition, substantially all disclosures and the statements of cash flows and comprehensive income required by GAAP (or OCBOA, if applicable) may be omitted.

Rule 7: Supplementary information must be identified. If supplementary information is presented (e.g., schedule of operating expenses), that information should be identified as supplementary information in the engagement letter. Sample language to be included in the engagement letter reads:

> The other data accompanying the financial statements in the schedule of operating expenses are presented only for supplementary analysis purposes and were compiled from information that is the representation of management, without audit or review, and we do not express an opinion or any other form of assurance on such data.

The same legend placed on the pages of the financial statements (e.g., *Restricted for Management Use Only*) should be placed on the pages of supplementary information.

OBSERVATION

Although supplementary information may be included in management-use only financial statements, it is not likely to be used for most of management-use engagements. The reason is because the CPA is likely to prepare financial statements using the client's financial statement format, which typically does not include supplementary information. A client's financial statements are likely to include a balance sheet and income statement, but not a separate schedule of operating expenses. Instead, the operating expenses will probably be included directly on the income statement with no need for a supplementary information schedule. In cases when supplementary information is included, the engagement letter must reference the information similar to the way a compilation report would reference it.

Rule 8: Management-use only financial statements are not reasonably expected to be used by a third party. If the accountant becomes aware that the financial statements have been distributed to third parties, he or she should discuss the situation with the client and request that the client have the statements returned. If the client does not comply with the request within a reasonable period of time, the accountant, preferably in

MODULE 2 — CHAPTER 4 — Compilation and Review Issues **97**

consultation with an attorney, should notify all known third parties that the financial statements are not intended for third-party use.

SSARS No. 8 defines third parties as all parties *except for members of management* who are generally knowledgeable and understand the nature of the procedures applied and the basis of accounting and assumptions used in the preparation of the financial statements.

If one looks at this definition, only certain members of management can receive management-use only financial statements. Those members comprise only individuals who are familiar with the procedures and basis of accounting and assumptions used to prepare financial statements—that is, individuals who are knowledgeable enough about the business function to be able to assess the financial information contained in the management-use only financial statements. In many organizations, this definition could apply to only a few employees, and in some case, not all of the owners are eligible to receive management-use financial statements.

To be considered a member of management (not a third party) who can receive management-use only financial statements under SSARS No. 8, the AICPA Guide states that two requirements must be met:

- The person must be a member of management.
- The person must be generally knowledgeable and understand the nature of the procedures applied and the basis of accounting and assumptions used in the preparation of the financial statements.

In determining whether a person is a member of management (requirement 1), reference should be made to the definition found in FASB No. 57, *Related Parties,* which states:

> Persons who are responsible for achieving the objectives of the enterprise and who have the authority to establish policies and make decisions by which those objectives are to be pursued.

FASB No. 57 lists the following persons normally included as members of management:

- Members of the board of directors
- Chief executive officer
- Chief operating officer
- Vice presidents in charge of principal business functions
- Other persons who perform similar policymaking functions
- Persons without formal titles but meet the criteria of members of management

Once a person is considered a member of management, he or she must satisfy the second test in order to be eligible to receive management-use financial statements. The second requirement is that the person must be generally

TOP AUDITING ISSUES FOR 2005 CPE COURSE

knowledgeable and understand the nature of the procedures applied and the basis of accounting and assumptions used in the preparation of the financial statements. That is, the person must have enough of an understanding of the business to put the information contained in management-use only financial statements into a proper context.

This requirement generally will "weed out" most of management, particularly those in sales and marketing who are not privy to financial information. Further, in some instances, board members may not qualify as members of management if they do not have the prerequisite knowledge necessary to receive management-use only financial statements.

The Guide provides the following examples, as adapted here, to illustrate the parameters of the members of management definition:

EXAMPLE

XYZ Company is a small, closely held business, owned and managed by John, its sole shareholder.

Conclusion: Absent other evidence, John would have the requisite knowledge of this business and would not be considered a third party.

EXAMPLE

ABC Corporation is a small, closely held business managed by one of its ten shareholders, Jane. The other nine shareholders live out of state and are not involved in the management of the business.

Conclusion: Absent other evidence, Jane would have the requisite knowledge of the business and would not be considered a third party. However, the other nine shareholders would be considered third parties.

EXAMPLE

Assume the same facts as in the previous example, except that the other nine shareholders live in state and are involved in the management of the business.

Conclusion: Jane and the other nine shareholders would probably have the requisite knowledge of the business and would not be considered third parties. Thus, all ten persons would qualify to receive management-use only financial statements.

MODULE 2 — CHAPTER 4 — Compilation and Review Issues 99

> **EXAMPLE**
>
> MLB Corporation is a small, closely held business. The management team consists of Joe, the president; Mary the controller; Sue, the operations manager; and Jim, the sales manager. Joe, Mary, and Sue are all involved in the financial operations and are knowledgeable about the accounting principles and practices used. Jim, the sales manager, has no finance background and is not involved in the financial operation of the company.
>
> **Conclusion:** Joe, Mary, and Sue would not be considered third parties, but Jim would be considered a third party even though he is a member of management. This is the case because Jim does not have the requisite knowledge of the accounting practices of the business and would be considered a third party under the SSARS No. 8 definition.

> **OBSERVATION**
>
> The AICPA Guide makes an important point that the financial statements are intended to be restricted for management use, not internal use. If internal use were the threshold, all employees of a company would be eligible to receive the financial statements. However, because the threshold is management use, only certain members of management with a requisite knowledge of the financial statements and principles use are eligible to receive the financial statements. Thus, many members of management such as those engaged in sales and marketing are considered third parties, not eligible to receive management-use only financial statements.

Will members of a board of directors that are not employees qualify to receive management-use only financial statements? Generally, board members who are not employees, will qualify as members of management under the definition in FASB No. 57. If members of the board of directors are active in the management of the business, they probably will qualify to receive management-use only financial statements even if they are not formal employees of the company.

If, however, the board members merely meet intermittently and do not participate in the management of the business, they probably will not have the requisite knowledge necessary to receive such statements. The determination is based on the facts and circumstances surrounding each board member with some members qualifying and others not.

Will members of the board of directors of a not-for-profit organization typically qualify to receive management-use only financial statements? Generally not. The board members may be considered members of management under FASB No. 57. But, they are not *generally knowledgeable and do not understand* the nature of the procedures applied and the basis of accounting and assumptions used in the preparation of the financial statements. In instances where they meet the second requirement, rarely will they meet the first requirement, which is being members of management.

TOP AUDITING ISSUES FOR 2005 CPE COURSE

Can a member of management who is ineligible to receive management-use only financial statements, subsequently become eligible to receive them? Certain employees can become eligible to receive management-use only financial statements if they are educated about the company's accounting practices and principles used, thus removing them from the third-party status.

SSARS No. 8 does not address what evidence the CPA must obtain to ensure that the financial statements are not reasonably expected to be used by a third party. However, The Guide states that the CPA may rely on management's representation in the engagement letter, without further inquiry, *unless* information comes to the CPA's attention that contradicts management's representation.

The financial statements may be restricted to specific members of management even if others qualify to receive the financial statements. The illustrative engagement letter in Appendix C of SSARS No. 8 provides optional language whereby the CPA can restrict issuance of management-use only financial statements to specific members of management, even though other members are eligible to receive them. The optional language reads:

The financial statements are intended solely for the information and use of [include list of specified members of management] and are not intended to be and should not be used by any other party.

> **EXAMPLE**
>
> Company X is owned by Harry Jones, its president. The company also has other members of management who have the requisite knowledge to qualify to receive management-use only financial statements. Although other members are eligible to receive the financial statements, Harry wants the financial statements to be issued only to him.
>
> **Conclusion:** The CPA can place a restriction in the engagement letter as follows: The financial statements are intended solely for the information and use of Harry Jones, President and are not intended to be and should not be used by any other party.

STUDY QUESTIONS

9. For management-use only financial statements, the CPA must document a written understanding with the client using an engagement letter, which must be signed by management. *True or False?*

10. The required items to be included in an engagement letter for management-use only financial statements include the fact that a compilation report will be issued in accordance with SSARS No. 1. *True or False?*

11. Each page of the management-use only financial statements must include a reference such as Restricted for Management's Use Only. *True or False?*

> **12.** The performance requirements for a compilation engagement found in SSARS No. 1 are applicable to management-use only financial statements. The performance requirements state that the CPA must prepare the financial statements and have them reviewed by an independent person to consider whether they are free from obvious material errors. ***True or False?***
>
> **13.** With respect to management-use only financial statements, disclosures are required. ***True or False?***
>
> **14.** A bookkeeper is a person normally included as a member of management under FASB No. 57. ***True or False?***
>
> **15.** In order for the CPA to consider issuing management-use only financial statements, the CPA should consider several key factors, including the third-party needs for the statements' use. ***True or False?***

OTHER ISSUES FOR MANAGEMENT-USE ONLY FINANCIAL STATEMENTS

Peer Review Considerations

he AICPA Code of Conduct states that a member is subject to peer review if he or she is reporting on financial statements. The management-use only financial statement does not include a report because the engagement letter is not considered a report.

The Peer Review Board has concluded that if a firm's only accounting and auditing service performed is the issuance of management-use only financial statements, the firm would not be required to enroll in the AICPA's Practice Monitoring (peer review) Program. If, however, the firm is already enrolled in the Program because it performs other accounting and auditing engagements (e.g., audits, reviews, compilations with reports), any management-use only financial statement engagements would also be included as part of the firm's accounting and auditing practice, and included within the scope of the peer review. That is, once a firm is subject to peer review, all accounting and auditing engagements are subject to selection during the peer review.

The reality is that if the management-use only financial statement engagement is selected in a peer review, the reviewer would have very little to actually review. The reviewer's time would be spent inspecting the engagement letter, whether signed or not signed, and whether a *restricted for management-use only* legend was placed on each page of the financial statements. Presumably, the reviewer would not be concerned with deficiencies in GAAP or OCBOA because SSARS No. 8 permits such deficiencies in a management-use only financial statement engagement.

Changes in the Level of Service

Occasionally, an accountant is engaged to perform a management-use only compilation engagement, and subsequently, the client needs compiled or reviewed financial statements for use by a third party. If the accountant has issued management-use only financial statements, he or she can subsequently issue compiled or reviewed financial statements for the same financial statement period. However, the engagement would be a different one that might require additional procedures, particularly in the case of a review engagement.

If the accountant merely issues a compilation report for distribution to third parties when previously, management-use only financial statements had been issued for the same period, the additional work needed to complete the new engagement should be minimal particularly where substantially all disclosures and the statement of cash flows have been omitted for both engagements.

If, however, a review engagement will be conducted, the engagement is a new one and the accountant will be required to complete all review procedures required by SSARS No. 1 including conducting analytical review procedures and inquiries.

The Guide suggests that the accountant include language in the engagement letter for the management-use only engagement alerting the client to the fact that if he or she needs financial statements for third party use, the accountant can provide that service as a separate engagement. This sample language is appropriate:

> Should you require financial statements for third-party use, we would be pleased to discuss with you the requested level of service. Such engagement would be considered separate and not deemed to be part of the services described in this engagement letter.

An accountant may issue management-use only financial statements (e.g., monthly and quarterly) and then issue a standard compilation report on the year-end financial statements.

However, the year-end compilation engagement would be considered a separate engagement and would be subject to both the performance standards and reporting standards of SSARS No. 1. (SSARS No. 8, Appendix A). Further, the CPA should obtain a separate engagement letter for the year-end compilation engagement.

An accountant who is engaged to perform a standard compilation engagement may also subsequently change the engagement to a management-use only engagement. Appendix A of SSARS No. 8 states that the accountant should carefully consider the reason for the request for the change in the engagement. For example, the accountant should ensure that he or she does not reasonably expect the financial statements to be issued to any third parties.

An accountant who is engaged to perform a management-use only engagement may subsequently change the engagement to a standard compilation. However, again, the accountant should consider the reasons for the change.

Management-use only financial statements may *not* be issued for a prescribed form under SSARS No. 3. Appendix A of SSARS No. 8 states that because the intended user of prescribed form financial statements is generally a third party (e.g., a bank), the management-use only financial statements option would not be appropriate.

MODULE 2 — CHAPTER 4 — Compilation and Review Issues **103**

An accountant may issue a standard compilation report on comparative financial statements when the prior period financial statements were restricted to management-use only. However, the accountant must comply with the reporting requirements of SSARS No. 1 for both periods before issuing the report on comparative statements. That is, the compilation report would have to cover both periods, not just the most recent period.

STUDY QUESTION

> **16.** If the accountant has issued management-use only financial statements, he or she can subsequently issue compiled or reviewed financial statements for the same financial statement period. *True or False?*

EXEMPTIONS FROM THE SSARSS

Changes were made by the ARSC to the definition of *submission* by SSARS No. 8 that became effective for financial statements issued after December 31, 2000. This section discusses the exemptions from the SSARSs that exist under current compilation and review literature and can be used in conjunction with the chapter's Overview of the SSARSs and Interpretations.

Overview of the SSARSs and Interpretations

Since the adoption of SSARS No. 1 in 1979, the codification of the SSARSs has been rather limited in comparison with other changes in the accounting profession. Specifically, from 1979 to 2003, only 9 SSARSs have been issued, in comparison to many other accounting-related documents. The following table illustrates the point that changes in compilation and review have been made at a much slower pace than other accounting documents.

Comparison of Volume of Documents Issued: 1979 to Present

FASB statements	150+
Statements on Auditing Standards (SASs)	101+
Statements on Attestation Engagements (SSAEs)	11
Internal Revenue Code and related regulations (estimate)	100,000 + pages
Statements on Standards for Accounting and Review Services (SSARSs)	9+

Source: Steven Fustolo's research.

The following is a summary of the SSARSs issued to date along with all interpretations.

SSARS No. 1, *Compilation and Review of Financial Statements* (issued December 1978, as amended by SSARS No. 8 in 2000): The basis of compilation and review services, providing guidance to CPAs concerning the standards and procedures applicable to compilation and review engagements.

SSARS No. 2, *Reporting on Comparative Financial Statements* (issued October 1979): Relates to reporting on comparative financial statements that include the current year compiled or reviewed financial statements of any nonpublic entity.

SSARS No. 3, *Compilation Reports on Financial Statements Included in Certain Prescribed Forms* (Issued December 1981): Amends SSARS No. 1 and 2 to provide for another form of a compilation report on prescribed forms (standard, preprinted forms designed or adopted by the body to which it is submitted) that required GAAP departures.

SSARS No. 4, *Communications Between Predecessor and Successor Accountants* (issued December 1981): Provides guidance to the successor in communicating with a predecessor accountant. Unlike an audit engagement, the successor accountant is not required to communicate with the predecessor but the predecessor is required to respond if authorized by the client.

SSARS No. 5, *Reporting on Compiled Financial Statements* (issued July 1982): Superseded by the issuance of SSARS No. 7.

SSARS No. 6, *Reporting on Personal Financial Statements Included in Written Personal Financial Plans* (issued September 1986): Provides an exemption from SSARS No. 1 for financial statements used to assist the client and his or her advisors in developing a personal financial plan, and not used to obtain credit or for any other purpose.

SSARS No. 7, *Omnibus Statement on Standards for Accounting and Review Services* (issued November 1992): Provides numerous technical changes including changes to the compilation and review report language and the requirement that the accountant obtain a management representation letter for a review engagement.

SSARS No. 8, *Amendment to Statement on Standards for Accounting and Review Services No. 1* (issued 2000): Amends SSARS No. 1 to change the definition of submission of financial statements, and introduces new management-use only financial statements.

SSARS No. 9, *Omnibus Statement on Standards for Accounting and Review Services 2002* (issued November 2002): Provides various technical changes to SSARS No. 1 including clarifying reporting responsibility with respect

MODULE 2 — CHAPTER 4 — Compilation and Review Issues **105**

to a statement of retained earnings, comprehensive income, as well as changing required provisions of the management representation letter for review engagements.

SSARS Interpretations

1. *Omission of Disclosures in Reviewed Financial Statements* (December 1979)
2. *Financial Statements Included in SEC Filings* (December 1979)
3. *Reporting on the Highest Level of Service* (December 1979)
4. *Discovery of Information After the Date of the Accountant's Report* (November 1980)
5. *Planning and Supervision* (August 1981)
6. *Withdrawal From Compilation or Review Engagement* (August 1981)
7. *Reporting When There Are Significant Departures from Generally Accepted Accounting Principles* (August 1981)
8. *Reports on Specified Elements, Accounts, or Items of a Financial Statement* (November 1981)
9. *Reporting When Management Has Elected to Omit Substantially All Disclosures* (May 1982)
10. *Reporting on Tax Returns* (November 1982)
11. *Reporting on Uncertainties* (December 1982)
12. *Reporting on a Comprehensive Basis of Accounting Other Than Generally Accepted Accounting Principles* (November 1992)
13. *Additional Procedures* (March 1983)
14. This Interpretation was withdrawn.
15. *Differentiating a Financial Statement Presentation from a Trial Balance (September 1990)*
16. This Interpretation was withdrawn.
17. *Submitting Draft Financial Statements* (September 1990)
18. *Special-Purpose Financial Presentation to Comply with Contractual Agreements or Regulatory Provisions* (September 1990)
19. *Reporting When Financial Statements Contain a Departure from Promulgated Accounting Principles That Prevents the Financial Statements from Being Misleading* (February 1991)
20. *Applicability of Statements on Standards For Accounting and Review Services to Litigation Service* (May 1991)
21. *Application of SSARS No. 1 When Performing Controllership or Other Management Services* (July 2002)
22. *Use of "Selected Information-Substantially All Disclosures Required by Generally Accepted Accounting Principles Are Not Included."* (2002)
23. *Application of Statements on Standards for Accounting and Review Services When an Accountant Engaged to Perform a Business Valuation Derives Information From an Entity's Tax Return* (2003)

106 TOP AUDITING ISSUES FOR 2005 CPE COURSE

24. *Reference to the Country of Origin in a Review or Compilation Report* (2003)
25. *Omission of the Display of Comprehensive Income in a Compilation* (2003)

General Rules

To review, the general rules in SSARS No. 1, as revised by SSARS No. 8 states:

> A CPA should not submit unaudited financial statements of a nonpublic entity to his or her client or a third party unless, as a minimum, he or she complies with the provisions of SSARS No. 1 (as amended by SSARS No. 8) applicable to a compilation engagement.

SSARS No. 1 states that an accountant is associated with financial statements if he or she has *submitted* them to the client or third party. SSARS No. 8 changed the definition of submission to the following:

> *Presenting* to a client or third parties financial statements that the accountant has *prepared* either manually or through the use of computer software.

Specifically, in order for an accountant to have submitted financial statements and, thus, have a reporting responsibility under the SSARSs, the accountant must *prepare* financial statements, and then must *present* them to a client or third party. If the accountant does not *both* prepare and present financial statements, he or she has no reporting responsibility under the SSARSs—that is, no compilation or review report is required.

Services Exempt from the SSARS No. 1 Requirements

The SSARSs (and related interpretations) list services that do not constitute a submission of financial statements and, therefore, are *exempt* from SSARS No. 1 requirements, described here:

- Reading client-prepared financial statements
- Proposing correcting entries or disclosures either orally or in written form as long as the CPA does not directly modify the client-prepared financial statements
- Preparing standard monthly entries such as depreciation, prepaid expenses
- Providing a client with a financial statement format, without dollar amounts, to be used by the client to prepare statements
- Advising a client about the selection or use of computer software that the client will use to prepare statements
- Typing or reproducing client-prepared financial statements, without modification, as an accommodation to a client
- Providing the client with the use of or access to computer hardware or software that the client will use to generate statements

MODULE 2 — CHAPTER 4 — Compilation and Review Issues **107**

- Providing manual or automated bookkeeping services, in which a CPA keeps the client's books up-to-date either manually or by use of computer software
- Preparing a trial balance, provided that a trial balance—not a financial statement—is prepared

> **OBSERVATION**
>
> Interpretation No. 14 of SSARS No. 1, *Differentiating a Financial Statement Presentation from a Trial Balance,* provides examples comparing a financial statement with a trial balance. A trial balance differs from a financial statement as follows:
>
> - A financial statement combines general ledger accounts to create account groups.
> - Trial balances do not contain labels such as statement of income.
> - Financial statements present integrated captions and numbers in equations, such as assets equal liabilities plus equity.
> - Financial statements present the balance sheet in the order of liquidity.
> - Net income is presented in a set of financial statements, but not a trial balance.

- Preparing a tax return. Interpretation 10 of SSARS 1 states that any information presented on a tax return is exempt from SSARS No. 1 provided the information relates to the same period as the tax return. This includes all tax return schedules including Schedule L (balance sheet). For example, a CPA submits a client's tax return to the banker.

> **OBSERVATION**
>
> If a CPA prepares financial statements based on tax return information (e.g., OCBOA statements), he or she must comply with SSARS No. 1.

> **OBSERVATION**
>
> Given the fact that our society is becoming more and more paperless, the fact that information is conveyed via an electronic format or by diskette does not change the reporting responsibility. Information distributed by a medium other than paper is treated with the same reporting requirements as had a paper medium been employed.

108 TOP AUDITING ISSUES FOR 2005 CPE COURSE

The Four Exemptions for Financial Statements from the SSARSs

Presently, there are four exemptions from SSARS No. 1 for historical financial statements in addition to those noted in the previous section:

- Financial statements included in a written personal financial plan (per SSARS No. 6)
- Financial statements involved in certain litigation services (per Interpretation 20 of SSARS No. 1)
- Financial statements included in certain prescribed forms (per SSARS No. 3)
- Certain information included in a business valuation (per Interpretation 23, SSARS No. 1)

Otherwise, the SSARSs apply to any engagement where the accountant has submitted financial statements.

Financial Statements Included Within Consulting Reports

The SSARSs do not provide any exemption for historical financial statements included within consulting reports. The general rule is the SSARSs apply to any financial statements submitted to a client.

Absent the three exemptions from SSARS No. 1 noted, the CPA must either compile or review the financial statements included in the consulting report. The exception is where the financial statements are prepared by another CPA or the client prepares the statements and the CPA has not submitted the statements. In such a case, the CPA would not be required to comply with SSARS No. 1.

If the financial statements are prepared by the client, the CPA might wish to include a reference to those statements in his or her consulting report, such as:

> The financial statements presented on pages x and x were prepared by XYZ Company. We have not compiled, reviewed, or audited the financial statements and, accordingly, we assume no responsibility for them.

Financial Information Included in a Written Business Valuation

In 2003, the ARSC issued Interpretation 23 of SSARS No. 1, *Applicability of Statements on Standards for Accounting and Review Services When an Accountant Engaged to Perform a Business Valuation Derives Information from an Entity's Tax Return.*

The Interpretation addresses the accountant's responsibility when he or she performs a business valuation that derives information from a client's tax return, or audited, reviewed or compiled financial statements, whether issued by the accountant or another accountant.

When an accountant is engaged to perform a business valuation of an entity, it may be necessary for the accountant to derive financial information to be used in that business valuation from the client's tax return. This is particularly true if the entity does not have audited, reviewed, or compiled financial statements.

MODULE 2 — CHAPTER 4 — Compilation and Review Issues **109**

If an accountant derives financial information from an entity's tax return, and such information is presented as part of the business valuation report, SSARS No. 1 does not apply.

As discussed in paragraph 4 of SSARS No. 1, under the definition of a financial statement, "*Financial forecasts, projections and similar presentations, and financial presentations included in tax returns are not financial statements for purposes of this Statement.*" Therefore, even if the accountant has prepared the tax return, he or she has not prepared financial statements in accordance with SSARS and the financial information derived from the tax return and presented as part of a business valuation is not deemed to be submission of financial statements as contemplated by SSARS No. 1.

When an accountant, in the course of performing a business valuation engagement, derives financial information from the client's tax return, or another accountant's audited, reviewed, or compiled financial statements, or client-prepared financial statements, the accountant should refer to the source of the financial information and include an indication in the business valuation report that the accountant has not audited, reviewed, or compiled the financial information and that the accountant assumes no responsibility for the information. (See paragraph 3 of SSARS No. 1.)

The following is sample wording that may be included in the business valuation report that incorporates the requirements of paragraph 3 of SSARS No. 1:

In preparing our business valuation report, we have relied upon historical financial information provided to us by management and derived from [refer to the appropriate source of the information, such as tax return, audit report issued by another auditor, and so on].

This financial information has not been audited, reviewed, or compiled by us and accordingly we do not express an opinion or any form of assurance on this financial information.

However, if the accountant submits financial statements in the course of performing a business valuation as defined in paragraph 4 of SSARS No. 1, then, at a minimum, the accountant should comply with the provisions of SSARS applicable to a compilation engagement.

STUDY QUESTIONS

17. A trial balance differs from a financial statement in that a financial statement combines general ledger accounts to create account groups. *True or False?*

18. The exemptions from SSARS No. 1 include financial statements that are part of a written personal financial plan. *True or False?*

19. When an accountant preparing a business valuation derives information from the client's tax return or financial statements prepared by another accountant but does not submit such statements, the accountant should so indicate, plus indicate:

a. That the other accountant audited the financial statements.

b. That the accountant does not express an opinion or assurance on the information.

c. That the business valuation report is compliant with requirements for a compilation engagement.

CONTROLLERSHIP ISSUES: WHAT IS GOING ON IN PRACTICE?

For years, accountants have performed write-up services for clients in addition to performing a compilation, review, or even an audit engagement. More recently, those services have expanded to part-time controllership. Because bookkeeping and controllership functions, by themselves, do not necessarily entail issuing a report, many accountants take it for granted that such engagements are risk-free. Yet, recent statistics obtained from major insurance carriers reach a different conclusion:

■ Malpractice cases against accountants in write-up services have risen dramatically in recent years. Undetected fraud is the number one charge against accountants in write-ups and involving cash and accounts receivable. Accountants in part-time controllership cases are being held to a higher standard than acting as an internal accountant.

■ Accountants may have a lack of independence depending on the degree of services provided.

The following suggestions may mitigate some of the risks associated with these engagements:

■ Obtain an engagement letter for both write-up services and part-time controllership engagements.

■ Malpractice insurance should cover controllership because the service could be construed as an employer-employee relationship rather than a professional-client relationship.

■ In planning to issue a report, the preparer should watch out for independence issues.

■ Part-time controllers should consider whether they need to issue a report and the impact of their position on the ability to do so.

Independence Issues

This section discusses the present developments about the controllership issue.

A CPA in public practice is permitted to issue a compilation report even if he or she is not independent provided the report identifies the fact that he or she is not independent. Yet, many CPAs provide part- or full-time controllership services, including:

- Maintaining the accounting books and records
- Preparing financial statements
- Performing certain management functions for clients, such as hiring employees, authorizing purchases, investing idle cash, and signing checks, or serving as an officer or director of a company

Ethics Interpretation 101-3 provides that if a CPA performs certain activities, he or she has impaired his or her independence. The list of activities consists of the following. Does the CPA:

- Have the authority to *authorize, execute, or consummate* a transaction, or otherwise exercise authority on behalf of a client (for example, negotiate a transaction)?
- Prepare source documents or originate data, in electronic or other form, evidencing the occurrence of a transaction (for example, purchase orders, payroll time records, and customer orders)?
- Have custody of client assets?
- Supervise client employees in the performance of their normal recurring activities?
- Determine which recommendations of the member should be implemented?
- Report to the board of directors on behalf of management?
- Serve as a client's stock transfer or escrow agent, registrar, general counsel, or its equivalent?

If the CPA does any of these activities on behalf of a client, he or she is not independent.

Prior to April 2002, there was confusion about the extent to which CPAs could avoid issuing compilation reports on financial statements. On one side of the issue, there were CPAs in public accounting who also provided management services (as listed above) for their clients.

Some CPAs in this situation argued that because they were both engaged in public accounting and performing management services, they could choose to issue financial statements in the capacity as a member of management, not public accounting. Thus, they argued that requirements to issue a compilation report under SSAR No. 1 did not apply. The result was that the compilation report was replaced with the issuance of a transmittal letter sent to the third party along with the financial statements.

On the other side of the issue, there were CPAs in industry who were issuing financial statements for their employers. Instead of issuing the financial statements with a transmittal letter, they were issuing them with a compilation report noting a lack of independence in the report.

Thus, CPAs in public accounting who performed management services were bypassing the requirements of SSARS No. 1 (compilation report), and CPAs in industry were issuing compilation reports for their employer companies.

What was the authority to deal with this situation? There simply was no authority to deal with the crossover among CPAs in industry and public accounting. For CPAs in industry who issued a compilation report for their employer, nothing in SSARS No. 1 precluded them from doing so provided they noted the lack of independence.

For CPAs in public accounting who issued merely a transmittal letter in the capacity as a member of management, AICPA Ethics Ruling No. 10 gave some guidance for a CPA in industry who was also a stockholder, partner, director, officer, or employee of an entity for which he or she prepared financial statements to be transmitted to a third party, as follows:

> If the member (CPA) submits financials statements in his or her capacity as a stockholder, partner, director, officer, or employee to a third party, the member (CPA) clearly communicate, preferably in writing, the relationship of the member to the entity and should not imply that the member is independent of the entity...

The Ethics Ruling essentially indicated that a CPA could issue financial statements in his or her capacity as a member of management provided he or she indicated his or her relationship to the entity; that is, indicated an employment title or the fact that the CPA was a "part-time controller."

Thus, existing authority appeared to authorize the crossover of activities by CPAs in industry and public accounting. Yet many observers took the position that, although not stated in SSARS No. 1, a compilation report was supposed to be issued by a CPA in public accounting, not industry. And use of a transmittal letter and the avoidance of the issuance of a compilation report should be set aside for CPAs that were truly part of management, exclusive of CPAs that provided part-time controllership work.

SSARS Interpretation No. 21, Applicability of SSARS No. 1 When Performing Controllership or Other Management Services

Finally, in July 2002, the ARSC offered some authoritative guidance as to the reporting responsibilities for accountants offering controllership services as well as those in industry seeking to issue compilation reports for their companies.

MODULE 2 — CHAPTER 4 — Compilation and Review Issues **113**

> **EXAMPLE**
>
> An accountant is in the practice of public accounting and provides an entity with controllership or other management services that entail the submission of financial statements. Is the accountant required to follow the requirements of SSARS No. 1?
>
> **Conclusion:** If the accountant is in the practice of public accounting as defined by AICPA Code of Conduct and *is not a stockholder, partner, director, officer, or employee of the entity,* the accountant is required to follow the performance and communication requirements of SSARS No. 1, including any requirement to disclose a lack of independence.

If the accountant is in the practice of public accounting and *is also* a stockholder, partner, director, officer, or employee of the entity, the accountant may either comply with the requirements of SSARS No. 1, or communicate, preferably in writing, the accountant's relationship to the entity (for example, stockholder, partner, director, officer, or employee).

The following is the type of communication that may be used by the accountant:

> The accompanying balance sheet of Company X as of December 31, 20XX, and the related statements of income and cash flows for the year then ended have been prepared by (name of accountant), CPA. I have prepared such financial statements in my capacity (describe capacity, for example, as director) of Company X.

If an accountant is not in the practice of public accounting, the issuance of a report under SSARS would be inappropriate; however, the above communication may be used.

The following table summarizes the requirements of Interpretation 21 of SSARS No. 1 when a CPA performs management or controllership services for a client.

Description	Acceptable Action
CPA in public accounting does not provide management or controllership services. However, he or she is not independent for other reasons (client relationship, unpaid fees, etc).	Must issue a compilation report with a separate paragraph indicating lack of independence per SSARS No. 1.
CPA in public accounting performs management or controllership services. He or she is not a stockholder, partner, director, officer, or employee of the entity.	Required to follow SSARS No. 1 (compilation report) and disclose lack of independence in report.

114 TOP AUDITING ISSUES FOR 2005 CPE COURSE

Description	Acceptable Action
CPA in public accounting performs management or controllership services. He or she is a stockholder, partner, director, officer, or employee of the entity.	CPA has a choice to either comply with the requirements of SSARS No. 1 or to communicate, preferably in writing, the accountant's relationship to the entity (for example, stockholder, partner, director, officer, or employee).
CPA is not in the practice of public accounting and provides management or controllership services to a company.	CPA is not allowed to issue a compilation report under SSARS No. 1.

EXAMPLE

John Mercury, CPA, is in public practice and is the brother of his client, clearly lacking independence. He is not a stockholder, partner, director, or employee of the company.

Conclusion: Under existing rules found in SSARS No. 1, the CPA may issue a compilation report provided the report states that he is not independent.

EXAMPLE

Justin Wood, CPA, is in public accounting. He performs part-time controllership services for a client. The CPA is not a stockholder, partner, director, officer, or employee of the entity. In fact, Wood receives a Form 1099 for his services. The client's entity needs to issue financial statements to the bank.

Conclusion: Under Interpretation 21 of SSARS No. 1, a CPA in public accounting who is not a stockholder, partner, director, officer, or employee of an entity must comply with SSARS No. 1. Thus, Wood's only option is to issue a compilation report. Sending financial statements with a transmittal letter in the capacity as a part-time controller is not permitted.

EXAMPLE

Assume the same facts as in the previous example, except the CPA, Melissa Jackson, is also a director of the company.

Conclusion: Under Interpretation 21 of SSARS No. 1, a CPA in public accounting who is also a stockholder, partner, director, officer, or employee of an entity has a choice of reporting: One option is to comply with SSARS No. 1 by issuing a compilation report, noting lack of independence. Another option is to issue financial statements in the capacity as a director of the company and communicate that his relationship with the company—that is, issue a transmittal letter indicating that she is a director of the company. The Interpretation recommends, but does not require, that the communication be in writing.

MODULE 2 — CHAPTER 4 — Compilation and Review Issues   **115**

> **EXAMPLE .**
>
> Alexandra Barton, CPA, is a CFO for a company and wishes to issue a compilation report on the company. She is not in public accounting.
>
> **Conclusion:** Interpretation 21 states that where a CPA is not in public accounting, the issuance of a report under SSARS No. 1 (e.g., compilation report) is not appropriate. Thus, the CFO's only option is to issue financial statements in her capacity as an officer of the company.

STUDY QUESTION

> **20.** In considering whether a controller may issue compiled financial statements, a CPA who is not in public accounting is precluded from issuing a compilation under SSARS No. 1. *True or False?*

Descriptions of Terms in the AICPA Code of Ethics

The AICPA Code of Ethics explores several terms relevant to compilation and review engagements.

Practice of Public Accounting

The practice of public accounting consists of the performance for a client, by a member or a member's firm, while holding out as CPAs, of the professional services of accounting, tax, personal financial planning, litigation support services, and those professional services for which standards are promulgated by designated by Council, [such as Statements of Financial Accounting Standards, Auditing Standards, Accounting and Review Services, Consulting Services, Governmental Accounting Standards, and Attestation Engagements].

Defining *Employee*

The interpretation references that a CPA in public practice who is also an stockholder, partner, director, officer, or employee has the choice between issuing a compilation report under SSARS No. 1 or giving financial statements to a third party with a communication (such as a transmittal letter).

The Interpretation does not define the term *employee*. For example, is a CPA who receives a Form 1099 for working as a part-time controller for one day per week deemed to be an employee? The definition of an employee is not based on the definition found in the Internal Revenue Code but rather one that is based on the substance of the relationship and the degree to which the CPA is engaged in management and controllership services.

Thus, a CPA who works four days a week as a part-time controller and receives a Form 1099 for her services still might be considered an employee due to the breadth of her services. Thus, a practitioner must follow a flowchart-like decision path to clarify when to issue a transmittal letter versus a compilation report.

Hierarchy: Accountants in Public Accounting Serving Also as Stockholders, Partners, Directors, Officers, or Employees

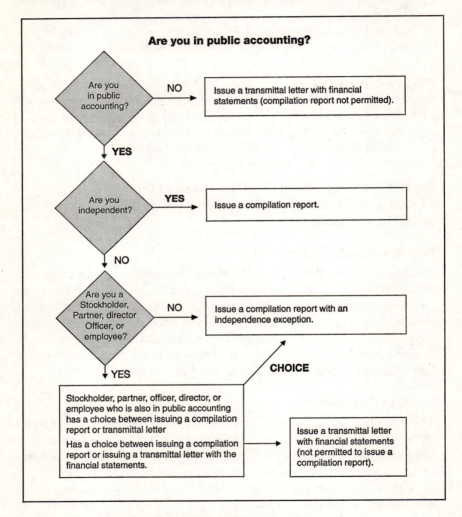

Form of a Communication Made to a Third Party by a CPA in Industry and Not Public Accounting

Interpretation 21 gives some recommended language to use when a CPA in industry is either permitted or required to issue a communication to accompany financial statements.

Further, Ethics Rulings 65 and 10 give guidance in situations in which a CPA wishes to issue financial statements with a transmittal letter to a third party. Ethics Ruling 65 states:

> If the member uses the CPA designation in a manner to imply that he or she is independent of the employer, the member would be knowingly misrepresenting facts in violation of Rule 102. Therefore, it is advisable that in any transmittal within which the member uses his or her CPA designation, he or she *clearly indicate the employment title.* In addition, if the member states affirmatively in any transmittal that a financial statement is presented in conformity with generally accepted accounting principles, the member is subject to Rule 203.

Ethics Ruling 10 further states:

> If the member (CPA) submits financials statements in his or her capacity as a stockholder, partner, director, officer, or employee to a third party, the member (CPA) clearly communicate, preferably in writing, the relationship of the member to the entity and should not imply that the member is independent of the entity.

In addition, if the communication states affirmatively that the financial statements are presented in conformity with generally accepted accounting principles, the member is subject to Rule 203 of the Code of Professional Conduct.

If the member prepares financial statements as a member in public practice and/or submits them using the member's public practitioner's letterhead or other identification, the member should comply with applicable standards including the requirement to disclose a lack of independence.

If a CPA in industry wishes to issue a communication (transmittal letter) to accompany financial statements to be given to a third party, the following rules apply:

- The communication must be on the entity's letterhead.
- The CPA can use his or her CPA designation provided he or she notes his or her title related to the entity (stockholder, partner, director, employee).
- If the CPA does mention in his or her letter that the financial statements are presented in conformity with GAAP, the CPA is subject to Ethics Rule 203 which states that he or she shall not knowingly state that statements are in conformity with GAAP when they are not.

Appendix A-6 contains a sample that shows how the transmittal letter may be phrased and how the accompanying financial statements are prepared, as well as samples of an internally generated balance sheet and income statement.

Regarding these documents, first notice that the transmittal letter is printed on the company's letterhead and references Robert Reilly's employment title.

TOP AUDITING ISSUES FOR 2005 CPE COURSE

Second, there is a reference to GAAP in the transmittal letter. This is not a requirement under any of the authoritative literature. However, if the CPA does mention in his or her letter that the financial statements are presented in conformity with GAAP, the CPA is subject to Ethics Rule 203, which states that he or she shall not knowingly state that statements are in conformity with GAAP when they are not. Any transmittal letter should probably remain silent on the GAAP or OCBOA format to provide maximum financial reporting flexibility.

Third, it may be advisable to stamp each statement *Internally Generated Financial Statements* to ensure that the third party fully understands that these statements were generated internally and not with the assistance of an outside CPA. If the above internally generated financial statement format is followed, it would not be appropriate to apply any SSARS No. 1 requirements such as a *See Accountant's Compilation Report* legend.

A CPA who is also a stockholder, partner, director, officer, or employee is advised to consider the risk associated with issuing financial statements with a transmittal letter. Logically, if a transmittal letter is issued, the CPA should be protected under the entity veil as being a stockholder, partner, director, officer, or employee of that entity. However, the CPA might wish to consult with legal counsel as to legal liability.

For example, could a third party who knows that a CPA is in public accounting as well as being a director, attempt to sue the CPA in his capacity as a member of public accounting, rather than as a director? The CPA should review his or her malpractice insurance policy and/or consult with legal counsel to consider whether such services are covered under the policy and place the CPA at personal risk with respect to the financial statement issued with a transmittal letter.

MODULE 2 — CHAPTER 5

Compilation and Review Update

LEARNING OBJECTIVES

At the completion of this chapter you should be able to:

- Understand the latest developments affecting compilation and review engagements.
- Answer client questions regarding the impact of SSARS No. 9.
- Identify changes made to the management representation letter.

INTRODUCTION

This chapter reviews updated information concerning compilation and review engagements, including SSARS No. 9 and other recently issued interpretations of SSARS No. 1. SSARS No. 9, in particular, cleans up various inconsistencies and confusions that exist under the present SSARS standards.

Among other topics, this chapter explains when an accountant's name may be included in written communications that also contain unaudited financial statements of a nonpublic entity; clarifies the report dates to be used for compilation and review reports; addresses changes to the elements that should be included in a management representation letter; covers when to include a separate report on supplementary information in a compilation engagement; integrates Statements on Quality Control Standards (SQCSs) into the SSARSs, showing how those standards relate to the SSARSs, and offers additional guidance on the successor-predecessor accountant communications.

SSARS NO. 9: *OMNIBUS STATEMENT ON STANDARDS FOR ACCOUNTING AND REVIEW SERVICES* 2002

In November 2002, the ARSC issued SSARS No. 9, Omnibus Statement on Standards for Accounting and Review Services- 2002. Like other omnibus statements, SSARS No. 9,cleans up various inconsistencies and confusions that exist under the present SSARS standards. Generally, an omnibus statement does not encompass one particular theme. Instead, it deals with a series of individual issues that require change or clarification and, that, individually, is not significant enough to warrant issuing separate statements for each issue.

SSARS No. 9, addresses changes to the following items, each of which is discussed below:

- Offers guidance in situations in which an accountant's name is included in a written document or communication containing unaudited financial statements.
- Clarifies the reporting requirements related to a statement of retained earnings and comprehensive income.
- Addresses whether an accountant's signature is required to be on a compilation or review report and the date that should be placed on report.
- Codifies specific representations that must be included in a management representation letter for a review engagement.
- Modifies SSARS No. 1, to deal with the issuance of a separate report on supplementary information.

TOP AUDITING ISSUES FOR 2005 CPE COURSE

- Integrates language into SSARS No. 1,regarding the requirement to adopt and maintain a quality control system.
- Provides guidance on communications between a predecessor and successor accountant.

SSARS No. 9, Change 1: An Accountant's Name that is Included in a Written Document or Communication Containing Unaudited Financial Statements.

There may be instances in which an accountant's name may be included in a document or written communication that also contains unaudited financial statements of a nonpublic entity.

> **EXAMPLE**
>
> A client prepared a financial package to be submitted to a bank or other third party. The package included various legal and financial documents including tax returns, client-prepared cash flows, and client-prepared financial statements that have not been audited, reviewed or compiled by the accountant. The client also includes the accountant's name and address in the package as a contact person.

For publicly held entities, auditing literature offers language that can be included with the unaudited information. Yet, the SSARSs do not include similar language. SSARS No. 9 amends SSARS No. 1 as follows:

> An accountant should not consent to the use of his or her name in a document or written communication containing unaudited financial statements of a nonpublic entity unless one of the following is the case:
> - The accountant has compiled or reviewed the financial statements in compliance with the provisions of SSARS No. 1.
> - The financial statements are accompanied by an indication that the accountant has not compiled or reviewed the financial statements and that the accountant assumes no responsibility for them.

For example, the indication may be worded as follows:

> The accompanying balance sheet of X Company as of December 31, 20X1, the related statements of income, and cash flows for the year then ended were not audited, reviewed, or compiled by us and, accordingly, we do not express an opinion or any other form of assurance on them.

If the accountant becomes aware that his or her name is being used improperly in a client-prepared document containing unaudited financial statements, the accountant should advise the client that the use of his or her name is inappropriate and should consider taking other actions, including consulting with his or her attorney.

> **OBSERVATION**
>
> The SSARS does not indicate where the report should be placed within the communications or document. Logically, the report should be positioned immediately before the financial statements similar to the placement of other reports.

One situation in which the above report might be needed is where a client submits a financial package to the bank or other third party. The package includes two years of financial statements compiled by the accountant. Additionally, the package includes a current six-month statement that has not been compiled or reviewed by the accountant. In fact, the accountant has no association with the statements. In such a case, the accountant should ask the client to insert the report immediately before the six-month financial statements to ensure that the bank or other third party is fully aware that he or she has nothing to do with the six-month financial statements.

SSARS No. 9, Change 2: Reporting Responsibility Related to the Statements of Retained Earnings and Comprehensive Income

The second change made by SSARS No. 9 is a clarification as to the reporting requirements with respect to the statements of retained earnings and comprehensive income when a compilation or review report is issued.

Retained Earnings

There is confusion in practice as to whether the change in retained earnings must be presented in the financial statements or related notes; moreover, if presented, whether the report must reference the statement.

A statement of retained earnings is not required by GAAP. However, APB No. 12, *Omnibus Opinion,* requires that all changes in capital must be disclosed. The change can be presented in one of three ways:

- Separate statement of retained earnings
- Combination statement of income and retained earnings
- Disclosure of the change in the notes to financial statements

SSARS No. 9 amends SSARS No. 1 to state that:

- A statement of retained earnings is not a required statement.
- If a statement of retained earnings is not presented, reference to the statement is not required in the compilation and review report.

122 TOP AUDITING ISSUES FOR 2005 CPE COURSE

If the change is presented in statement form either as a separate statement or as the statement of income and retained earnings, the statement should be referenced in the compilation or review report.

If the change in retained earnings is not presented in statement form, APB No. 12 still requires that the change be disclosed in the notes, in which case, there is still no need to reference the statement of retained earnings in the compilation report.

OBSERVATION

Although disclosing the change in retained earnings (either in statement or footnote format) is useful to the reader, there are instances in practice where not presenting the change may be useful. Assume for example, that a compilation report is issued whereby substantially all disclosures are omitted. The accountant may wish to merely issue a compilation report, balance sheet and statement of income all of which are generated from a computer program. The program may not present the change in retained earnings on the statement of income, thus requiring the accountant to override the program and insert the change manually. In such cases, the accountant may wish to not present the change in retained earnings on the statement of income. If so, no reference to retained earnings needs to be made in the compilation report. Note, however, the in a review engagement, disclosure of the change in retained earnings (in financial statement or footnote format) is required and, not to do so results in a GAAP departure.

Question: What if the accountant issues a compilation report in which management omits substantially all disclosures required by GAAP?
Question: Is the accountant required to present the change in the financial statements?
Response: No. APB No. 12 requires that the change in capital be disclosed. If management elects to omit substantially all disclosures, presumably one of those disclosures is the change in capital (retained earnings). Absent the footnotes, the accountant is not required to present the change in financial statement form such as a separate statement of retained earnings or a statement of income and retained earnings.

Question: Should the change in retained earnings be disclosed if OCBOA (income tax basis) statements are presented?
Response: Yes. Interpretation 14 of SAS No. 62, *Special Reports,* states that if OCBOA financial statements are presented, all disclosures that are similar to GAAP should be presented. Therefore, with OCBOA statements, the change in capital (retained earnings) must be either disclosed or presented in financial statement format. However, if, using OCBOA statements, management elects to omit substantially all disclosures required for

MODULE 2 — CHAPTER 5 — Compilation and Review Update **123**

OCBOA statements, one of the disclosures omitted is the change in capital (retained earnings).

Following are three examples of reports that illustrate the application of the SSARS No. 9 requirements with respect to the change in retained earnings.

EXAMPLE

XYZ Corporation discloses the change in retained earnings in the form of a statement of income and retained earnings.

Conclusion: Because the change in retained earnings is presented in a statement form, it should be presented in the compilation report.

EXAMPLE

XYZ Corporation discloses the change in retained earnings in the form of a footnote.

Conclusion: Because the change in retained earnings is presented in a footnote and not in a statement form, there is no requirement to mention it in the report.

EXAMPLE

The accountant for XYZ Corporation issues a compilation report in which management elects to omit substantially all disclosures and the statement of cash flows and does not disclose the change in retained earnings in a footnote or financial statement format.

Conclusion: APB No. 12 requires that the change in capital (retained earnings) be disclosed either in statement form or in the notes to financial statements. However, because management has elected to omit substantially all disclosures, one of those disclosures would have been the change in retained earnings. Thus, there is no disclosure of the change in retained earnings either in statement or footnote form and no reference to the change anywhere in the compilation report.

EXAMPLE

XYZ Corporation discloses the change in retained earnings in the form of a footnote. A review report is issued.

Conclusion: Because the change in retained earnings is presented in a footnote and not in a statement form, there is no requirement to mention in the report.

124 TOP AUDITING ISSUES FOR 2005 CPE COURSE

> **EXAMPLE**
>
> XYZ Corporation does not disclose the change in retained earnings in the form of a footnote or in a statement form. A review report is issued.
>
> **Conclusion:** Because the change in retained earnings is not presented in a footnote or statement form and a review report is being issued, there is a GAAP violation of APB No. 12. Thus, a report modification should be presented.

Comprehensive Income

SSARS No. 9 also makes a change to SSARS No. 1 with respect to the statement of comprehensive income.

In June 1997, FASB No. 130 *Reporting on Comprehensive Income,* was issued. The Statement requires that a company must present all components of comprehensive income in a financial statement format if a full set of financial statements is presented. The definition of comprehensive income is stated as follows:

Net income	xx
Other comprehensive income items: [separately presented based on their nature]	
Foreign exchange gains and losses	xx
Unrealized gains and losses on securities available for sale	xx
Loss on excess of pension liability over unrecognized prior service cost	xx
Unrealized gains and losses arising from certain derivative transactions	<u>xx</u>
Total Comprehensive Income	**xx**

The formula includes four components of other comprehensive income:
- Foreign exchange gains and losses
- Unrealized gains/losses on securities available for sale
- The loss on excess pension liability
- Changes in the market value of futures contracts

FASB No. 130 requires that comprehensive income be presented in a financial statement format. The three options available are:
- Present a separate statement of comprehensive income.
- Combine the statement of income and comprehensive income.
- Present comprehensive income as a section within the statement of stockholder's equity.

The following are three examples of financial statements.

Option 1: Separate Statement of Comprehensive Income

XYZ Corporation
Statement of Comprehensive Income
For The Year Ended December 31, 20X2

Net income	$120,000
Other comprehensive income:	
Unrealized gain on securities available for sales (net of tax effect of $20,000)	$30,000
Foreign currency translation adjustments (net of tax effect of $16,000)	<u>$24,000</u>
Other comprehensive income	<u>$54,000</u>
Comprehensive income	<u>$174,000</u>

See Accountants' Review Report

Option 2: Combined Statement of Income and Comprehensive Income

XYZ Corporation
Statement of Income and Comprehensive Income
For The Year Ended December 31, 20X2

Revenue	$1,000,000
Expenses	<u>$800,000</u>
Income from operations	$200,000
Income taxes	<u>$80,000</u>
Net income	$120,000
Other comprehensive income:	
Unrealized gain on securities available for sale (net of tax effect of $20,000)*	$30,000
Foreign currency translation adjustments (net of tax effect of $16,000)	<u>$24,000</u>
Other comprehensive income *	<u>$54,000</u>
Comprehensive income	<u>$174,000</u>

See Accountants' review Report

126 TOP AUDITING ISSUES FOR 2005 CPE COURSE

* Alternatively, the tax effect of other comprehensive income could be presented as follows:

Unrealized gain	$50,000
Foreign currency adjustments	$40,000
Other comprehensive income, before taxes	$90,000
Income tax expense allocated	($36,000)
Other comprehensive income	$54,000

Option 3: Present Comprehensive Income As Part of the Statement of Stockholder's Equity

XYZ Corporation
Statement of Stockholders' Equity
For The Year Ended December 31, 20X2

	Total	Retained earnings	Accumulated Other Comprehensive Income		Common Stock
			Unrealized gains on securities	Foreign currency adjustments	
Beginning balance	$2,525,000	$200,000	$10,000	$15,000	$500,000
Comprehensive income:					
Net income	$120,000	$120,000			
Other comprehensive income:					
Unrealized gain on securities available for sale (net of tax effect of $20,000)	$30,000		$30,000		
Foreign currency translation adjustments (net of tax effect of $16,000)	$24,000			$24,000	
Other comprehensive income	$54,000				
Comprehensive income	$174,000				
Ending balance	$2,699,000	$2,120,000	$40,000	$39,000	$500,000

See Accountant's Review Report

OBSERVATION

If option 1 or Option 2 is selected, the title of the financial statement will be changed to either "Statement of Comprehensive Income" or "Statement of Income and Comprehensive Income."

For most companies, unrealized gains and losses on securities available for sale is the most likely component of comprehensive income. FASB No. 115 requires that unrealized gains and losses on securities available for sale must be presented in stockholder's equity as a separate component, net of the tax effect. The unrealized gains or losses are presented under the caption, accumulated other comprehensive income.

If a company does not have any of the four components of other comprehensive income, FASB No. 130 does not apply and a presentation of comprehensive income is not required.

SSARS No. 9 amends SSARS No. 1 to state that if the statement of comprehensive income is presented, reference to the statement should be made in the appropriate paragraphs. Thus, if a statement of comprehensive income is required, the compilation and review reports should be modified to include reference to the statement.

Interpretation No. 25, SSARS No. 1: Omission of the Display of Comprehensive Income in a Compilation

FASB No. 130 has a special rule whereby if a full set of financial statements is not presented, a statement of comprehensive income does not have to be displayed in a financial statement format even though the company has one of the four components of other comprehensive income.

Question: How does this exemption impact the language found in the third paragraph of a compilation that omits substantially all disclosures and the statement of cash flows?
Response: The statement of comprehensive income is not required unless a full set of financial statements is presented.

If management elects to omit the statement of cash flows in a compilation engagement, a full set of financial statements is not present and the statement of comprehensive income is not required.

In 2003, the ARSC issued Interpretation No. 25 of SSARS No. 1: Omission of the Display of Comprehensive Income in a Compilation, to deal with the reporting requirements for a compilation engagement in which a statement of comprehensive income is omitted.

Question: When an element of comprehensive income is present, can the display of comprehensive income be omitted when issuing a compilation report with substantially all disclosures omitted?
Response: Yes. FASB Statement No. 130, Reporting Comprehensive Income, requires the display of comprehensive income when a full set of financial statements is presented in conformity with generally accepted accounting principles. However, the display of comprehensive income may be omitted by identifying the omission in the compilation report or engagement letter (SSARS No. 8, Amendment to Statement on Standards

for Accounting and Review Services No. 1, Compilation and Review of Financial Statements). The following is suggested modified wording (shown in italic) to the standard compilation report found in AR section 100.18:

> Management has elected to omit substantially all the disclosures, the statement of cash flows, *and the display of comprehensive income* required by generally accepted accounting principles. If the omitted disclosures, the statement of cash flows, *and the display of comprehensive income* were included in the financial statements, they might influence the user's conclusions about the company's financial position, results of operations, and cash flows. Accordingly, these financial statements are not designed for those who are not informed about such matters.

In addition, if the accountant issues a compilation report on financial statements that omit substantially all disclosures and the display of comprehensive income but includes the statement of cash flows, the following suggested modified wording (shown in italic) to the compilation report found in AR section 100.18:

> Management has elected to omit substantially all the disclosures *and the display of comprehensive income* required by generally accepted accounting principles. If the omitted disclosures *and the display of comprehensive income* were included in the financial statements, they might influence the user's conclusions about the company's financial position, results of operations, and cash flows. Accordingly, these financial statements are not designed for those who are not informed about such matters.

If the accountant compiles financial statements that include all disclosures, but omit the display of comprehensive income the omission should be treated as a departure from generally accepted accounting principles.

Additionally, if an element of comprehensive income has not been computed, for example, unrealized gains and losses arising from investments in marketable securities classified as "available for sale" then the accountant should consider a departure from generally accepted accounting principles and follow the guidance in AR sections 100.41-.43.

SSARS No. 9, Change 3: Changes
to the Compilation and Review Reports

SSARS No. 9 changes some of the requirements related to the compilation and review reports.

Presently, the SSARSs doe not specifically require that the signature of the accounting firm or the accountant be included on a compilation or review report. SSARS No. 9 addresses the signature issue and clarifies the report dates for compilation and review reports. SSARS No. 9 revises SSARS No. 1 to require the following:

MODULE 2 — CHAPTER 5 — Compilation and Review Update **129**

- A signature of the accounting firm or accountant must be included in the compilation or review report. The signature can be manual, stamped, electronic or typed.
- Dates of reports:
  - *Compilation report:* The date of the compilation report is the date of completion of the compilation.
  - *Review report:* The date of the review report is the date of the completion of the accountant's review procedures.

Question: Must the accountant's report be printed on the firm's letterhead?
Response: No. The SSARSs do not require the accountant's report to be printed on the firm's letterhead. However, letterhead does add a level of formality to the presentation. Further, if the report does not appear on letterhead, a heading such as CPA's Report may be useful to reduce any misunderstanding about the document.

Question: To whom should the accountant's report be addressed?
Response: Although the SSARSs are silent on this issue, generally, the report (review or compilation) should be addressed to the owner, manager, board or directors, board of stockholders, or each, in a corporate setting.

Question: Who should sign the report?
Response: The SSARSs do not stipulate who should sign the report. Usually the firm's signature rather than the individual's signature should accompany the report. However, some state boards of accountancy require the individual shareholder's or partner's signature if the firm is a professional corporation or LLC.

SSARS No. 9, Change 4: Changes to Management's Representation Letter

SSARS No. 9 makes changes to the elements that should be included in a management representation letter.

SSARS No. 7, *Omnibus Statement on Standards for Accounting and Review Services,* amended SSARS No. 1 to require that an accountant obtain a management representation letter for all review engagements. The letter is not required for compilation engagements; however, an accountant may choose to obtain one.

However, SSARS No. 7 does not give guidance as to the specific content, dating of the letter, and the current management's responsibility regarding previous years. In 1999, the ARSC did issue a revised representation letter. Yet, that letter was not codified within the SSARS standards.

SSARS No. 9 amends SSARS No. 1 to:

- Require specific representations to be included in the management representation letter for a review engagement

TOP AUDITING ISSUES FOR 2005 CPE COURSE

- Provides guidance on the dating of the representation letter
- Addresses the issue of obtaining representations from current management when they were not present during all periods covered by the accountant's report

Specific changes are as follows:
- Written representations should be obtained for all financial statements and periods covered by the accountant's review report:
  - If comparative financial statements are reported on, the representations at the completion of the most recent review should address all periods being reported on.
- Specific written representations will depend on the circumstances and the nature and basis of the financial statement presentations.
- For a review of financial statements, specific representations should relate to the following matters:
  - Management's acknowledgement of its responsibility for the fair presentation in the financial statements in conformity with GAAP (or OCBOA, if applicable)
  - Management's belief that the financial statements are fairly presented in conformity with GAAP (or OCBOA, if applicable)
  - Management's full and truthful response to all inquiries
  - Completeness of information
  - Information concerning subsequent events
  - Other information on matters specific to the entity's business or industry.
- The representation should be addressed to the accountant.
- The letter should be signed by those members of management whom the accountant believes are responsible for and knowledgeable about the matters covered in the letter, directly or through others in the organization. These could include the CEO, CFO, or others with equivalent positions.
  - If the current management was not present during all periods covered by the accountant's report, the accountant should nevertheless obtain written representations from the current management on all such periods.
- The representations should be made as of a date no earlier than the date of the accountant's report (date of completion of the accountant's review procedures).

Each of the above SSARS No. 9 requirements is discussed below but not necessarily in the order presented.

Obtaining Representation Letters for All Periods Reported

SSARS No. 9 amends SSARS No. 1 to require that an accountant obtain a representation letter for all periods covered by the accountant's report.

Question: What happens when current management was not present in the previous period?

Response: The SSARS does not provide an exception when current management was not present in a prior year. In fact, management might reasonably be reluctant not to sign a letter for a period during which it was not present.

> **EXAMPLE**
>
> In 20X2, Harry purchases the common stock of Company X. The CPA is planning to issue comparative reviewed financial statements for 20X2 and 20X1. Harry was not involved in the operations in 20X1.
>
> **Conclusion:** The CPA must obtain a representation letter for both 20X2 and 20X1. However, Harry might be reluctant to sign the representation letter for 20X1 since it was before he was involved in the company.

Question: Assuming the CPA received a representation letter from the previous owner for 20X1, doesn't that satisfy the need to obtain a representation letter for the 20X1 financial statements?

Response: Apparently not. Even though a representation letter was obtained in 20X1 from the previous owner, a new representation letter covering both 20X2 and 20X1 must be obtained since the 20X1 financial statements are presented along with the 20X2 statements.

One solution is to present reviewed financial statements for 20X2 only without 20X1 information. By doing so, the new owner must sign a representation letter only for 20X2.

> **OBSERVATION**
>
> One way to convince management to sign a representation letter for a previous period during which management was not involved with the company is by pointing out the degree of representation. Additional language can be inserted into the letter to protect an absent management concerning representations that relate to a period during which it was not present such as, "To the best of my knowledge or belief." If the current owner/manager refuses to sign a representation letter, a review report may not be issued.

Question: If management refuses to sign a representation letter that covers a period of time during which accountant was not present, may the accountant step down the engagement to a compilation to solve the issue?

Response: No. Stepping down to a compilation engagement is not appropriate in accordance with SSARS No. 1, paragraph 47 guidance which states:

TOP AUDITING ISSUES FOR 2005 CPE COURSE

If in an audit or a review engagement a client does not provide the accountant with a signed representation letter, the accountant would be precluded from issuing a review report on the financial statements and would ordinarily be precluded from issuing a compilation report on the financial statements.

Question: If an accountant issues a review report for interim periods (e.g., three- or six-month statements), must he or she obtain a representation letter for each interim financial statement?

Response: Yes. The accountant must obtain a representation letter for each interim period.

EXAMPLE.

An accountant prepares monthly reviewed financial statements for a client.

Conclusion: The accountant must obtain twelve representation letters, one for each monthly financial statement issued.

OBSERVATION

Usually most firms prepare monthly compiled rather than reviewed statements. Therefore, the issue of obtaining interim representation letters is not applicable

---

The Date of the Representation Letter

SSARS No. 9 amends SSARS No. 1 to require that management's representations be made as of a date no earlier than the date of the accountant's report. The date of the accountant's review report is generally the date that the accountant completes his or her review procedures (inquiry and analytical procedures).

However, representations made as of the date of the report may not be adequate to cover events that might occur after the completion date of the review and the date the report is issued.

EXAMPLE

An accountant performs a review engagement on a company for the year ended December 31, 20X2. The accountant completes her review procedures (e.g., inquiry and analytical procedures) on February 14, 20X3 and issues the report on April 26, 20X3.

A subsequent event occurs between February 14 and April 26, 20X3. Management does not disclose the event to the accountant and the letter does not cover it because it occurred after February 14.

MODULE 2 — CHAPTER 5 — Compilation and Review Update **133**

Conclusion: Customarily, the firm obtains a representation letter dated and signed as of February 14, 20X3 and does not obtain an updated letter close to April 26, 20X3. In this case, because the letter is signed as of February 14, management could claim that it is not responsible for the representation because it occurred after the date of the letter, February 14, 20X3.

OBSERVATION

SSARS No. 9 stipulates that the date of the letter should be no earlier than the date of the report. In the previous example, that means a date that is no earlier than February 14, 20X2. The result is that CPA firms should delay the receipt of representation letters to a date that is as close to the date that the report is issued. In the previous example, the author believes that the letter date and the date on which the letter is signed should both be April 26, 20X2. Alternatively, the CPA could obtain a representation letter as of February 14 with an updated letter signed through April 26.

One way to ensure the timing of this letter is to fax a copy of the letter to the client for signature on the day the report and financial statements are ready to be issued. Once the signed and dated letter is received back, you can mail out the report and financial statements even though an original signed letter has not been received. Remember that in most jurisdictions, receipt of a plain-paper faxed document is a legally binding document.

EXAMPLE

An accountant completes her fieldwork on February 14, 20X3 for a December 31, 20X2 year-end review engagement. The report is issued on April 26, 20X3.

Conclusion: The accountant should obtain a representation letter from management that is dated and signed on or near the April 26, 20X3 date.

Following the letter are additional representations that are available depending on the situation, an example of which is in Appendix B-1.

OBSERVATION

In designing an effective representation letter, a CPA may wish to consider the following:

- Avoid the use of technical terms and, instead, use terms that are understandable to the client.
- It is good practice to review the representation letter with the client before the letter is signed. By reviewing the letter in person, it may act as a "memory jogger" for the client concerning additional matters that may affect the financial statements. Discussions may make the client feel more comfortable about signing the letter.

134 TOP AUDITING ISSUES FOR 2005 CPE COURSE

> ■ In litigation, a more thorough explanation in person has helped some firms defend against management's claim that they did not understand the level of service being performed.

Additional Illustrative Representations

See Appendix B-2 for examples of additional illustrative disclosures that may be added into the basic representation letter. Some of these representations are recommended by the ARSC in SSARS No. 9 while the remainder are disclosures that are included in SAS 85, Management Representations, for audits that the author believes are relevant to reviews. Those representations followed by "***" are thought to be particularly important and should be included in representation letters, depending on the circumstances.

> **OBSERVATION**
>
> The additional list of representations is not authoritative and certainly not all-inclusive. The author believes that management representation letters can become voluminous and intimidating for clients to sign. Therefore, it is important that the accountant balance the need for full management disclosure with the need to make the letter concise and relevant to the client. In practice, many firms have handled representation letters for reviews (and audits) in one of two extreme ways—either by using an old insufficient letter, not updated for recent pronouncements, or by using a letter that is unnecessarily verbose-just short of a *New York Times* Best Seller. Most of the representations provide little assistance to a accountant who wishes to use representations as a substitute for performing adequate fieldwork. For audits, SAS No. 85, *Management Representations,* specifically states that management representations should not be a substitute for performing substantive tests. The same should hold true for review engagements whereby representations should not replace the accountant's responsibility to perform adequate analytical procedures or inquiries.

SSARS No. 9, Change 5: Changes to Supplementary Information Reporting

SSARS No. 1 includes guidance on reporting for supplementary information. However, the guidance is unclear related to separate reporting on supplementary information in a compilation engagement.

SSARS No. 9 amends SSARS no. 1 to allow for a separate report on supplementary information in a compilation engagement. Specific changes to the language in SSARS No. 1 follows:

> When the accountant has compiled both the basic financial statements and other data presented only for supplementary analysis purposes, the compilation report should refer to the other data or the accountant can

issue a separate report on the other data. If the separate report is issued, the report should state that the other data accompanying the financial statements are presented only for supplementary analysis purposes and that the information has been compiled from information that is the representation of management, without audit or review, and the accountant does not express an opinion or any other form of assurance on such data.

Other Issues Related to Supplementary Information

The changes in SSARS No. 9 address some of the more important issues that appear related to supplementary information in a compilation or review engagement.

Reporting Options

According to the AICPA's Peer Review Committee, one of the significant errors detected in peer reviews is the mishandling of the reporting on supplementary information. As a result, the author believes it is important to identify the rules associated with presenting supplementary information and the reporting thereon as it relates to compilation and review engagements.

The rules for dealing with supplementary information in compilation and review engagements are found in paragraph 43 of SSARS No. 1 that states:

> When the basic financial statements are accompanied by information presented for supplementary analysis purposes, the CPA should clearly indicate the degree of responsibility, if any, he is taking with respect to such information.

The accountant has two options in dealing with supplementary information. The first option is to review the supplementary information. Report that:

> The additional information is presented for supplementary analysis and has been subjected to the inquiry and analytical procedures applied in the review of the financial statements, and the CPA did not become aware of any material modifications that should be made to the data.

The second option is to compile the supplementary information. Report that:

> The additional information is presented for supplementary analysis and has been subjected to the inquiry and analytical procedures applied in the review of the financial statements, but were compiled from information that is the representation of management, without audit or review, and the CPA does not express an opinion or any other form of assurance on such data.

Supplementary information should not be reviewed when the basic financial statements have been compiled. The following table summarizes the options.

TOP AUDITING ISSUES FOR 2005 CPE COURSE

Review Engagements	Compilation Engagements
Review the supplementary information and report on it.	Supplementary information may not be reviewed in a compilation engagement.
Compile the supplementary information	Compile the supplementary information

> **OBSERVATION**
>
> In a review engagement, most accountants will perform analytical procedures on supplementary information as part of the engagement. For example, analytical procedures are performed on many of the individual operating expenses listed in the operating expense schedule. Therefore, it is rare that an accountant compiles, rather than reviews supplementary information in a review engagement.

Alternatively, a separate report on supplementary information may be presented after the basic reviewed financial statements and notes to financial statements. Another option is that the accountant can issue a separate report on the compiled supplementary information, as authorized by SSARS No. 9.

What is Supplementary Information?

SSARS No. 1 does not define supplementary information. However, paragraph 43 of SSARS No. 1 describes such information as information presented for supplementary analysis purposes. There is no authority defining what SSARS No. 1 means. But SAS No. 29, Reporting on Information Accompanying the Basic Financial Statements in Auditor-Submitted Documents defines supplementary information to include the following categories of information as modified by the author:

- Additional details of items in or related to the basic financial statements, unless the information has been identified as being part of the basic financial statements. Attached schedules that relate to line items on the financial statements including:
  - Operating expense schedule(s)
  - Schedule of cost of sales
  - Schedule of selling and G&A expenses
  - Details of marketable securities
  - Schedule of property and equipment
  - Aging analysis of accounts receivable
  - Detailed analysis of sales by product line, territory, or salesman
- Modifications to basic financial statements, for example, budgeted financial information presented along side an historic income statement

- Graphs and charts of the information presented on the financial statements, such as pie charts, etc.
- Schedule of financial data for individual companies within a consolidated group
- Condensed financial statements for previous years
- Statistical data including divisions analyses
- Detailed analysis of inventories and accounts receivable
- Supplementary information related to specialized industries (e.g., common interest realty association supplementary information)
- Other material, some of which may be from sources outside the accounting system or outside the entity

Question: Are percentages that accompany an income statement considered supplementary information?

Response: Although statistical data is usually considered supplementary information, most practitioners do not treat financial statement percentages as supplementary information. For example, an income statement may present percentages in a separate column. Generally, this information would not be considered supplementary information and the author believes there is no additional reporting requirement in connection with this information.

Question: Are charts and graphs considered supplementary information?

Response: The advent and availability of easy-to-use computer software capable of generating graphs has resulted in an increase in the inclusion of graphs in financial statement presentations. As a result, many CPAs continue to inquire about their reporting responsibility for graphs that accompany financial statements in compilation and review engagements. Graphs may depict information:

- Identified in the financial statements such as a pie chart depicting various components of sales, cost of sales and operating expenses
- Derived from the accounting records such as a bar graph depicting sales by product line
- Derived from sources outside the financial statements and accounting records, such as a pie chart depicting square feet of selling space by product line

Presently, SSARS No. 1 does not address the reporting on graphs accompanying financial statements. Yet, SSARS No. 1, paragraph 43 does make reference to supplementary information accompanying the basic financial statements. Absent authority, a CPA may wish to consider the graphs and charts as supplementary information and report on them as such.

138 TOP AUDITING ISSUES FOR 2005 CPE COURSE

Procedures for Reviewing or Compiling Supplementary Information

Although SSARS No. 1 does not identify procedures to follow in compiling or reviewing supplementary information, it would appear prudent to follow the same procedures that are utilized to compile or review the underlying financial statements.

Although not binding, the AICPA recommends that supplementary information in the form of graphs and charts be compiled regardless of whether the underlying financial statements are compiled or reviewed. By doing so, the CPA takes a more practical and conservative approach given the absence of authoritative standards and criteria for these presentations.

Examples of procedures that might be employed to compile supplementary information charts and graphs include:

- Reading the title, captions, and numerical information included in the graph to determine whether that information agrees with the information presented in the financial statements
- Considering whether the graph's pictorial representation agrees with the quantities and relationships it purports to represent

---

EXAMPLE

Consider one misrepresentation of a graph. Comparative financial statements might indicate that the increase in net income from 20X1 to 20X2 is ten percent, and the captions in the accompanying bar graph might accurately identify the amount of net income in each year consistent with the income statement. However, the graph is drawn so that the increase in the height of the bar is significantly greater than ten percent.

Conclusion: If a CPA concludes that there is a material inconsistency between the graph and the financial statements, the CPA should determine whether the financial statements, the graph, or both require revision, and, if appropriate, should ask the client to revise the incorrect or misleading information. If the information is not revised to eliminate the problem, the CPA should consider revising the report to describe the inconsistency or misleading information or should consider withdrawing from the engagement.

How to Present Supplementary Information

There is no authority on how supplementary information should be presented. However, the author recommends that the pages of supplementary information be easily identified versus the financial statement pages. In order to do so, the author believes the following is good form:

Page Legend

Make sure each page of supplementary information makes reference to the Accountant's report.

Condition	Recommended Legend
If the report on supplementary information is included in the report on financial statements	*See Accountant's Report* or *See Accountant's Review Report*
If there is a separte report on supplementary information	*See Accountant's Report on Supplementary information*

Titles on Pages

Although not authoritative, titles should be selected that ensure that the reader clearly differentiates the supplementary information from the primary financial statements.

> **EXAMPLE**
>
> ABC Company
> Schedule of Operating Expenses
> For the Year Ended December 31, 20X1
> (See Accountant's Report on Supplementary Information)
>
> ABC Company
> Supplementary Analysis of Operating Expenses
> For the Year Ended December 31, 20X1
> (See Accountant's Report on Supplementary Information)

In addition to the above legends and titles, some practitioners include a separate introductory title page for supplementary information that follows the notes to financial statements. The author does not believe this is necessary provided the reader can differentiate between the financial statements and supplementary information.

Reporting on Budgets Presented Alongside Historic Statements

At times, a CPA will be asked to present financial statements for the fiscal year along with budgeted financial statements on a comparative basis.

> **EXAMPLE**
>
> Actual financial statements for the year ended June 30, 20X1 are presented with the budget for the year ended June 30, 20X1.

If a CPA is engaged to report on such a presentation, the budgeted information for the expired period should be treated as supplementary information in accordance with paragraph 43 of SSARS No. 1.

140 TOP AUDITING ISSUES FOR 2005 CPE COURSE

> **EXAMPLE**
>
> A CPA must identify responsibility for the supplementary information in his or her report.

> **OBSERVATION**
>
> Although the budgeted information was once prospective information, it is no longer prospective information once the period has expired.

Sample Statement of Income
Actual and Expired Budgeted Income Statement

NXJ Company
Statement of Income-Historical and Budgeted
For The Six Months Ended June 30, 20X1
(See Accountant's Compilation Report)

	Actual	Budgeted	Variance
Net sales	$xx	$xx	$xx
Cost of sales	xx	xx	xx
Gross profit on sales	xx	xx	xx
Operating expenses	xx	xx	xx
Net operating income	xx	xx	xx
Other income	xx	xx	xx
Net income before income taxes	xx	xx	xx
Income taxes	xx	xx	xx
Net income	$xx	$xx	$xx

SSARS No. 9, Change 6: Relationship of Quality Control Standards with the SSARSs

The SSARSs presently do not refer to the Statements on Quality Control Standards (SQCSs) and how those standards relate to the SSARSs. Rule 202 of the AICPA's Code of Professional Conduct requires that members comply with associated reviewed or compiled financial statements. SSARS No. 9 amends SSARS No. 1 to integrate the SQCSs into the SSARSs as follows:

MODULE 2 — CHAPTER 5 — Compilation and Review Update **141**

- An accountant is responsible for compliance with the SSARSs in a review or compilation engagement.
- An accountant has the responsibility to adopt a system of quality control in conducting an accounting practice and should establish quality control policies and procedures to provide it with reasonable assurance that its personnel comply with SSARS in its review and compilation engagements.
  - The nature and extent of the policies and procedures depend on factors such as The firm's size, the degree of operating autonomy allowed to its personnel and offices, nature of the practice, its organization, and appropriate cost-benefit considerations.
- The SSARSs relate to the conduct on individual review and compilation engagements. SQCSs relate to the conduct of a firm's accounting practice. Thus, SSARSs and SQCSs are related, and the quality control policies and procedures that a firm adopts may affect both the conduct of the engagement and the firm's accounting practice.
- Deficiencies in or instances of noncompliance with a firm's quality control policies and procedures do not, in and of themselves, indicate that a particular review or compilation engagement was not performed in accordance with SSARSs.

OBSERVATION

The most important aspect of the introduction of the SQCSs to the SSARSs is the fact that the revision specifically confirms that if an accountant can still perform a compilation or review engagement in accordance with the SSARSs even though the individual or firm either does not have a quality control system or is not in compliance with such a system.

SSARS No. 9, Change 7: Communications Between Predecessor and Successor CPAs

With respect to audits, SAS No. 84, Communications Between Predecessor and Successor Auditors requires that a successor auditor communicate with a predecessor auditor prior to accepting an audit engagement.

For compilation and review engagements, SSARS No. 4, Communications Between Predecessor and Successor CPAs provides guidance on communications between accountants when the successor accountant decides to communicate with the predecessor accountant regarding the acceptance of an engagement.

Unlike an audit engagement, SSARS No. 4 does not require successor CPAs to communicate with or obtain access to working papers of predecessor CPAs in accepting compilation or review engagements. However, SSARS No. 4 does not prevent a CPA from making a communication and, in certain circumstances, it may be helpful. SSARS No. 9 amends SSARS No. 4 by providing additional guidance on the successor-predecessor accountant communication process. SSARS No. 9 does the following:

- Defines a predecessor and successor accountant
- Includes a sample successor accountant acknowledgement letter which a predecessor accountant might want to have the successor sign before allowing the successor access to working papers

The following is a detail of the new SSARS No. 4 rules, as amended by SSARS No. 9, related to the predecessor-successor accountant relationship.

Definitions of *Successor Accountant* and *Predecessor Accountant*

SSARS No. 9 modifies the definitions of the *successor* and *predecessor* accountant.

The successor accountant is an accountant who has been invited to make a proposal for an engagement to compile or review financial statements and is considering accepting the engagement or an accountant who has accepted the engagement.

The predecessor accountant is an accountant who:

- Has reported on the most recent compiled or reviewed financial statements or was engaged to perform but did not complete a compilation or review of the financial statements
- Has resigned, declined to stand for reappointment, or been notified that his or her services have been or may be terminated

A successor accountant is not required to communicate with a predecessor accountant in connection with acceptance of a compilation or review engagement. But, he or she may believe it is beneficial to obtain information that will assist in determining whether to accept the engagement.

The successor may consider making inquiries of the predecessor accountant when circumstances such as one of the following exist:

- The information obtained about the prospective client and its management and principals is limited or appears to require special attention.
- The change in accountants takes place substantially after the end of the accounting period for which statements are to be compiled or reviewed.
- There have been frequent changes in accountants.

The successor accountant should be aware that the predecessor accountant and the client may have disagreed about accounting principles, procedures applied by the predecessor accountant, or similarly significant matters.

The successor should request permission from the prospective client to make any inquiries of the predecessor accountant.

> **OBSERVATION**
>
> Except as allowed by the AICPA *Code of Professional Conduct,* the accountant is precluded from disclosing any confidential information obtained in the course of the engagement unless the client specifically consents.

If the successor accountant decides to communicate with the predecessor, the successor accountant should request the client to:

- Permit the successor accountant to make inquiries of the predecessor accountant.
- Authorize the predecessor accountant to respond fully to those inquiries.

If the prospective client refuses to permit the predecessor accountant to respond or limits the response, the successor should inquire about the reasons and consider the implications of that refusal in determining whether to accept the engagement.

If the successor decides to communicate with the predecessor, the inquiries should be specific and reasonable regarding matters that will assist the successor in determining whether to accept the engagement. Examples of such matters include:

- Information that might bear on the integrity of management or the owners
- Disagreements with management or the owners about accounting principles or the necessity for the performance of certain procedures or similarly significant matters
- The cooperation of management or the owners in providing additional or revised information
- The predecessor's knowledge of any fraud or illegal acts perpetrated within the client
- The predecessor's understanding of the reason for the change of accountants

The predecessor is required to respond promptly and fully to the inquiries on the basis of known facts. If the predecessor decides, due to unusual circumstances, such as impending, threatened, or potential litigation, disciplinary proceedings, or other circumstances, not to respond fully to the inquiries, the predecessor should indicate that the response is limited. The successor should consider the effect of such limited responses on his or her decision to accept the engagement.

> **OBSERVATION**
>
> The SSARS indicates that unpaid fees are not considered to be an unusual circumstance for which the predecessor refuses to respond to inquiries.

TOP AUDITING ISSUES FOR 2005 CPE COURSE

If the successor wishes to review the predecessor's working papers, the successor should request the client to authorize the predecessor to allow access. The predecessor should determine which working papers are to be made available for review and which may be copied.

Usually, the predecessor should provide the successor with access to certain working papers related to matters of continuing accounting significance and contingencies.

Valid business reasons, including, but (not limited to unpaid fees) may lead the predecessor to decide not to allow access to the working papers.

The predecessor may wish to reach an agreement with the successor as to the use of the working papers. Such an agreement may be in writing in the form of a Successor Accountant Acknowledgement Letter. The predecessor should not be expected to make the working papers available until the client has designated an accountant as a successor.

> **OBSERVATION**
>
> The SSARSs do not address the form and content of working papers for a review or compilation.

The successor is not permitted to reference the predecessor's report or work in his or her own report except if financial statements for the prior year are presented comparatively and those statements were compiled or reviewed by the predecessor.

In such a case, the successor should include the following language in his report for the current period. Review report for 20X3 would include language related to 20X2 as follows:

> The 20X2 financial statements of XYZ Company were reviewed by other accountants whose report dated March 1, 20X3, stated that they were not aware of any material modifications that should be made to those statements in order for them to be in conformity with generally accepted accounting principles.

Compilation report for 20X3 would include language related to 20X2 as follows:

> The 20X1 financial statements of XYZ Company were compiled by other accountants whose report dated March 1, 20X3, stated that they did not express an opinion or any other form of assurance on those statements.

If, during an engagement, the successor becomes aware of information that leads him or her to believe that the financial statements reported on by the predecessor may require revision, the successor should request the client to communicate this information to the predecessor.

MODULE 2 — CHAPTER 5 — Compilation and Review Update **145**

If the client refuses to communicate with the predecessor or if the successor is not satisfied with the predecessor's course of action, the successor should evaluate possible implications for the current engagement and whether to resign. Also, the accountant may wish to consult with legal counsel about the appropriate course of action.

Question: What if the previous year's financial statements were audited and the current year will be compiled or reviewed?

Response: There is no requirement for the successor accountant to communicate with the predecessor auditor if the previous year was audited and the current year will be compiled or reviewed.

SSARS No. 4 does not require any communication in this situation. And, from the auditing side, SAS No. 84 applies only when both the previous and current year statements involve an audit. The same answer would apply if the opposite were true with the prior year statements compiled or reviewed with an upgrade to a current year audit.

See Appendix B-3 for a sample letter to be signed by successor accountant before having access to the predecessor's working papers.

STUDY QUESTIONS

> **1.** The second change made by SSARS No. 9 is a clarification as to the reporting requirements with respect to the statements of retained earnings when a compilation or review report is issued. *True or False?*
>
> **2.** A representation letter is required for all review engagements, but not required for compilation engagements. *True or False?*
>
> **3.** In designing an effective representation letter, an accountant may wish to consider making the letter very technical in nature so that it will be binding in the event of litigation. *True or False?*
>
> **4.** When dealing with supplementary information, in a compilation engagement, supplementary information may be reviewed. *True or False?*

SELECTED INFORMATION: "SUBSTANTIALLY ALL DISCLOSURES REQUIRED BY GENERALLY ACCEPTED ACCOUNTING PRINCIPLES ARE NOT INCLUDED"

In December 2002, the ARSC issued Interpretation 22 of SSARS No. 1, Use of "Selected Information-Substantially All Disclosures Required by Generally Accepted Accounting Principles Are Not Included." This Interpretation clarifies the practice of disclosing selected information as required by GAAP.

146 TOP AUDITING ISSUES FOR 2005 CPE COURSE

In some instances, a client may wish to include only selected disclosures in compiled financial statements. For example, the bank may accept compiled financial statements that include only long-term debt, fixed asset and lease footnotes, thereby excluding the remainder of disclosures required by GAAP (or OCBOA).

Question: If this is the case, may the CPA issue a compilation report indicating that substantially all of the disclosures and the statement of cash flows have been omitted?

Response: Paragraph 19 of SSARS No. 1 states:

> An entity may request a CPA to compile financial statements that omit substantially all of the disclosures required by generally accepted accounting principles, including disclosures that might appear in the body of the financial statements .... The CPA may compile such financial statements provided the omission of substantially all disclosures is clearly indicated in his report and is not, to his knowledge, undertaken with the intention of misleading those who might reasonably be expected to use such financial statements.

Question: What is meant by *substantially all disclosures?*

Response: SSARS No. 1 does not elaborate; however, it does appear that the SSARS No. 1 exception is not an all or nothing situation. Meaning, a client may select certain disclosures to accompany the financial statements provide certain criteria are met and come under the guise of the *substantially all* criteria. Paragraph 19 of SSARS No. 1 continues by stating:

> When the entity wishes to include disclosures about only a few matters in the form of notes to such financial statements, such disclosures should be labeled, "Selected Information—Substantially All Disclosures required by Generally Accepted Accounting Principles Are Not Included."

EXAMPLE

Harry's client, Fred asks Harry to compile financial statements. Fred has little need for a statement of cash flows and most of the disclosures required by GAAP except that the local bank wants a disclosure of the long-term debt and operating leases.

Conclusion: Harry may issue a compilation report as follows along with the attached notes to financial statements.

MODULE 2 — CHAPTER 5 — Compilation and Review Update **147**

XYZ CORPORATION
SELECTED INFORMATION
Substantially All Disclosures Required
by General Accepted Accounting
Principles Are Not Included
December 31, 20X1

Note 1: Long-term debt

A summary of long-term debt at December 31, 20X1 follows:

No Loan Bank: Term loan with monthly payments of $10,000 plus interest at nine percent per annum through the year 20X6. Secured by a first mortgage on certain corporate real estate	$1,000,000
Installment loans: Serveral installment loans relating to the purchase of certain manufacturing equipment. The terms of these loans require monthly principlal payments of $5,000 plus interest at 10% per annum through the year 20X6	$300,000
	$1,300,000
Less current portion	($100,000)
	$1,200,000

Interest expense was $118,000

A summary of the annual maturities of long-term debt for the five years subsequent to 20X1 follows:

20X2	$100,000
20X3	$120,000
20X4	$140,000
20X5	$160,000
20X6	$180,000

Note 2: Leases

The Company leases its principal operating facility under a five-year non-cancelable operating lease. The terms of the lease require monthly payments of $15,000 with periodic increases through June 20X5. The company has a five-year option for renewal for the years 20X6 to 20X9 at an increased monthly rental rate.

The following consists of the future minimum rental payments due under this operating lease.

Year	Amount
20X2	$180,000
20X3	$190,000
20X4	$200,000
20X5	$105,000

Question: What if all disclosures are included except one. Does the "substantially all" paragraph apply?

Response: Prior to December 2002, the answer was not clear. To resolve the confusion, in December 2002, the ARSC issued Interpretation 22, SSARS No. 1, *Use of "Selected Information-Substantially All Disclosures Required by Generally Accepted Accounting Principles Are Not Included."*

Interpretation 22, SSARS No. 1, *Use of "Selected Information—Substantially All Disclosures Required by Generally Accepted Accounting Principles Are Not Included."*

Question: Can an accountant label notes to the financial statements "Selected Information—Substantially All Disclosures Required by Generally Accepted Accounting Principles Are Not Included" when the client includes more than a few required disclosures?

Response: No. As discussed in paragraph 16 of SSARS No. 1, when the entity wishes to include disclosures about only a few matters in the form of notes to the financial statements, such disclosures should be labeled "Selected Information—Substantially All Disclosures Required by Generally Accepted Accounting Principles Are Not Included."

When the financial statements include more than a few disclosures, this guidance is not appropriate. The omission of one or more notes, when substantially all other disclosures are presented, should be treated in a compilation or review report like any other departure from GAAP, and the nature of the departure and its effects, if known, should be disclosed.

The label "Selected Information—Substantially All Disclosures Required by Generally Accepted Accounting Principles Are Not Included" should not be used in situations where substantially all disclosures are included. The label "Selected Information—Substantially All Disclosures Required by Generally Accepted Accounting Principles Are Not Included" is not intended to be used for the omission of (intentionally or unintentionally) one or more disclosures and the accountant should use his or her judgment in determining the appropriateness of the label.

EXAMPLE

A client wishes to include all notes to financial statements except a disclosure of risks and uncertainties as required by SOP 94-6.

Conclusion: Because all but one required disclosure are included in the notes, the use of "Selected Information—Substantially All Disclosures Required by Generally Accepted Accounting Principles Are Not Included" is not appropriate. Instead, the missing disclosure should be treated as a GAAP departure.

MODULE 2 — CHAPTER 5 — Compilation and Review Update **149**

Question: May disclosures be omitted in a review engagement?

Response: No. Interpretation No. 1 of SSARS No. 1 states that the exception only applies when financial statements have been compiled, not reviewed. Therefore, generally, a CPA would not accept an engagement to review financial statements that omit substantially all of the GAAP disclosures.

REFERENCE TO THE COUNTRY OF ORIGIN IN A REVIEW OR COMPILATION REPORT

SAS No. 93, *Omnibus Statement on Auditing Standards—2000,* made modifications to the audit report by requiring that the auditor's report include reference to the country of origin of the accounting principles and auditing standards the auditor followed in performing the audit.

The auditor report language is as follows:

Paragraph 2:

We conducted our audit in accordance with auditing standards generally accepted in the United States of America. Those standards require that we plan and perform the audit to obtain reasonable assurance about whether the financial statements are free of material misstatement. An audit includes examining, on a test basis, evidence supporting the amounts and disclosures in the financial statements. An audit also includes assessing the accounting principles used and significant estimates made by management, as well as evaluating the overall financial statement presentation. We believe that our audit provides a reasonable basis for our opinion.

Paragraph 3:

In our opinion, the financial statements referred to above present fairly, in all material respects, the financial position of X Company as of December 31, 20XX, and the results of its operations and its cash flows for the year then ended in conformity with accounting principles generally accepted in the United States of America.

Since the issuance of SAS No. 93, there has been speculation that the ARSC would amend the SSARSs requiring a similar reference to the country of origin in a compilation and report. In 2003, the ARSC issued Interpretation No. 24 of SSARS No. 1, Reference to the Country of Origin in a Review or Compilation Report to address the issue.

Interpretation No. 24: Reference to the Country of Origin in a Review or Compilation Report

Question: When issuing a review or compilation report, should there be a reference to the country of origin of the accounting principles used to prepare the financial statements, similar to the requirement when issuing audited financial statements?

150 TOP AUDITING ISSUES FOR 2005 CPE COURSE

Response: SSARS do not require the reference to the country of origin as review and compilation reports refer to the American Institute of Certified Public Accountants. However, there is no prohibition of the reference if the accountant believes it is appropriate under the circumstances to include it in the report.

> **OBSERVATION**
>
> The ARSC's Interpretation was the correct response to the issue. Specifically, the Interpretation does not require that reference to the country of origin be included in the compilation or review report, but does not preclude an accountant from doing so.

SAS No. 93 inserted the country of origin in the auditor's report to deal with the confusion found with companies issuing financial statements on an international basis. Prior to SAS No. 93, the traditional auditor's report referenced GAAP and GAAS but did not indicate the country or origin to which GAAP and GAAS applied. Thus, a reader of a company's financial statements had no idea whether GAAP and GAAS related to accounting principles and auditing standards issued in the United States or United Kingdom. The problem was exacerbated by the posting of SEC companies' financial statements on the Internet.

A similar challenge does not exist with compilation and review engagements. In most cases, compilation and review reports are issued within the United States and they are rarely posted on the Internet. Thus, the need to reference the country of original is not important.

STUDY QUESTIONS

5. Supplementary information includes an operating expense schedule. *True or False?*

6. With respect to page legends for supplementary information, make sure each page of supplementary information makes reference to the Accountant's report. *True or False?*

7. For compilation and review engagements, SSARS No. 4, Communications Between Predecessor and Successor CPAs provides guidance on communications between accountants when the successor accountant decides to communicate with the predecessor accountant regarding the acceptance of an engagement. *True or False?*

ANSWERS TO STUDY QUESTIONS — Module 1 — Chapter 1   **151**

TOP AUDITING ISSUES FOR 2005 CPE COURSE
Answers to Study Questions

MODULE 1 — CHAPTER 1

1. True. *Correct.* In 2004, the AICPA published its annual Top 10 list of technology issues. On the top of that list is information security, which has been on the list for several years. Information security involves using the hardware, software, processes and procedures in place that protect an entity's systems, including firewalls, anti-virus, password management, patches, and locked facilities.

False. *Incorrect.* Information security is on the Top 10 list so that the statement is correct. With the concern over security, including hackers and viruses, it is no surprise that information security is on the top of the list. Interestingly, newcomers to the list include spam technology, digital optimization, database and application integration, data mining, virtual office, business exchange technology, and message applications.

2. True. *Correct.* In addition to the AICPA's Top 10 Technologies list, the AICPA published a Top 5 Emerging Technologies list. The Emerging Technologies include those technologies that may not have a current commercial impact, but may do so in the next few years. Third on the list is the development of 3G wireless. 3G wireless is used for high-speed multi-media data and voice. As multi-media grows, wireless communications will be a major segment for that new form of technology.

False. *Incorrect.* 3G Wireless is, in fact, on the Top 5 list so that the statement is correct. Others on the list include a) ID/Authentication, which includes verifying either the identity of a user who is logging onto a computer system or the integrity of a transmitted message, b) Radio Frequency Identification (RFID), which consists of silicon chips and an antenna that can transmit data to a wireless receiver, and could be used to track the geographic location of anything, c) Simple Object Access Protocol (SOAP), which is a message-based protocol based on XML for accessing services on the Internet, and d) Autonomic Computers which consist of tools and strategies to manage and maintain all systems across an entity with the goal toward self-managing computer systems.

3. False. *Correct.* The statement is not correctly stated in that the profession's public image has, in fact, improved from 2002 to 2003. After the Enron crisis at the end of 2001, the accounting profession's image plummeted from 2001 to 2002. Now, after some reforms have been put in place coupled with the passage of time, the accounting profession's image has significantly improved from 2002 to 2003. Based on the 2003 survey, 45% of the respondents had a positive image of accountants, with only 14% having a negative one.

152 TOP AUDITING ISSUES FOR 2005 CPE COURSE

True. *Incorrect.* The Poll shows just the opposite result. That is, the image of accountants has actually improved from 2002 to 2003. In the poll, Americans were asked to rate their overall view of each of 25 industries ranging from very positive to very negative. The results of the 2003 poll were quite positive for the accounting profession, showing a 14% increase in positive image, while showing a 17% decrease in negative image. Computer, restaurant, and grocery businesses had the most positive images, while the oil and gas, healthcare, and legal industries had the most negative images.

4. False. *Correct.* The statement is not correctly stated in that SAS No. 99 does supersede SAS No. 82. Specifically, SAS No. 99 makes significant changes to SAS No. 82 among which it a) emphasizes that an auditor must exercise professional skepticism during the audit, b) requires that the auditor conduct a brainstorming session with audit engagement personnel to discuss the risks of material misstatement due to fraud and set the tone of the audit, and, c) expands information gathering required to identify fraud risks, among other changes.

True. *Incorrect.* SAS No. 99 supersedes SAS No. 82, Consideration of Fraud in a Financial Statement Audit, and establishes expanded requirements for auditors to consider fraud in a financial statement audit. It applies to audits of both public and non-public entities.

5. True. *Correct.* The statement is correctly stated in that the auditor must enhance his or her degree of professional skepticism. Professional skepticism is an attitude based on having a questioning mind and performing a critical assessment of all audit evidence received, and possessing a "show me" mindset that recognizes the distinct possibility that a material misstatement due to fraud could be present.

Further, an auditor that displays professional skepticism evaluates information received by management without any bias to past experience with the entity and regardless of the auditor's belief about management's honesty and integrity. Professional skepticism does not assume that management or employees are guilty or innocent of committing fraud. Instead, it is based on a mandatory degree of neutrality. In gathering and evaluating evidence, the auditor should not be satisfied with less-than-persuasive evidence because of his or her belief that management is honest.

False. *Incorrect.* A major change in SAS No. 99 is the emphasis on auditors maintaining a high degree of professional skepticism throughout the audit. SAS No. 1, Codification of Auditing Standards and Procedures, volume 1, Due Professional Care in the Performance of Work, requires an auditor to exercise professional skepticism in conducting his or her engagement. SAS No. 99 reemphasizes the auditor's responsibility under SAS No. 1 and the fact that auditors must overcome any bias they have toward a client in conducting an audit.

6. False. *Correct.* The statement is incorrectly stated because there are generally considered two types of fraud: fraudulent financial reporting and misappropriation of assets. Fraudulent financial reporting is likely to be performed by higher-level management who has a stake in altering the financial statement results. Alternatively, misappropriation of assets (e.g., theft) can be performed at all levels from the lowest employment position to the highest. Statistically, 80% of all fraud involves the misappropriation of assets, while only 20% consists of fraudulent financial reporting. Regarding employee theft, reasons for committing the crime vary from employee revenge for corporate restructurings to changes in technology making it easier to conceal fraud.

True. *Incorrect.* There are two types of misstatements due to fraud: fraudulent financial reporting (cooking the books) and misappropriation of assets (theft or defalcation). Both types of fraud can occur in any organization.

7. True. *Correct.* Fraudulent financial reporting involves the intentional misstatements or omissions of amounts or disclosures in financial statements. designed to deceive financial statement users where the effect causes the financial statements not to be presented in accordance with GAAP (or another comprehensive basis of accounting, if used).

False. *Incorrect.* The statement is correct in that fraudulent financial reporting involves an intentional misstatement or omission of amount or disclosures. It is designed to deceive the users. Fraudulent financial reporting is accomplished in several ways such as:

- Manipulation, falsification, or alteration of accounting records or supporting documents from which financial statements are prepared
- Misrepresentation in or intentional omission from the financial statements of events, transactions, or other significant information
- Intentional misapplication of accounting principles relating to amounts, classification, manner of presentation, or disclosure.

8. True. *Correct.* Misappropriation of assets involves the theft of an entity's assets where the effect of the theft causes the financial statements not to be presented in conformity with GAAP. Misappropriation of assets usually involves the personal enrichment of the perpetrator. In contract, fraudulent financial reporting may involve a person who performs the fraudulent act on behalf of the company without any personal enrichment.

False. *Incorrect.* The statement is correctly stated in that misappropriation of assets involves the theft of assets and the effect of the theft results in the financial statements not being presented in accordance with GAAP. It is usually accomplished by false or misleading records or documents, possibly created by circumventing controls. Misappropriation of assets is accomplished in several ways, including embezzling receipts, stealing assets, or causing the entity to pay for goods or services not received.

154 TOP AUDITING ISSUES FOR 2005 CPE COURSE

9. False. *Correct.* Cash is not a common asset manipulated in fraudulent financial reporting because its manipulation will usually not change the financial statements enough to achieve the objective of falsely presenting financial position and results of operations. Thus, the statement is not correct. Instead, cash is most commonly involved in the misappropriation of assets (theft) because cash is so portable. In fraudulent financial reporting, revenue is the most common account manipulated followed by inventories. Both can easily over- or under-state results of operations.

True. *Incorrect.* Fraudulent financial reporting involves manipulating the financial statements. Typically, this type of fraud involves not cash, but rather revenue, accounts receivable, and inventories. Further, management is typically the perpetrator of this type of fraud.

10. True. *Correct.* There are three factors usually present when a fraud occurs. These three factors are commonly referred to by fraud examiners as the fraud triangle. The three factors are:

- Incentive or pressure: Management or other employees have an incentive or are under pressure (financial or otherwise), which provides a reason to commit fraud.
- Opportunity: Circumstances exist, such as the absence of controls, ineffective controls, or the ability of management to override controls, that provide an opportunity for a fraud to be perpetrated.
- Rationalization or attitude: Individuals involved in the fraud are able to rationalize committing the fraud. Some individuals possess an attitude, character, or set of ethical values that allow them to knowingly and intentionally commit a dishonest act.

False. *Incorrect.* There are three factors that make up the fraud triangle, as correctly stated. Although all three conditions may help contribute to the perpetuation of fraud, the most important one is opportunity. Where there is incentive and rationalization to commit a fraud, such a fraud cannot occur unless the system of internal control allows it to happen.

The number one reason why fraud occurs is due to poor internal controls, thus creating the opportunity for it to occur. Even though the three conditions of the fraud triangle are typically present in a perpetuation of a fraud, there are circumstances when only one, or even two of the conditions may not be present. The author also notes that the three conditions of fraud needed to be considered in light of the size, complexity and ownership attributes of the entity. For example a larger entity might have controls that constrain improper conduct by management, while a smaller, closely held entity will not have any of the same constraints placed on the management of a larger entity, as noted above.

11. True. *Correct.* The new Board has five (5) full-time members, each appointed by the SEC in consultation with the Secretary of the Treasury and the Chairman of the Federal Reserve.

ANSWERS TO STUDY QUESTIONS — Module 1 — Chapter 1   **155**

False. *Incorrect.* The statement is correctly stated at five full-time members. A maximum of two (2) members must be or have been CPAs. If one of the two CPAs is the chairperson, he or she must not have practiced in public accounting format within five years from his or her appointment to the Board.

Additionally, a Board member may not serve for more than two, five-year terms, regardless of whether those terms are consecutive. Members are selected from among prominent individuals of integrity and reputation who have demonstrated commitment to investors and the public, understand the responsibilities and nature of financial disclosures, and, understand the obligations of accountants in the issuance of audit reports.

12. False. *Correct.* The statement is not correctly presented in that a seven-year retention period is required under the Act, not four years. The Act adds other requirements to auditors including a) a concurring or second partner review, and b) the requirement for the auditor to report on internal control.
True. *Incorrect.* The Act adds significant responsibilities and restrictions to auditors of SEC companies (referred to as registered accounting firms). One of those restrictions is that auditors must adopt a minimum retention period of seven years for workpapers.

13. False. *Correct.* The Act does not have a mandatory firm rotation, but it does have a mandatory partner rotation every five consecutive fiscal years. The Act provides that a firm may not perform audit services where the lead or review partner has performed audit services for the issuer client for five (5) consecutive fiscal years. The mandatory partner rotation, instead of the firm rotation, was included to ensure that one partner would not become too familiar with his or her client, similar to the situation that existed during Enron.
True. *Incorrect.* The Act has no mandatory firm rotation. During the deliberation of the Sarbanes-Oxley Act, one suggestion was for mandatory firm rotation. That suggested provision was not included in the final Act.

14. False. *Correct.* The five-year cooling off period does not exist and, instead, consists of a one-year period. The theory behind the one-year period was to eliminate any bias that may exist with a firm whose previous employee or principal is now a senior executive (e.g., CEO or CFO) of an audit client. After one year it is assumed that the bias has diluted. Five years would have been unnecessarily long.
True. *Incorrect.* There is no five-year cooling off period. Instead, the Act provides a one-year cooling off period. A firm is precluded from auditing an issuer if the issuer's CEO, controller, CFO, CAO, or any person serving in an equivalent position for the issuer, was employed by the firm and participated in any capacity in the audit of that issuer during the one-year period preceding the date of the initiation of the audit.

The cooling-off provision applies only to those officers that served on the audit in the preceding year. If, instead, the officer served elsewhere in the firm, such as in the tax or consulting department, the preclusion would not apply.

15. True. *Correct.* The Act prohibits any issuer directly or indirectly (including through an affiliate) from extending or maintaining credit, arranging for the extension of credit, or renewing credit, in the form of a personal loan to or for any executive officer or director, or the equivalent thereof, of the issuer. Credit cards issued by a company to an executive or officer are not prohibited under the Act.

False. *Incorrect.* Credit cards are not prohibited under the Act thereby making the statement correctly stated. Although the Act prohibits certain loans to officers and executives, there are certain loans that are not prohibited include home improvement and manufactured home loans, an extension of credit under an open end credit plan, credit cards, and certain extensions of credit by a broker or dealer to an employee of that broker or dealer to buy, trade, or carry securities.

MODULE 1 — CHAPTER 2

1. True. *Correct.* SAS No. 101 does make note of the fact that fair value measurements for which observable market prices are not available are inherently imprecise because those fair value measurements may be based on assumptions about future conditions, transactions, or events whose outcome is uncertain and will therefore be subject to change over time. For example, if fair value is based on expected cash flows under Concept Statement No. 7, those expected cash flows are probability weighted. The weighting is very subjective.

False. *Incorrect.* Although observable market prices are precise measurements, other measurements may be imprecise because they are based on assumptions. Auditing such measurements can be difficult. If observable market prices are not available, GAAP requires that valuation methods reflect assumptions that marketplace participants would generally use in estimating fair value, whenever that information is available without undue cost and effort. If information about market assumptions is not available, an entity may use its own assumptions as long as there is no contrary data indicating that marketplace participants would use different assumptions. The auditor's consideration of such assumptions is based on information available to the auditor at the time of the audit. Further, the auditor is not responsible for predicting future conditions, transactions, or events that, had they been known at the time of the audit, may have had a significant effect on management's actions or management's assumptions underlying the fair value measurements and disclosures.

2. False. *Correct.* The auditor is not responsible for the financial statements of any entity it audits. That responsibility belongs to management.

Moreover, in fulfilling its responsibility, management should develop an accounting and financial reporting process for determining the fair value measurements and disclosures; select appropriate valuation methods, identify and adequately support any significant assumptions used; prepare the valuation; and make sure that the presentation and disclosure of the fair value measurements are in accordance with GAAP.

True. *Incorrect.* Management, not the auditor, is ultimately responsible for making the fair value measurements and disclosures included in the financial statements. After all, management is responsible for the financial statements issued.

3. True. *Correct.* SAS No. 55, *Consideration of Internal Control in a Financial Statement Audit,* as amended, requires the auditor to obtain an understanding of each of the five components of internal control sufficient to plan the audit. In connection with SAS No. 101, the auditor should obtain such an understanding related to the determination of the entity's fair value measurements and disclosures in order to plan the nature, timing, and extent of the audit procedures. In obtaining an understanding of the entity's process for determining fair value measurements and disclosures, the auditor should considers various factors that include the types of controls in existence over the process used to determine fair value measurements, including, for example, controls over data and the segregation of duties between those committing the entity to the underlying transactions and those responsible for undertaking the valuations.

False. *Incorrect.* The auditor should consider various factors as noted in the statement. Thus he statement is true. Factors that should be considered include: the expertise and experience of persons involved in determining the fair value measurements; the use of information technology in the valuation process; the accounts or transactions requiring fair value measurements or disclosures (such as, whether the accounts arise from the recording of routine and recurring transactions or whether they arise from non-routine or unusual transactions); and the extent to which service organizations are used that impact the fair value measurements or the data that supports the measurement. When an entity uses a service organization, the auditor should also consider the requirements of SAS No. 70, *Service Organizations.*

4. True. *Correct.* GAAP requires that certain items be measured at fair value, such as investments under FASB No. 115. The SAS requires that the auditor obtain sufficient audit evidence to provide reasonable assurance that the fair value measurements and disclosures used are in conformity with GAAP.

False. *Incorrect.* For purposes of auditing fair value, Financial Accounting Standards Board (FASB) Statement of Financial Accounting Concepts No. 7, *Using Cash Flow Information and Present Value in Accounting Measurements,* defines the fair value of an asset (liability) as: "the amount

158 TOP AUDITING ISSUES FOR 2005 CPE COURSE

at which that asset (or liability) could be bought (or incurred) or sold (or settled) in a current transaction between willing parties, that is, other than in a forced or liquidation sale."

5. False. _Correct._ SAS requires the auditor to evaluate the adequacy of the disclosures. When auditing fair value measurements and related disclosures included in the notes to the financial statements, whether required by GAAP or disclosed voluntarily, the auditor ordinarily performs essentially the same types of audit procedures as those employed in auditing a fair value measurement recognized in the financial statements.

The auditor obtains sufficient competent audit evidence that the valuation principles are appropriate under GAAP and are being consistently applied, and that the method of estimation and significant assumptions used are adequately disclosed in accordance with GAAP. The auditor evaluates whether the entity has made adequate disclosures about fair value information.

If an item contains a high degree of measurement uncertainty, the auditor assesses whether the disclosures are sufficient to inform users of such uncertainty. When disclosure of fair value information under GAAP is omitted because it is not practicable to determine fair value with sufficient reliability, the auditor evaluates the adequacy of disclosures required in these circumstances. If the entity has not appropriately disclosed fair value information required by GAAP, the auditor evaluates whether the financial statements are materially misstated.

True. _Incorrect._ SAS No. 101 does, in fact, require an auditor to evaluate whether disclosures about fair values are in conformity with GAAP. Disclosure of fair value information is an important aspect of financial statements. Often, fair value disclosure is required because of the relevance to users in the evaluation of an entity's performance and financial position. In addition to the fair value information required under GAAP, some entities disclose voluntary additional fair value information in the notes to the financial statements.

6. True. _Correct._ SAS No. 101 states that the auditor should evaluate whether an entity's method of measurement is appropriate when there are no observable market prices and the entity estimates fair value using a valuation method. Such an evaluation requires the use of professional judgment as well as obtaining an understanding of management's rationale for selecting a particular method by discussing with management its reasons for selecting the valuation method.

False. _Incorrect._ The statement is correctly stated in that the SAS requires the auditor to make an evaluation of the method of measurement under the noted situation. In doing so, the auditor considers whether management has sufficiently evaluated and appropriately applied the criteria, if any, provided by GAAP to support the selected method; the valuation method is appropriate in the circumstances given the nature of the item being valued; and the valuation method is appropriate in relation to the business, industry, and environment in which the entity operates. Note further that management may have determined that different valuation methods results in a range of significantly different fair value measurements. In such cases, the auditor evaluates how the entity has investigated the reasons for the differences in establishing its fair value measurements.

7. True. *Correct.* The SAS does deal with the auditor's consideration of whether to engage a specialist with respect to fair value measurements. The auditor may have the necessary skill and knowledge to plan and perform audit procedures related to fair values or may decide to use the work of a specialist. If the use of such a specialist is planned, the auditor should consider the guidance in SAS No. 73, *Using the Work of a Specialist.*
False. *Incorrect.* The auditor needs to consider whether he or she should engage a specialist to assess fair value. When planning to use the work of a specialist in auditing fair value measurements, the auditor considers whether the specialist's understanding of the definition of fair value and the method that the specialist will use to determine fair value are consistent with those of management and with GAAP. SAS No. 73 provides that, while the reasonableness of assumptions and the appropriateness of the methods used and their application are the responsibility of the specialist, the auditor obtains an understanding of the assumptions and methods used. However, if the auditor believes the findings are unreasonable, he or she applies additional procedures as required in SAS No. 73.

8. True. *Correct.* SAS No. 101 specifically mentions that the auditor's understanding of the reliability of the process used by management to determine fair value is an important element in support of the resulting amounts and therefore affects the nature, timing, and extent of audit procedures, in testing management's significant assumptions, the valuation model, and the underlying data. When testing the entity's fair value measurements and disclosures, the auditor evaluates whether management's assumptions are reasonable and reflect, or are not inconsistent with, market information; the fair value measurement was determined using an appropriate model, if applicable; and management used relevant information that was reasonably available at the time.
False. *Incorrect.* The statement is correctly stated thereby making the statement true. As part of the auditor's understanding of the reliability of the process, estimation methods and assumptions, and the auditor's consideration and comparison of fair value measurements determined in prior periods, if any, to results obtained in the current period, may provide evidence of the reliability of management's processes. However, the auditor also considers whether variances from the prior-period fair value measurements result from changes in market or economic circumstances.

160 TOP AUDITING ISSUES FOR 2005 CPE COURSE

Moreover, where applicable, the auditor should evaluate whether the significant assumptions used by management in measuring fair value, taken individually and as a whole, provide a reasonable basis for the fair value measurements and disclosures in the entity's financial statements.

9. True. *Correct.* SAS No. 85 does, in fact, require an independent auditor to obtain written representations from management. The auditor ordinarily should obtain written representations from management regarding the reasonableness of significant assumptions, including whether they appropriately reflect management's intent and ability to carry out specific courses of action on behalf of the entity, where relevant to the use of fair value measurements or disclosures.

False. *Incorrect.* SAS No. 85 requires that the auditor obtain written representations. With respect to fair value, depending on the nature, materiality, and complexity of fair values, management representations about fair value measurements and disclosures contained in the financial statements may include representations about the appropriateness of the measurement methods and related assumptions used in determining fair value, the consistency in application of the methods, the completeness and adequacy of disclosures related to fair values, and whether subsequent events require adjustment to the fair value measurements and disclosures included in the financial statements.

10. False. *Correct.* The statement is not correct in that the SAS requires, rather than recommends, that the auditor communicate certain matters to the audit committee. Certain accounting estimates are particularly sensitive because of their significance to the financial statements and because of the possibility that future events affecting them may differ markedly from management's current judgments. The auditor should determine that the audit committee is informed about the process used by management in formulating particularly sensitive accounting estimates, including fair value estimates, and about the basis for the auditor's conclusions regarding the reasonableness of those estimates.

True. *Incorrect.* SAS No. 61 requires, not recommends, that auditors determine that certain matters related to the conduct of an audit are communicated to audit committees.

MODULE 1 — CHAPTER 3

1. b. *Correct.* Failure to disclose a pending lawsuit would, by omission of material facts, mislead financial statement users.

a. *Incorrect.* An employee theft of inventory would be an example of misappropriation of assets.

c. *Incorrect.* Incorrectly estimating the life of a patent, unless deliberate, would simply constitute an estimation error.

ANSWERS TO STUDY QUESTIONS — Module 1 — Chapter 3 **161**

2. a. *Correct.* Altering the date of a sales invoice to enable the sale to be recorded in an earlier period would constitute fraudulent financial reporting, not misappropriation of assets.
b. *Incorrect.* Theft of inventory is an example of a misappropriation of assets.
c. *Incorrect.* Paying twice to a related supplier is an example of a misappropriation of assets.

3. c. *Correct.* SAS No. 1, *Codification of Auditing Standards,* requires the auditor to exercise professional skepticism.
a. *Incorrect.* The auditor should exercise professional skepticism in conducting the entire audit.
b. *Incorrect.* Exercising professional skepticism does not imply that all material transactions be examined, and auditing standards do not envision the auditor examining all such transactions.

4. b. *Correct.* Professional skepticism would require a knowledge that past results do not necessarily lead to current results.
a. *Incorrect.* Such an expectation would constitute cynicism, not skepticism.
c. *Incorrect.* Challenging all management's assertions for veracity would require auditing every transaction.

5. b. *Correct.* The audit team is required to discuss the potential for fraud.
a. *Incorrect.* The audit team is not just strongly encouraged, but is required to discuss the potential for fraud.
c. *Incorrect.* The audit team is required to discuss the potential for fraud before any assessment is made of the likelihood of fraud.
d. *Incorrect.* SAS No. 99 does not so state. The SAS makes no distinction between large and small companies regarding the need to discuss the potential for fraud.

6. d. *Correct.* Management should be asked a number of questions, including whether it is aware of allegations of fraud.
a. *Incorrect.* The SAS has not designated the order in which management, the audit committee, employees and others should be contacted regarding fraud.
b. *Incorrect.* The auditor is not expected to ask management to give an opinion as to the likelihood of fraud, but rather whether they have knowledge of fraud or are aware of allegations of fraud, as well as other pertinent questions related to fraud.
c. *Incorrect.* In addition to asking management about its knowledge of actual or suspected fraud, management should be asked if they are aware of allegations of fraud, as well as other pertinent questions related to fraud.

162 TOP AUDITING ISSUES FOR 2005 CPE COURSE

7. b. *Correct.* The SAS does not require auditors to contact suppliers about the risks of fraud.

a. *Incorrect.* Internal auditors should be contacted regarding their views about the risks of fraud.

c. *Incorrect.* The SAS suggests that auditors may want to contact in-house legal counsel about the risks of fraud.

d. *Incorrect.* The SAS requires auditors to contact the audit committee about the risks of fraud.

8. c. *Correct.* The fact that such data is often highly aggregated, making it difficult to draw specific conclusions, is mentioned as a limitation in their use in assessing the risks of fraud.

a. *Incorrect.* Analytical procedures are a form of substantive testing and always involve quantitative data.

b. *Incorrect.* Analytical procedures are a form of substantive tests, not compliance tests of controls.

9. a. *Correct.* The SAS notes that reviews of interim financial statements may help in identifying the risks of fraud

b. *Incorrect.* The SAS does not specify the time period during the audit in which reviews of interim financial statements should be conducted.

c. *Incorrect.* The SAS does not state that reviews of interim financial statements are helpful in identifying the risks of misappropriation of assets. Such risks are identified by examining the three fraud risk factors; i.e., incentives/pressures, opportunities, and attitudes/rationalizations.

d. *Incorrect.* The risks of fraud from deficient internal control components would be identified by studying the system of internal controls, and by performing compliance tests of such controls.

10. True. *Correct.* For example, management may emphasize the importance of ethical behavior.

False. *Incorrect.* Although formal internal controls are more important in large companies, in smaller companies the culture of management may discourage fraud.

11. d. *Correct.* Equity ownership in a supplier constitutes an example of investment assets which the SAS notes are high risk assets because measurement of the value of the asset is subjective.

a. *Incorrect.* Plant and equipment are relatively difficult to misappropriate and have fewer subjective measurement problems than many assets.

b. *Incorrect.* Notes receivable are generally valued at face value and are not easy to misappropriate.

c. *Incorrect.* There are no valuation issues with prepaid insurance, and the asset would be difficult to misappropriate.

ANSWERS TO STUDY QUESTIONS — Module 1 — Chapter 3 **163**

12. True. *Correct.* For example, if the auditor's study of internal controls reveal strong controls, and compliance tests indicate the controls are being followed, the auditor would consider such controls to have lessened the risks of fraud.

False. *Incorrect.* Examining internal controls can help the auditor determine whether the risks of fraud are increased or decreased; i.e., weak internal controls would increase the risks of fraud.

13. a. *Correct.* The SAS describes a code of ethics as a broad control.

b. *Incorrect.* Specific controls are those that address particular risks, such as controls to prevent theft.

c. *Incorrect.* A company's code of ethics would not affect the pervasiveness of a possible risk of material misstatement of assets. Instead the nature of the particular misrepresentation or misappropriation would determine the pervasiveness of the risk.

14. False. *Correct.* The SAS notes that "applying professional skepticism" might lead the auditor to get third party confirmations of management's assertions.

True. *Incorrect.* An auditor exercising professional skepticism may respond to a perceived high risk of material misstatement by using a high quality evidential procedure such as third party confirmations.

15. b. *Correct.* The SAS notes that the auditor may wish to change the predictability of auditing procedures in response to an identified high risk of fraud.

a. *Incorrect.* A perceived high risk of fraud may lead the auditor to change the predictability of audit tests; e.g., she may conduct a surprise count of cash.

c. *Incorrect.* Audit programs must be sufficiently flexible to respond to new events/changed conditions such as a higher assessment of risk than previously expected.

d. *Incorrect.* The auditor's assessment of internal controls is only one of many factors governing the risks of fraud, which in turn may cause the auditor to change the predictability of auditing procedures performed.

16. c. *Correct.* Changing the conclusions drawn from the analysis of a statistical sample would be improper and is not a recommended response to identified risks of fraud.

a. *Incorrect.* The SAS states that changing the timing of substantive tests (e.g., more year-end tests) is one appropriate response to identified risks of fraud.

b. *Incorrect.* Changing the extent of audit procedures such as increasing the sample size is another appropriate response to identified risks of fraud.

164 TOP AUDITING ISSUES FOR 2005 CPE COURSE

d. Incorrect. The SAS notes that it may be appropriate to change the types of auditing procedures performed (e.g., it may be more critical to observe inventory).

17. True. Correct. The SAS notes that accounting principles/practices do vary among industries (e.g., the percentage of completion method used by contractors). Therefore, auditing procedures are often tailored to the entity being audited.
False. Incorrect. Audit programs are tailored to the entity, especially so for procedures relating to revenue.

18. d. Correct. Although there are circumstances in which the auditor would decide to suspend compliance tests of controls (e.g., the controls are ineffective or it is not cost effective to conduct the tests), an increase in the risks of fraud would not be one of those circumstances.
a. Incorrect. For example, an auditor might discover a journal entry recording the sale of assets to a related party. Such a discovery would likely increase the auditor's judgment of the risks of fraud. may necessitate using a specialist during the observation of inventory.
b. Incorrect. The SAS states that certain analytical tests may need to be performed in responses to an increase in fraud risks with respect to inventory.
c. Incorrect. Observing inventory on a surprise basis is an example of a specific procedure that the SAS indicates may be necessary.

19. True. Correct. The SAS notes that fraud is often perpetuated through inappropriate journal entries.
False. Incorrect. Management override with respect to journal entries is of concern to the auditor because the non-routine nature of journal entries makes them more susceptible to override. The auditor can help control for this by testing journal entries.

20. False. Correct. The SAS cautions that the indication of good internal controls in an entity does not remove the need for substantive testing.
True. Incorrect. Effective internal controls can be defeated by employee collusion. Therefore, substantive testing is necessary.

21. False. Correct. The SAS notes that accounts that have been error prone in the past constitute a higher risk and should be examined closely.
True. Incorrect. Accounts that were error prone in the past would carry a higher risk of misstatement. Because one of the factors affecting the required sample size is risk of misstatement, a larger sample size would be necessary to obtain the same confidence level.

ANSWERS TO STUDY QUESTIONS — Module 1 — Chapter 3 **165**

22. False. *Correct.* The SAS specifically states that the purpose is not to call into question the auditor's judgment regarding the prior year.
True. *Incorrect.* The purpose of the retrospective review of the prior year is to help assess the risks of fraud in the current year.

23. a. *Correct.* A transaction with a large customer would not necessarily lead the auditor to exercise professional skepticism over the business purpose of a transaction. Indeed, the transaction on its face is more likely to be routine and have a business purpose.
b. *Incorrect.* Transactions with unconsolidated related parties such as special purpose entities constitute unusual transactions that would merit professional skepticism over the business purpose.
c. *Incorrect.* The SAS notes that extremely complicated transactions (e.g., hedging transactions) would warrant professional skepticism about the business purpose.
d. *Incorrect.* Transactions where a party lacks financial strength to do the transaction constitute transactions in which the SAS requires the auditor to look for a business purpose to the transactions.

24. False. *Correct.* The SAS notes that certain events or circumstances, such as discovering last- minute adjustments, could change the judgment of the risks of fraud.
True. Incorrect. For example, an auditor might discover a journal entry recording the sale of assets to a related party. Such a discovery could change the auditor's assessment of the risks of fraud.

25. True. *Correct.* Comparing net income to cash flow may detect transactions such as "swaps" that are designed to inflate revenue.
False. *Incorrect.* The SAS notes that comparing net income to cash flow may be useful because it is difficult to manipulate cash.

26. b. *Correct.* The SAS notes that the higher the level at which fraud is committed, the more likely it is that the fraud constitutes a pervasive problem.
a. *Incorrect.* Uncovering fraud that is not material to the financial statements would not necessarily require the auditor to withdraw from the engagement.
c. *Incorrect.* Discovery of possible material fraud could, if the fraud is committed at a high enough level, require communication directly with the board of directors.

27. False. *Correct.* The auditor should if requested, communicate such information to the successor auditor. However, permission of the client must be obtained.
True. *Incorrect.* If the client denies permission, the auditor cannot communicate such evidence to the successor auditor.

166 TOP AUDITING ISSUES FOR 2005 CPE COURSE

28. False. *Correct.* Documenting the auditor's consideration of fraud is required by the SAS.

True. *Incorrect.* Documenting the auditor's consideration of fraud would show evidence of compliance with GAAS. Failure to do so would be a "red flag" to plaintiff's attorneys.

MODULE 2 — CHAPTER 4

1. True. *Correct.* The ARSC modified SSARS No. 1 to simplify financial statement reporting.

False. *Incorrect.* The modifications exempt some business activities from the reporting process.

2. True. *Correct.* SSARS No. 8 changes the definition of submission. A submission occurs when financial statements are prepared and presented to third parties.

False. *Incorrect.* SSARS No. 8 does change the definition of submission to be based on preparing and presenting financial statements, which differs from the previous definition found in SSARS No. 1. To prepare financial statements, you must use your knowledge, education, and experience to create financial statements that would not have existed otherwise. SSARS No. 8 does not define the term *presenting*.

3. False. *Correct.* There are two elements that are "prepare" and "present" financial statements. Prior to the issuance of SSARS No. 8, the definition of submission was based on who "generated" the financial statements. Because that definition was ambiguous, the ARSC replaced it with the two-element definition, based on preparing and presenting financial statements.

True. *Incorrect.* There are two, not three elements. The two elements are preparing and presenting financial statements.

4. False. *Correct.* Knowledge, education, and experience are used to create financial statements, not expertise. Logically, some general expertise may be required, but SSARS No. 8 does not identify expertise as necessary to prepare financial statements.

True. *Incorrect.* Expertise is not used to create financial statements.

5. False. *Correct.* Giving a client a trial balance is not among the modes of communications that satisfy the definition of present. A financial statement, rather than a trial balance, must be given to a client or third party.

A trial balance differs from a financial statement in several ways including the fact that a financial statement combines general ledger accounts to create account groups, while a trial balance does not.

ANSWERS TO STUDY QUESTIONS — Module 2 — Chapter 4 **167**

True. *Incorrect.* Giving a client a trial balance is not a mode of communication under SSARS No. 8. SSARS No. 1 specifically exempts the issuance of a trial balance from the application of the SSARSs.

6. False. *Correct.* If the CPA prints out and delivers financial statements to a client, the statements have been presented. In fact, the statements do not have to be printed out. They can be given to the client on a CD-ROM or diskette, or can be sent electronically.
True. *Incorrect.* Even if the CPA did not prepare the financial statements, if he or she prints them out and delivers them to the client, they have been presented.

7. True. *Correct.* SSARS No. 8 introduces management-use only financial statements as an alternative to a traditional compilation report when the third party user is management.
False. *Incorrect.* SSARS No. 8 introduces management-use only financial statements as an alternative to a traditional compilation report. However, the alternative only works if the end user is management, and not external third parties. For external third parties (such as bankers and investors), the management-use only financial statements are not appropriate. Instead, a traditional compilation, review, or audit engagement is required.

8. b. *Correct.* The CPA must consider whether third parties will require the financial statements and whether the engagement offers a client cost savings compared with a traditional compilation engagement.
a. *Incorrect.* Management-use only financial statements generally offer the CPA a more, not less, profitable engagement. Also, such statements have a greater, not lower, risk because third parties may receive and rely on the statements.
c. *Incorrect.* The duration of the engagement or contract is not a major issue in creating management-use only financial statements. The number of third parties requiring the financial statements is not an issue, but rather whether even one third party must obtain the statements.

9. False. *Correct.* SSARS No. 8 recommends, but does not require, that the engagement letter to be signed. Of course, if the letter is not signed, the accountant has no evidence that the letter was received and that the client agreed to the terms and conditions of the engagement.
True. *Incorrect.* The letter is not required to be signed by management.

10. False. *Correct.* A compilation report is never issued on management-use only financial statements. One of the advantages of management-use only financial statements is that there is no reporting requirement. Thus,

168 TOP AUDITING ISSUES FOR 2005 CPE COURSE

unlike a traditional compilation engagement, a report is not issued on management-use only financial statements.

True. *Incorrect.* The engagement letter for management-use financial statements does not state that a compilation report will be issued in accordance with SSARS No. 1. No report is issued for management-use only financial statements.

11. True. *Correct.* SSARS No. 8 requires that each page include a reference such as *Restricted for Management's Use Only.*

False. *Incorrect.* SSARS No. 8 requires that each page include a reference such as *Restricted for Management's Use Only.* Because a report is not issued, the user of the financial statements must be aware that the financial statements are restricted for management use only. The footer *Restricted for Management's Use Only* is an effective way to put the reader of the financial statements on notice.

12. False. *Correct.* SSARS No. 1 has no such requirement as to have the financial statements reviewed by an independent person. However, SSARS No. 1 does have several performance requirements including that the CPA must establish an understanding about the services to be performed, and he or she must possess a level of knowledge of the accounting principles and practices of the industry in which the entity operates.

True. *Incorrect.* There is no such requirement noted in the statement. There are several performance standards; however, having the financial statements reviewed by an independent person is not one of them.

13. False. *Correct.* SSARS No. 8 does not require disclosures, but permits them. If disclosures are not included, the engagement letter should include language stating so. Moreover, if both the statement of cash flows and substantially all disclosures are omitted, the engagement letter should also be modified to state this fact.

True. *Incorrect.* There is no disclosure requirement in SSARS No. 8. SSARS No. 8 permits, but not does require, disclosures. Generally, a CPA prepares management-use only financial statements without notes because management does not need a full set of financial statements.

14. False. *Correct.* A bookkeeper is not a person normally included as members of management under FASB No. 57. Examples of members of management covered by FASB No. 57 include: members of the board of directors, CEO, CFO, vice presidents in charge of principal business functions, and other persons who perform similar policymaking functions.

True. *Incorrect.* A bookkeeper is not a person normally included as members of management under FASB No. 57. FASB No. 57, *Related*

ANSWERS TO STUDY QUESTIONS — Module 2 — Chapter 4   **169**

Parties, includes persons who are responsible for achieving the objectives of the enterprise and who have the authority to establish policies and make decisions. Generally, a bookkeeper does not fit that definition.

15. False. *Correct.* Management-use only financial statements are not issued to third parties and their needs are not a consideration to the CPA. However, if third parties need financial statements, a better choice of engagement might be a compilation, review, or audit of the entity's financial statements.
True. *Incorrect.* Management-use only financial statements are not used by third parties. By definition, management-use only financial statements are limited to use by members of management. Thus, the third-party needs for use are irrelevant.

16. True. *Correct.* SSARS No. 8 permits compiled or reviewed financial statements to be subsequently issued for the same period.
False. *Incorrect.* SSARS No. 8 specifically allows compiled or reviewed financial statements to be subsequently issued for the same period. In some instances, the CPA may wish to issue compiled or reviewed financial statements for the same period.
For example, a bank or third party may require financial statements. Management-use financial statements may not be issued to third parties.

17. True. *Correct.* One difference between a trial balance and financial statement is that accounts are combined for a financial statement.
False. *Incorrect.* Interpretation 14 of SSARS No. 1 provides examples comparing a financial statement with a trial balance. One such difference is that accounts are combined for a financial statement. Another is that a trial balance does not contain labels such as a statement of income, etc.

18. True. *Correct.* SSARS No. 1 exempts financial statements included in a written personal financial plan from its application.
False. *Incorrect.* SSARS No. 1 provides four exemptions, one of which is financial statements included in a written personal financial plan from its application. Other exemptions include financial statements involved in certain litigation services, certain prescribed forms, and financial information included in a business valuation.

19. b. *Correct.* An accountant solely preparing a business valuation for which information is derived from statements and information he or she has not submitted should state that he or she is not expressing an opinion or offering assurance about the statements.
a. *Incorrect.* The accountant providing the business valuation should make no statement about auditing the financial statements.

170 TOP AUDITING ISSUES FOR 2005 CPE COURSE

c. Incorrect. The business valuation report is not compliant with compilation engagement requirements if it is dependent on sources the valuation accountant has not submitted.

20. True. Correct. Interpretation 21 of SSARS No. 1 precludes a CPA who is not in public accounting from issuing a compilation report under SSARS No. 1. A CPA in public practice must, at a minimum, issue a compilation report if he or she wishes to report on financial statements. Conversely, a CPA in industry may submit financial statements using a transmittal letter. **False. Incorrect.** Interpretation 21 of SSARS No. 1 precludes a CPA who is not in public accounting from issuing a compilation report under SSARS No. 1. Only a CPA who is in public accounting may issue a compilation report. Interpretation 21 clarifies an issue that has been ambiguous for some time.

MODULE 2 — CHAPTER 5

1. True. Correct. SSARS No. 9 clarifies the reporting requirements with respect to the statement of retained earnings. There is confusion in practice as to whether the change in retained earnings must be presented in the financial statements or related notes; moreover, if presented, whether the report must reference the statement. SSARS No. 9 resolves this issue. **False. Incorrect.** The statement is correct in that SSARS No. 9 does clarify the reporting requirements for the statement of retained earnings. Specifically, SSARS No. 9 states that a statement of retained earnings is not required by GAAP. However, APB No. 12, Omnibus Opinion, requires that all changes in capital must be disclosed. The change can be presented in one of three ways including 1) Separate statement of retained earnings, 2) Combination statement of income and retained earnings, and 3) Disclosure of the change in the notes to financial statements. SSARS No. 9 amends SSARS No. 1 to state that a statement of retained earnings is not a required statement, and, if a statement of retained earnings is not presented, reference to the statement is not required in the compilation and review report.

2. True. Correct. A representation letter is required for all review engagements, but not for compilation engagements. SSARS No. 7 requires a representation letter. **False. Incorrect.** A representation letter is required for all review engagements. Although a representation letter is not required for a compilation engagement, an accountant may choose to obtain one. Further, SSARS No. 9 amends the standard representation letter to reflect various changes.

3. False. Correct. The accountant should make the letter easy to understand rather than technical in nature. It should also spell out those specific representations deemed necessary by the accountant.

ANSWERS TO STUDY QUESTIONS — Module 2 — Chapter 5 **171**

True. *Incorrect.* The accountant should consider making the letter easy to understand and not technical. One of the criticisms of the accounting profession is that it does not easily convey what it is it does to clients and third parties. The average client does not understand very technical information. Consequently, a easy-to-understand letter is more meaningful to the client.

4. False. *Correct.* In a compilation engagement, supplementary information must be compiled. Conversely, in a review engagement, supplementary information may be reviewed or compiled.
True. *Incorrect.* In a compilation engagement, supplementary information may not be reviewed, it must be compiled.

5. True. *Correct.* Supplementary information usually includes an operating expense schedule even though SSARS No. 1 does not specifically define supplementary information.
False. *Incorrect.* Supplementary information includes an operating expense schedule among other information. Other examples of supplementary information include a schedule of cost of sales, selling and G&A expenses, aging analysis, and schedule of property and equipment.

6. True. *Correct.* The SSARSs require that each page of supplementary information make reference to the Accountant's Report. Usually a footer such as "See Accountant's Report" or See Accountant's Report on Supplementary Information" is appropriate.
False. *Incorrect.* The SSARSs require that each page of supplementary information make reference to the Accountant's Report. The reason is so that the reader becomes fully aware of the accountant's responsibility with respect to the supplementary information.

7. True. *Correct.* SSARS No. 4 does provide guidance on communications between accountants and does not require successor CPAs to communicate with or obtain access to working papers of predecessor CPAs in accepting compilation or review engagements. However, SSARS No. 4 does not prevent a CPA from making a communication and, in certain circumstances, it may be helpful.
False. *Incorrect.* SSARS No. 4 does correctly provide guidance on communications between accountants when the successor accountant decides to communicate with the predecessor. SSARS No. 9 amends SSARS No. 4 by providing additional guidance on the successor-predecessor accountant communication process. SSARS No. 9 also defines a predecessor and successor accountant, and includes a sample successor accountant acknowledgement letter which a predecessor accountant might want to have the successor sign before allowing the successor access to working papers.

A-1a Scenarios That Clarify the SSARS No. 8 Guide

Scenario	Pre-pared	Pre-sented	Sub-mitted	Explanation
1. At the client's office, the CPA makes material adjustments to the client's accounting database (e.g., general ledger), which automatically updates the client's financial statements that are embedded in the software. The CPA doesn't look at or make any changes to the financial statements. The CPA prints out the adjusted general ledger and takes it with him or her. The client has the ability to access the adjusted general ledger and financial statements after the CPA leaves the client's office by choosing certain selection criteria (e.g., dates, format, basis of accounting, etc.)	No	No	No	The CPA is providing bookkeeping services, not preparing the financial statements. That is, the CPA did not use his or her knowledge, education, and experience to create the financial statements. In fact, the CPA has not even looked at the financial statements. The fact that the financial statements are automatically updated as the CPA makes entries to the general ledger is not a factor to consider in determining whether the financial statements were prepared. Second, the CPA did not present the financial statements to the client even though the client has the ability to generate financial statements by choosing certain selection criteria. Instead, a general ledger file that includes the potential for creating financial statements has been presented to the client. In order for financial statements to be created by the client, the client must take action such as select the specific dates, format, basis of accounting, etc. from the financial statement file. Therefore, the CPA has not presented financial statements to the client. **Conclusion:** Submission has not occurred under SSARS No. 1.
2. At the client's office, the CPA makes material adjustments to the client's accounting database (e.g., general ledger), which automatically update the client's financial statements. The CPA looks at the financial statements to see whether there are any changes to be made but does not make any changes. The CPA prints out the adjusted general ledger and financial statements, and takes the financial statements with him or her, but does not give the general ledger or financial statements to the client.	No	No	No	The CPA is providing bookkeeping services, and not preparing the financial statements. The CPA did not use his or her knowledge, education, and experience to create financial statements that would not have existed otherwise. The fact that the CPA looked at the financial statements or even made some changes to the financial statements does not mean the CPA prepared the financial statements. Second, similar to Scenario 1 above, the CPA did not present the financial statements to the client even though the client has the ability to create financial statements by choosing certain selection criteria. Instead, a general ledger file that includes the potential for creating financial statements has been presented to the client. In order for financial statements to be created by the client, the client must take action such as select the specific dates, format, basis of accounting, etc. from the financial statement file. Therefore, the CPA has not presented financial statements to the client. **Conclusion:** Submission has not occurred under SSARS No. 1.

APPENDIX A 173

A-1b

Scenario	Pre-pared	Pre-sented	Sub-mitted	Explanation
3. Assume the same facts as Scenario 2, except that the CPA also prints out a copy of the financial statements and presents them to the client.	No	Yes	No	The CPA is providing bookkeeping services and has not prepared the financial statements. The CPA did not use his or her knowledge, education, and experience to create the financial statements that would not have existed otherwise. The CPA has presented financial statements to the client, even though he or she has not prepared them. Therefore, the CPA has not met the definition of submission (e.g., prepare and present) and does not have to comply with SSARS No. 1. **Conclusion:** Submission has not occurred under SSARS No. 1.
4. Assume the same facts as Scenario 3, except the work is done at the CPA's office. The CPA receives the client's database in a diskette format and updates the database (general ledger) with adjusting entries that automatically update the financial statements. The CPA does not prepare the financial statements or even look at the financial statements. The diskette is sent back to the client with the updated database and the embedded financial statement file. Once the client receives the diskette from the CPA, the client can print out updated financial statements by choosing certain selection criteria (e.g., dates, format, basis of accounting).	No	No	No	The CPA is providing bookkeeping services, and has not prepared financial statements. The fact that the financial statements are automatically updated as the CPA makes entries to the general ledger is not a factor to consider in determining whether the financial statements were prepared. That is, the CPA did not use his knowledge, education, and experience to create financial statements that would not have existed otherwise. Second, the CPA has not presented financial statements to the client. Although financial statements are deemed to be presented to a client when they are delivered by diskette or electronically, in this case, the financial statements have not been delivered by diskette. Instead, only a general ledger file that includes the potential for creating financial statements has been delivered. In order for financial statements to be created by the client, the client must take action such as select the specific dates, format, basis of accounting, etc. from the financial statement file. Therefore, the CPA has not presented financial statements to the client. **Conclusion:** Submission has not occurred under SSARS No. 1.
5. Assume the same facts as Scenario 4 except that the accountant receives the client's general ledger (and embedded financial statements) electronically from the client, updates the general ledger with adjusting entries, and sends the file back to the client electronically. The CPA does not prepare or even look at the financial statements.	No	No	No	The same conclusion as Scenario 4. The CPA has not prepared financial statements and has not presented them. Regardless of whether the file is delivered by diskette or electronically, the financial statements have not been delivered to the client because the client is required to create the financial statements by choosing certain selection criteria such as dates, format, and basis of accounting. **Conclusion:** Submission has not occurred under SSARS No. 1.

174 TOP AUDITING ISSUES FOR 2005 CPE COURSE

A-1c

Scenario	Pre-pared	Pre-sented	Sub-mitted	Explanation
6. Using client information, the CPA prepares an adjusted trial balance and financial statements in the CPA's office for use in preparing a corporate income tax return. The financial statement preparation involves linking each trial balance account to each financial statement line and establishing account classifications on the financial statements (e.g., current versus long-term). The financial statements are used to prepare the tax return but are not attached to the tax return. The income tax returns are given to the client but the financial statements are not given to the client.	Yes	No	No	The accountant has prepared financial statements because he or she used his or her knowledge, education, and experience to link the general ledger accounts to the financial statement lines and establish account classifications on the financial statement. Although the financial statements have been prepared, they have not been presented to the client. **Conclusion:** Submission has not occurred under SSARS No. 1.
7. Assume the same facts as Scenario 6, except that a copy of the adjusting journal entries and trial balance is given to the client, along with the income tax return. The financial statements are not given to the client.	Yes	No	No	The accountant has prepared the financial statements because he or she used his or her knowledge, education, and experience to link the general ledger accounts to the financial statement lines and establish financial statement classifications. The accountant presented a trial balance to the client, which is not a financial statement. Therefore, financial statements were not presented to the client. **Conclusion:** Submission has not occurred under SSARS No. 1.
8. Assume the same facts as Scenario 7 above, except that a printed copy of the financial statements is given to the client, along with the income tax return.	Yes	Yes	Yes	The financial statements have been both prepared by the CPA and presented to the client. Delivering financial statements to a client in a paper form is considered presenting those financial statements to the client. **Conclusion:** Submission has occurred under SSARS No. 1.

APPENDIX A   **175**

A-1d

Scenario	Pre-pared	Pre-sented	Sub-mitted	Explanation
9. Assume the same facts as Scenario 6 above except that a diskette is given to the client, containing the general ledger and embedded financial statements prepared by the CPA. The client can print out the updated financial statements from the diskette only by choosing specific selection criteria such as the financial state-ment dates, format (comparative, percent-ages, etc), and basis of accounting.	Yes	No	No	The financial statements have been prepared by the accountant but they have not been presented to the client. Although financial statements are deemed to be presented to a client when they are delivered by diskette or electronically, in this case the financial statements have not been delivered by diskette. Instead, only a general ledger file that includes the potential for creat-ing financial statements has been delivered. In order for financial statements to be created by the client, the client must take action such as select the specific dates, format, basis of accounting, etc. from the financial statement file. Therefore, the CPA has not presented financial statements to the client. **Conclusion:** Submission has not occurred under SSARS No. 1.
10. Assume the same facts as Scenario 9 above except that the CPA receives the general ledger from the client electronically via modem, adjusts the general ledger, and prepares the financial statements, and sends the general ledger and embedded financial statements prepared by the accountant elec-tronically to the client.	Yes	No	No	The same conclusion as Scenario 8. That is, the CPA has prepared the financial state-ments, but has not presented them to the client. The financial statements are embed-ded in the database file and require that the client take action to create those financial statements. **Conclusion:** Submission has not occurred under SSARS No. 1.
11. Assume the same facts as Scenario 10 except that the CPA prepares the financial statements in a separate Word® file and sends the client two separate files: an adjusted general ledger file, and a Word® file containing the finan-cial statements for the particular period. When the client receives the file, the client can print out financial statements from the Word® file without performing any selection criteria.	Yes	Yes	Yes	The CPA has both prepared and presented the financial statements. First the CPA has prepared the financial statements, which is a given fact in this scenario. The CPA has pre-sented the financial statements to the client. If a CPA delivers financial statements by diskette or electronically, it is the same as if the finan-cial statements were delivered in a paper form. Therefore, by delivering the financial statements electronically in a Word® file, the CPA has pre-sented financial statements to the client. This conclusion is different from Scenarios 8 and 9 above because the financial statements are delivered in a separate file that does not require that the client perform selection criteria to create financial statements. Scenarios 8 and 9 had the financial statements embedded in the client file, requiring the client to choose selection criteria in order to create financial statements. **Conclusion:** Submission has occurred under SSARS No. 1.

A-1e

Scenario	Pre-pared	Pre-sented	Sub-mitted	Explanation
12. A CPA updates a client's general ledger. The client has prepared the balance sheet, income statement and statement of cash flows but has not prepared footnotes. The CPA looks at the client's financial statements and makes minor changes to the categorization of a few accounts between current and long-term. The CPA prepared a full set of footnotes to accompany the financial statements. The CPA prints out a full set of financial statements and presents them to the client in a paper form.	Yes	Yes	Yes	The CPA has both prepared and presented the financial statements. With respect to the "prepared" threshold, although the CPA has not prepared the core financial statements (e.g., balance sheet, income statement, statement of cash flows), he or she has prepared the accompanying footnotes, which are considered part of the financial statements. The SSARS No. 8 definition of "prepare" does not have a materiality threshold whereby the CPA must prepare a certain percentage of the overall financial statements. It is clear that the CPA used his or her knowledge, education, and experience to create a part of the financial statements (footnotes) that would not have existed otherwise. Clearly, the CPA has presented financial statements to the client in a paper form. **Conclusion:** Submission has occurred under SSARS No. 1.
13. In 20X1, a CPA (CPA No. 1) prepared financial statements by linking individual general ledger accounts to the financial statement lines and established financial statement classifications. In 20X2, a new CPA (CPA No. 2) is hired to replace CPA No. 1. CPA No. 2 updates the client's database that automatically updates the financial statements. The financial statement links are the same ones that were created by CPA No. 1 in 20X1. CPA No. 2 presents printed financial statements to the client.	No	Yes	No	CPA No. 2 has not prepared financial statements, but has presented them to the client. CPA No. 2 is providing bookkeeping services, and is not preparing financial statements. The fact that the CPA is updating the financial statements as he or she updates the general ledger, is not considered the preparation of financial statements. That is, CPA No. 2 did not use his or her knowledge, education, and experience to create financial statements in 20X2 that would not have existed otherwise. Instead, the 20X2 financial statements are based on financial statement links that were obtained from CPA No. 1. Had CPA No. 2 developed new financial statement links and classifications for 20X2, the 20X2 financial statements would have been prepared by CPA No. 2. CPA No. 2 has presented the 20X2 financial statements to the client but has not prepared them. Because CPA No. 2 has presented, but not prepared the financial statements, he or she has not submitted financial statements. However, CPA No. 2 may elect to issue financial statements even though he or she has not satisfied both submission criteria (e.g., present and prepare). **Conclusion:** Submission has not occurred under SSARS No. 1.

APPENDIX A   **177**

A-2   Sample Engagement Letter for Electronically Delivered Files

December 31, 20X0
XYZ Corporation
250 West Nowhere Street
Everywhere, MA, 03294

Dear Ladies and Gentlemen:

This letter is to confirm our understanding of the terms and conditions of our engagement and the nature of the limitations of the services we will provide:

We will perform the following bookkeeping services on a monthly basis for the months of January through November, 20XX.

1. You agree to send us an electronic version of your general ledger which has been prepared by you, on a monthly basis in a QuickBooks® format. We will assume that you will send your file from a secure website to ensure that your financial information is not received by unauthorized parties.

2. Prior to receiving the monthly general ledger from you:

    a. You will record all income and expenses to the appropriate general ledger accounts.

    b. You will be responsible for reconciling all cash accounts to bank balances.

    c. We take no responsibility for reviewing the accuracy of cash reconciliations.

3. We will record adjusting and correcting entries to adjust to general ledger to an accrual basis in accordance with generally accepted accounting principles. We will also reclassify any postings to the appropriate general ledger accounts as we believe appropriate.

4. We will send an adjusted general ledger back to you electronically. You agree to review this general-ledger report each month and approve any changes that we have made. Unless you tell us of the changes within 10 days, we will assume that you have approved all adjusting, correcting, and reclassifying entries that we have made.

5. We will not submit financial statements to you as defined in Statement on Standards for Accounting and Review Services 8, and assume no responsibility for any financial statements created by you from the adjusted general ledger file for your internal use or use by any third parties.

Etc.

Note: If the CPA wishes to maintain his or her independence, all adjustments listed in item 4 of the letter must be approved by the client in accordance with Ethics Interpretation 101-3.

178 TOP AUDITING ISSUES FOR 2005 CPE COURSE

A-3a Sample Engagement Letter for Management-Use Only Financial Statements

Mr. John Jason
President
Jason Distributing, Inc.
1 Johanson Road
Everywhere, Massachusetts 02174

Dear Mr. Jason:

Enclosed you will find the federal and state tax returns of Jason Distributing, Inc. for the year ended December 31, 20XX.

Please follow these instructions with respect to the filing of these tax returns.
   [insert standard tax return transmittal letter language here]

Enclosed you will also find compiled financial statements for the year ended December 31, 20XX.

This letter is to confirm our understanding of the terms and objectives of our engagement and the nature and limitations of the services we have provided in connection with these compiled financial statements.

1. We have performed the following services: We have compiled from information you provided, the (monthly, quarterly, or other frequency) financial statements of Jason Distributing, Inc. for the year 20XX. A compilation is limited to presenting in the form of financial statements information that is the representation of management. We did *not* review or audit the financial statements and accordingly, do not express an opinion or any other form of assurance on them. The financial statements will not be accompanied by a report.

Based upon our discussions with you, these financial statements have been designed to meet your needs in managing your business. Accordingly, these statements are for management's use only and are not intended for third-party use.

Material departures from GAAP exist and the effects of those departures, if any, on the financial statements are not be disclosed. In addition, substantially all disclosures and the statement of cash flows required by GAAP (or OCBOA, if applicable) have been omitted. Notwithstanding these limitations, you represent that you have knowledge about the nature of the procedures applied and the basis of accounting and assumptions used in the preparation of the financial statements that allows you to place the financial information in the proper context. Further, you represent and agree that the use of the financial statements will be limited to members of management with similar knowledge.

The financial statements are intended solely for the information and use of [include a list of specified members of management] and are *not intended to be and should not be used by any other party.* [optional].

A-3b

2. We have also *[discuss other services provided]* [optional]….

Our engagement cannot be relied upon to disclose errors, fraud, or illegal acts that may exist. However, we will inform the appropriate level of management of any material errors that come to our attention and any fraud or illegal acts that come to our attention, unless clearly inconsequential. No such acts came to our attention during the engagement.

We are not independent with respect to Jones Manufacturing, Inc. [insert if applicable].

The other data accompanying the financial statement in the schedule of operating expenses are presented only for supplementary analysis purposes and were compiled from information that is the representation of management, without audit or review, and we do not express an opinion or any other form of assurance on such data [if applicable].

In view of the limitations described above, you agree not to take, or assist in, any action seeking to hold us liable for damages due to any deficiency in the financial statements we prepare and you agree to hold us harmless from any liability and related legal costs arising from any third-party use of the financial statements in contravention of the terms of this agreement [optional, but recommended language].

Our fees for our services are $_____.

Should you require financial statements for third party use, we would be pleased to discuss with you the requested level of service. Such engagement would be considered separate and not deemed to be part of the services described in this engagement letter.

If the foregoing is not in accordance with your understanding, please notify me.

Sincerely,
Freddie, CPA
Date:

180 TOP AUDITING ISSUES FOR 2005 CPE COURSE

A-4a Sample Engagement Letter Option 1: Signed by Management

Ms. Mary Jones
President
Jones Manufacturing, Inc.
111 Smith Road
Notown, Massachusetts 02174

Dear Ms. Jones:

This letter is to confirm our understanding of the terms and objectives of our engagement and the nature and limitations of the services we will provide:

1. We will perform the following services: We will compile from information you provide, the (monthly, quarterly, or other frequency) financial statements of ABC Corporation for the year 20XX. A compilation is limited to presenting in the form of financial statements, information that is the representation of management. We will not review or audit the financial statements and accordingly, will not express an opinion or any other form of assurance on them. The financial statements will not be accompanied by a report.

Based upon our discussions with you, these financial statements have been designed to meet your needs in managing your business. Accordingly, these statements are *for management's use only and are not intended for third-party use.*

Material departures from GAAP (or OCBOA, if applicable) may exist and the effects of those departures, if any, on the financial statements may not be disclosed. In addition, substantially all disclosures and the statement of cash flows required by GAAP (or OCBOA, if applicable) may be omitted.[1] (The accountant may wish to identify known departures.) Notwithstanding these limitations, you represent that you have knowledge about the nature of the procedures applied and the basis of accounting and assumptions used in the preparation of the financial statements that allows you to place the financial information in the proper context. Further, you represent and agree that the use of the financial statements will be limited to members of management with similar knowledge.

The financial statements are intended solely for the information and use of [include a list of specified members of management of ABC Corporation] and are *not* intended to be and should not be used by any other party. [optional].

2. We will also [discuss other services provided] [optional]....

---

[1] The statement does not require that the known departure(s) be identified. In the exposure draft, the illustrative engagement letter included a suggestion that the accountant may wish to identify known departures. The final statement clarifies that the accountant is not required to identify known GAAP or OCBOA departures, but is permitted to do so.

A-4b

Our engagement cannot be relied upon to disclose errors, fraud, or illegal acts that may exist. However, we will inform the appropriate level of management of any material errors that come to our attention and any fraud or illegal acts that come to our attention, unless clearly inconsequential.

We are not independent with respect to Jones Manufacturing, Inc. [insert if applicable].

The other data accompanying the financial statement in the schedule of operating expenses are presented only for supplementary analysis purposes and were compiled from information that is the representation of management, without audit or review, and we do not express an opinion or any other form of assurance on such data [if applicable]

In view of the limitations described above, you agree not to take, or assist in, any action seeking to hold us liable for damages due to any deficiency in the financial statements we prepare and you agree to hold us harmless from any liability and related legal costs arising from any third-party use of the financial statements in contravention of the terms of this agreement [optional, but recommended language].

Our fees for our services are \$_____.

Should you require financial statements for third party use, we would be pleased to discuss with you the requested level of service. Such engagement would be considered separate and not deemed to be part of the services described in this engagement letter.

If the forgoing is in accordance with your understanding, *please sign the copy of this letter* in the space provided and return it to me.

Sincerely,

Billy Bob, CPA

Accepted and agreed to:

_____
Mary Jones, President
Jones Manufacturing, Inc.
Date:

182 TOP AUDITING ISSUES FOR 2005 CPE COURSE

A-5a Sample Engagement Letter Option 2: Not Signed by Management

Ms. Mary Jones
President
Jones Manufacturing, Inc.
111 Smith Road
Notown, Massachusetts 02174

Dear Ms. Jones:

This letter sets forth our understanding of the terms and objectives of our engagement and the nature and limitations of the services we will provide:

1. We will perform the following services: We will compile from information you provide, the (monthly, quarterly, or other frequency) financial statements of ABC Corporation for the year 20XX. A compilation is limited to presenting in the form of financial statements information that is the representation of management. We will not review or audit the financial statements and accordingly, will not express an opinion or any other form of assurance on them. The financial statements will not be accompanied by a report.

Based upon our discussions with you, these financial statements have been designed to meet your needs in managing your business. Accordingly, these statements are *for management's use only and are not intended for third-party use.*

Material departures from GAAP (or OCBOA, if applicable) may exist and the effects of those departures, if any, on the financial statements may not be disclosed. In addition, substantially all disclosures and the statement of cash flows required by GAAP (or OCBOA, if applicable) may be omitted.[1] (The accountant may wish to identify known departures.)

Notwithstanding these limitations, you represent that you have knowledge about the nature of the procedures applied and the basis of accounting and assumptions used in the preparation of the financial statements that allows you to place the financial information in the proper context. Further, you represent and agree that the use of the financial statements will be limited to members of management with similar knowledge.

The financial statements are intended solely for the information and use of [include a list of specified members of management of ABC Corporation] and are *not* intended to be and should not be used by any other party. [optional].

2. We will also [discuss other services provided] [optional]....

---

[1] The statement does not require that the known departure(s) be identified. In the exposure draft, the, the illustrative engagement letter included suggested that the accountant may wish to identify known departures. The final statement clarifies that the accountant is not required to identify known GAAP or OCBOA departures.

A-5b

Our engagement cannot be relied upon to disclose errors, fraud, or illegal acts that may exist. However, we will inform the appropriate level of management of any material errors that come to our attention and any fraud or illegal acts that come to our attention, unless clearly inconsequential.

We are not independent with respect to Jones Manufacturing, Inc. [insert if applicable].

The other data accompanying the financial statement in the schedule of operating expenses are presented only for supplementary analysis purposes and were compiled from information that is the representation of management, without audit or review, and we do not express an opinion or any other form of assurance on such data. [if applicable]

In view of the limitations described above, you agree not to take, or assist in, any action seeking to hold us liable for damages due to any deficiency in the financial statements we prepare and you agree to hold us harmless from any liability and related legal costs arising from any third-party use of the financial statements in contravention of the terms of this agreement. [optional, but recommended language]

Our fees for our services are $_____.

Should you require financial statements for third party use, we would be pleased to discuss with you the requested level of service. Such engagement would be considered separate and not deemed to be part of the services described in this engagement letter. If the foregoing is not in accordance with your understanding, please notify me.[2]

Sincerely,

Billy Bob, CPA

Date:

---

[2] Because the second letter is merely a transmittal letter not requiring a signature, the CPA should change the language requiring that the client notify him or her of any differences only if their client does not agree with the terms and conditions of the letter.

184 TOP AUDITING ISSUES FOR 2005 CPE COURSE

A-6a Sample Non-Authoritative Transmittal Letter

ACME Manufacturing Co.
Robert Reilly, CPA
Chief Financial Officer

Mr. William No, President   March 16, 200X
No Loan Bank and Trust
54 Everywhere Way
Nowhere, USA

Dear Mr. No:

Attached you will find the financial statements of ACME Manufacturing Co. for the month ended February 28, 20X1.

The accompanying balance sheet of ACME Manufacturing as of February 28, 20X1, and the related statements of income and cash flows for the year then ended have been prepared by Robert Reilly, CPA. I have prepared such financial statements in my capacity as Chief Financial Officer of the company.

These financial statements have been prepared in accordance with generally accepted accounting principles. (optional)

Very truly yours,

Robert Reilly, CPA
Chief Financial Officer
ACME Manufacturing Co.

APPENDIX A **185**

A-6b   Sample Internally Generated Balance Sheet

ACME Manufacturing Co.
Balance Sheet
February 28, 20X1

ASSETS

Current assets:

Cash	$xx	
Accounts receivable	xx	
Inventories		xx
Total current assets	xx	

Property and equipment:

Cost	xx
Less accumulated depreciation	xx
Total property and equipment	xx

$xx

LIABILITIES AND STOCKHOLDER'S EQUITY

Current liabilities:

Accounts payable	$xx	
Accrued expenses and taxes		xx
Short-term notes payable	xx	
Total current liabilities	xx	

Long-term debt: xx

Stockholders' equity:

Common stock	xx	
Retained earnings	xx	
Total stockholders' equity		xx

$xx

Internally Generated Financial Statements

A-6c Sample Internally Generated Income Statement

ACME Manufacturing Co.
Income Statement
For the Month Ended February 28, 20X1

Net sales	$xx
Cost of sales	xx
Gross profit on sales	xx
Operating expenses	xx
Net operating income	xx
Income taxes	xx
Net income	$xx

Internally Generated Financial Statements

APPENDIX B   **187**

B-1a   Revised Illustrative Representation Letter
Review Engagements: SSARS No. 9

Date: [No earlier than the date of the Accountant's Report]

To John Jones, CPA

We are providing this letter in connection with your review of the financial statements of XYZ Corporation as of December 31, 20X3 and 20X2 and for the years then ended for the purpose of expressing limited assurance that there are no material modifications that should be made to the statements in order for them to be in conformity with generally accepted accounting principles. We confirm, *to the best of our knowledge and belief,* that we are responsible for the fair presentation in the financial statements of financial position, results of operations, and cash flows in conformity with generally accepted accounting principles.

Certain representations in this letter are described as being limited to matters that are material. Items are material, regardless of size, if they involve an omission of a misstatement of accounting information that, in the light of surrounding circumstances, makes it probable that the judgment of a reasonable person relying on the information would be changed or influenced by the omission or misstatement.[1]

We confirm, to the best of our knowledge and belief, (as of [insert a date no earlier than the date of the review report]), the following representations made to you during your review:

1. The financial statements referred to above are fairly presented in conformity with generally accepted accounting principles.

2. We have made available to you all:

    a. Financial records and related data.

    b. Minutes of the meetings of stockholders, directors, directors, and committees of directors, or summaries of actions of recent meetings for which minutes have not yet been prepared.

3. There are no material transactions that have not been properly recorded in the accounting records underlying the financial statements.

4. We have no plans or intentions that may materially affect the carrying amounts or classification of assets and liabilities.

5. There are no material losses (such as obsolete inventory or purchase or sales commitments) that have not been properly accrued or disclosed in the financial statements.

6. There are no:

    a. Violations or possible violations of laws or regulations whose effects should be considered for disclosure in the financial statements or as a basis for recording a loss contingency

    b. Unasserted claims or assessments that our lawyer has advised us are probable of assertion that must be disclosed in accordance with Financial Accounting Standards Board (FASB) Statement No. 5, *Accounting for Contingencies.*

---

[1] The qualitative discussion of materiality used in this letter is adapted from FASB Concepts Statement No. 2, Qualitative Characteristics of Accounting Information.

B-1b

[Alternative language when management has not consulted a lawyer]

[*We are not aware of any pending or threatened litigation, claims, or assessments or unasserted claims or assessments that are required to be accrued or disclosed in the financial statements in accordance with Financial Accounting Standards Board Statement No. 5, Accounting for Contingencies, and we have not consulted a lawyer concerning litigation, claims, or assessments.*]

    c. Other material liabilities or gain or loss contingencies that are required to be accrued or disclosed by FASB Statement No. 5.

7. The company has satisfactory title to all owned assets, and there are no liens or encumbrances on such assets nor has any asset been pledged, [*except as disclosed in the financial statements*].

8. We have complied with all aspects of contractual agreements that would have a material effect on the financial statements in the event of noncompliance.

9. The following have been properly recorded or disclosed in the financial statements:

    a. Related party transactions including sales, purchases, loans, transfers, leasing arrangements, and guarantees, and amounts receivable from or payable to related parties.

    b. Guarantees, whether written or oral, under which the company is contingently liable.

    c. Significant estimates and material concentrations known to management that are required to be disclosed in accordance with AICPA's Statement of Position 94-6, *Disclosure of Certain Significant Risks and Uncertainties* [Significant estimates are estimates at the balance sheet date that could change materially within the next year. Concentrations refer to volumes of business, revenues, available sources of supply, or markets or geographic areas for which events could occur that would significantly disrupt normal finances within the next year.]

    d. [Add additional representations that are unique to the entity's business or industry-Sample additional disclosures are noted below.]

10. To the best of our knowledge and belief, no events have occurred subsequent to the balance-sheet date and through the date of this letter that would require adjustments to, or disclosure in, the aforementioned financial statements.

11. We have responded ***fully and truthfully*** to all inquiries made to us by you during your review.

Date: _____ Name of Owner or Chief Executive Officer and Title

Date: _____ Name of Chief Financial Officer and Title

APPENDIX B **189**

B-2a Additional Conditions and Illustrative Representations

Condition	Example of Additional Representation
The impact of a new accounting principle is not known.	We have not completed the process of evaluating the impact that will result from adopting Financial Accounting Standards Board (FASB) No. XXX, as discussed in Note X. The company is therefore unable to disclose the impact that adopting FASB Statement No. XXX will have on the financial statements and the results of operations when such Statement is adopted.
Change in accounting principle is made and management has justification making the change.	We believe that [*description of the newly adopted accounting principle*] is preferable to [*description of the former accounting principle*] because [*description of management's justification for the change in accounting principle*].
The entity has used the work of a specialist.	We agree with the findings of the specialist in evaluating the [description of the assertion] and have adequately considered the qualifications of the specialist in determining the amounts and disclosures used in the financial statements and underlying accounting records. We did not give or cause any instructions to be given to the specialist with respect to the values or amounts derived in an attempt to bias his or her work, and we are not otherwise aware of any matters that have had an impact on the independence or objectivity of the specialist.
Disclosure has been made regarding an entity's ability to continue as a going concern pursuant to paragraphs 10 and 11 of SAS No. 59.	The financial statements disclose all of the matters of which we are aware that are relevant to the company's ability to continue as a going concern, including significant conditions and events, and our plans.
Cash: Disclosure is required of compensating balances or other arrangements involving restrictions on cash balances, lines of credit, or similar arrangements.	Arrangements with financial institutions involving compensating balances or other arrangements involving restricted balances, lines of credit, or similar arrangements have been properly disclosed.
Trade and other receivables:	Receivables recorded in the financial statements represent valid claims against debtors for sales or other charges arising on or before the balance-sheet date and have been appropriately reduced to their estimated net realizable value.***
No allowance for uncollectible accounts has be used	No allowance for uncollectible accounts has been established for trade receivables because the amount of estimated uncollectible accounts is not material. ***
Inventories: Excess or obsolete inventories exist.	A provision in the amount of $XXX has been made to reduce excess or obsolete inventories to their estimated net realizable value.***
The year end inventory has been valued by the company.	Inventories, valued at LIFO lower of cost or market value were $XX at December 31, 20X2 and $XX at December 31, 20X1.***

190 TOP AUDITING ISSUES FOR 2005 CPE COURSE

B-2b

Condition	Example of Additional Representation
Investment securities: The entity has investment securities which have been categorized in accordance with FASB No. 115 into three (3) categories: held to maturity, trading, and available for sale.	Debt securities [with an amortized cost of $XXX and $XXX at December 31, 20X2 and 20X1, respectively], that have been classified as held to maturity have been so classified due to our intent to hold such securities to maturity and our ability to do so. All other debt securities have been classified as available-for-sale or trading.**
	Certain equity securities with a market value of $XXX and $XXX at December 31, 20X2 and 20X1, respectively, have been classified as trading securities as the company intends to sell such securities within the next operating cycle.
	Certain debt and equity securities with a market value of $XXX and $XXX at December 31, 20X2 and 20X1, respectively, have been classified as available for sale as the company does not intend to hold such securities to maturity or does not have a plan to sell such securities within the next operating cycle.
Management considers the decline in value of debt or equity securities to be temporary.	We consider the decline in value of debt or equity securities as either available-for-sale or held-to maturity to be temporary.**
Investments- non securities (not publicly traded):	The cost method is used to account for the company's invest-ment in the common stock of [*investee*] because the company does not have the ability to exercise significant influence over the investee's operating and financial policies.
Investments accounted for using the equity method:	The equity method is used to account for the company's investment in the common stock of [investee] because the company does have the ability to exercise significant influence over the investee's operating and financial policies.
Financial instruments (including investments): There are financial instruments with off-balance sheet risk	The following information about financial instruments with off-balance sheet risk has been properly disclosed in the financial statements: a) The extent, nature, and terms of financial instruments with off-balance-sheet risk.
	b) The amount of credit risk of financial instruments with off-balance-sheet risk and information about the collateral supporting such financial instruments.
The entity has the following financial instruments with concentrations of credit risk:	The entity has disclosed all significant concentrations of credit risk arising from all financial instruments and infor-mation about the collateral supporting such financial instruments.
The majority of the entity's trade receivables are due from customers concentrated within one geographic area.	

B-2c

Condition	Example of Additional Representation
Financial instruments - continued: The majority of the entity's cash is deposited in one commercial bank with balances which, from time to time, exceed FDIC insurable limits.	
Deferred charges: Significant expenditures have been deferred.	We believe that all significant expenditures that have been deferred to future periods will be recoverable.
Deferred tax asset: A deferred tax asset exists at the balance-sheet date.	A valuation allowance in the amount of $XXX at December 31, 20X2, has been determined pursuant to the provisions of FASB No. 109, *Accounting for Income Taxes*, including the company's estimation of future taxable income, if necessary, and is adequate to reduce the total deferred tax asset to an amount that will more likely than not be realized. *[Fill in with appropriate wording detailing how the entity determined the valuation allowance against the deferred tax asset.]* A valuation allowance against deferred tax assets at the balance-sheet date is not considered necessary because it is more likely than not the deferred tax asset will be fully realized.
Fixed assets and intangible assets: The Company has significant fixed assets and intangible assets.	We have reviewed long-lived assets and certain identifiable intangibles to be held and used for impairment in accordance with FASB No. 144, *Accounting for the Impairment or Disposal of Long-Lived Assets,* whenever events or changes in circumstances have indicated that the carrying value of its assets might not be recoverable, and have appropriately recorded the adjustment.*** We have tested goodwill and indefinite-lived intangibles for impairment in accordance with FASB Statement No. 142, *Goodwill and Other Intangible Assets*, and, when an asset has been impaired, we have appropriately recorded the adjustment to the carrying value of the impaired asset.***
All assets:	We believe that the carrying amounts of all material assets will be recoverable.***
Debt: Short-term debt is shown long-term because a) management intends to refinance it on a long-term basis and, b) it has the ability to do so. After the balance sheet date and before the issuance of the financial statements, term basis. the company receives a commitment letter from a bank for long-term financing.	The Company has excluded short-term obligations totaling $XXX from current liabilities because it intends to refinance the obligations on a long-term basis. On March 1, 20X1, Company received a commitment from NoLoan Bank for the purpose of refinancing the short-term obligations on a long-

TOP AUDITING ISSUES FOR 2005 CPE COURSE

B-2d

Condition	Example of Additional Representation
Taxes: The Company is an S Corporation.	At year-end, the Company has retained its S corporation tax status for federal and state tax purposes.
The Company is an LLC and elects to be taxed as a partnership.	At year-end, the Company has retained its election to be taxed as a partnership and not a corporation for federal and state tax purposes.
Contingencies: Estimates and disclosures have been made of environmental remediation liabilities and related loss contingencies.	We have recorded a provision for any material loss in connection with environmental remediation where it is probable that a loss has been incurred and we can reasonably estimate the amount.
	In particular, we have recorded a provision for loss in connection with Site X. We believe that such estimate is reasonable based on available information and that the liability and related loss contingency and the expected outcome of uncertainties have been adequately described in the company's financial statements.
There are no known environmental liabilities.	We are not aware of any asserted or unasserted claims remediation presented against the company by the EPA, governmental agencies or other third parties related to any environmental issues [SOP 96-1].
Agreement may exist to repurchase assets previously sold.	An agreement to repurchase assets previously sold has been properly disclosed.
Pension and postretirement benefits: An actuary has been used to measure pension liabilities and costs.	We believe that the actuarial assumptions and methods used to measure pension liabilities and costs for financial accounting purposes are appropriate in the circumstances.
There is involvement with a multi-employer plan.	We are unable to determine the possibility of a withdrawal liability in a multiemployer benefit plan, or,
	We have determined that there is the possibility of a withdrawal liability in a multiemployer plan in the amount of $XXXX.
Postretirement benefits have been eliminated.	We do not intend to compensate for the elimination of post-retirement benefits by granting an increase in pension benefits or We plan to compensate for the elimination of postretirement benefits by granting an increase in pension benefits in the amount of $XXX.

B-2e

Condition	Example of Additional Representation
Pension and postretirement benefits (continued):	
Employee layoffs that would otherwise lead to a curtailment of a benefit plan are intended to be temporary.	Current employee layoffs are intended to be temporary.
Management intends to either continue to make or not make frequent amendments to its pension or other postretirement benefit plans, which may affect the amortization period of prior service cost, or has expressed a substantive commitment to increase benefit obligations.	We plan to continue to make frequent amendments to its pension or other postretirement benefit plans, which may affect the amortization period of prior service cost or, We do not plan to make frequent amendments to its pension or other postretirement benefit plans.
Income statement: There may be a loss from sales commitments.	We have made provisions for losses to be sustained in the fulfillment of or from inability to fulfill, sales commitments.
There may be losses from purchase commitments.	Provisions have been made for losses to be sustained as a result of purchase commitments for inventory quantities in excess of normal requirements or at prices in excess of prevailing market prices.
Nature of the product or industry indicates the possibility of undisclosed sales terms.	We have fully disclosed to you all sales terms, including all rights of return or price adjustments and all warranty provisions.

194 TOP AUDITING ISSUES FOR 2005 CPE COURSE

B-3a Sample Successor Accountant Acknowledgment Letter

Roberts, Park and Roberts, CPA (Successor Accountant)
51 Main Street
Nowhere, MA, 49393

We have previously [reviewed or compiled], in accordance with Statements on Standards for Accounting and Review Services the December 31, 20X2, financial statements of XYZ Corporation (XYZ). In connection with your [review or compilation] of XYZ's 20X3 financial statements, you have requested access to our working papers prepared in connection with that engagement. XYZ has authorized our firm to allow you to review those working papers.

Our [review or compilation], and the working papers prepared in connection therewith, of XYZ's financial statements were not planned or conducted in contemplation of your [review or compilation]. Therefore, items of possible interest to you may not have been specifically addressed. Our use of professional judgment for the purpose of this engagement means that mattes may have existed that would have been assessed differently by you. We make no representation about the sufficiency or appropriateness of the information in our working papers for your purposes.

We understand that the purpose of your review is to obtain information about XYZ and our 20X2 results to assist you in your 20X3 engagement of XYZ. For that purposes only, we will provide you access to our working papers that relate to that objective.

Upon request, we will provide copies of those working papers that provide factual information about XYZ. You agree to subject any such copies or information otherwise derived from our working papers to your normal policy for retention of working papers and protection of confidential client information. Furthermore, in the event of a third-party request for access to your working papers prepared in connection with your (reviews or compilations of XYZ Corporation, you agree to obtain our permission before voluntarily allowing any such access to our working papers or information otherwise derived from our working papers, and to obtain on our behalf any releases that you obtain from such third party. You agree to advise us promptly and provide us a copy of any subpoenas, summons, or other court order for access

APPENDIX B **195**

B-3b

to your working papers that include copies of our working papers or information otherwise derived therefrom.

Because your review of our working papers is undertaken solely for the purpose described above and may not entail a review of all our working papers, you agree that (1) the information obtained from the review will not be used by you for any other purpose, (2) you will not comment, orally or in writing, to anyone as a result of that review about whether our engagement was performed in accordance with Statements on Standards for Accounting and Review Services, (3) you will not provide expert testimony or litigation services or otherwise accept an engagement to comment on issues relating to the quality of our engagement.

Please confirm your agreement with the foregoing by signing and dating a copy of this letter and returning it to us.

Very truly yours,

By: James J. Fox & Company, CPA [Predecessor Accountant]

Accepted:

By: _____

    Roberts, Park and Roberts, CPA (Successor Accountant)

Date: _____

TOP AUDITING ISSUES FOR 2005 CPE COURSE

Index

A

Accountants in public accounting serving also as stockholders, partners, directors, officers, or employees ... 111–116, 118

Accounting estimates, retrospective review of prior year's ... 61–62

Accounting principles
of client's industry, accountant's knowledge of ... 93
country of origin of ... 149, 150
disagreement between client and predecessor accountant about ... 142
intentional misapplication of ... 6

Accounting profession, public opinion of image of ... 4–5

Accounting records, manipulation, falsification, or alteration of ... 6

Accounting rules, aggressive interpretation of ... 7, 49

Accounts containing inherent risks, identifying ... 55

Accounts receivable
focusing audit on ... 12
fraudulent financial reporting of ... 7

Accounts susceptible to inappropriate entries... 61

Accruals, reducing audit time for ... 12

Additional evidence to determine commission of illegal acts ... 47

American Institute of Certified Public Accountants (AICPA)
Accounting and Review Services Committee (ARSC) of ... 69, 70, 71–72, 91, 129, 145
anti-fraud program of ... 46
Code of Ethics of ... 115
Code of Professional Conduct of ... 117, 143
Council of ... 69, 115
Peer Review Committee of ... 135

Analytical procedures
increased in lieu of account balance tests ... 11
relating to revenue recognition ... 64
results of, not consistent with expectations ... 50
role in identifying fraud risks of ... 52–53, 54

APB No. 12, Omnibus Opinion, disclosures required by ... 121, 122

Arthur Andersen clients, absorption statistics for ... 28

Assembly statement ... 71, 72

Attorney responsibility to report material violations of securities law ... 14

Audit committees
communication about fraud to ... 48
communication with ... 44
to constrain improper conduct and fraud ... 9, 14, 57
inquiries about risks of fraud to ... 53
requirements under Sarbanes-Oxley Section 301 for public company ... 22, 24

Audit evidence
evaluated throughout audit ... 64
learning how to evaluate ... 63
requirement to evaluate ... 48

Audit fees
increasing, client preparation for ... 12–13
of non-public companies, issues of implementing SAS No. 99 for ... 11–12
SAS No. 99 as increasing ... 10–11

Audit firm rotation, requirement for ... 14

Audit partner rotation, mandatory ... 13, 14

Audit procedures
additional, to obtain higher quality evidence ... 58
evaluating results of ... 43, 65
nature of ... 59

Audit report, SAS No. 93 changes to ... 149

Audit team
consideration of how and where fraud might exist required for ... 47, 51–52
discussion of plan to assess likelihood of fraud in ... 66
specialists included in ... 52

Audit tests for fraud ... 59

Audit time
for planning ... 10
reducing ... 11–12

Auditing Standards Board (ASB), former authority of ... 14

Auditing standards, country of origin of ... 149, 150

Auditors
assumptions about future conditions of ... 31

198 TOP AUDITING ISSUES FOR 2005 CPE COURSE

changes implemented under Sarbanes-Oxley for SEC company ... 16–17
documenting consideration of fraud by ... 66–67
fraud focus of ... 7
independence of. *See* Independence, auditor
professional skepticism of ... 5, 47, 50–51, 58
prohibited activities for SEC company ... 13
public opinion polls about ... 3–5
responsibilities under Sarbanes-Oxley Section 404 of ... 23–24
specialist engaged by ... 37
switching. *See* Public accounting firms
understanding of controls and process for fair value measurements of ... 32, 34

Auditors' responsibility for fraud assessment ... 12–13

Autonomic computers among AICPA top 5 emerging technologies ... 3

B

"Big 4" accounting firms
concentrations of industries among, table of ... 29
former Arthur Andersen clients absorbed by, statistics for ... 28
market shares of ... 27, 29
staff levels of ... 26

Board of directors, receipt of management-use only financial statements by members of ... 99

Budgets presented alongside historic financial statements ... 139–140

Business exchange technology among AICPA top 10 technologies ... 2

Business valuation
accountant's responsibility for information in ... 108–110
exemption from SSARSs of information in ... 108

C

Cash flows
discounted, forecasts using ... 41
risks associated with ... 41
trends in ... 65

CEO and CFO certification of financial statements ... 14
Sarbanes-Oxley Sections 302 and 906 for ... 24

Certification of disclosures in companies' quarterly and annual reports (Sarbanes-Oxley Sections 302 and 906) ... 22, 24

Changes in behavior or lifestyle as fraud risk factor ... 55

Charts in financial statements ... 137

Client perception of fraud assessment responsibility ... 12–13, 46–47

Client signature
for client's understanding in management-use only engagements ... 93
for engagement letter ... 90

Clients
consent to disclose confidential information required from ... 143
permission to make inquiries of predecessor accounts by ... 142
procedures for accepting and continuing with ... 55

Closely held businesses
effects of Sarbanes-Oxley on ... 14
misappropriation of assets in ... 7, 9–10

Code of conduct, enforcement of formal ... 9

Code of Professional Conduct rules for CPAs ... 117, 143

Collateral in measuring fair market value ... 38–39

Collusion of management, employees, or third parties in fraud ... 50, 67

Compilation and review ... 68–117
update to ... 118–150

Compilation and Review Alerts (AICPA)
generation of financial statements addressed in ... 74
modification of financial statements addressed in ... 74–75
as planning aid for accountants ... 69
presentation of financial statements addressed in ... 77

Compilation engagements. *See also* Review engagements
alternatives to traditional ... 70
changes in level of service for ... 101–103
as commodities for clients ... 69
peer review of ... 70
rules for dealing with supplementary information in ... 135
stepping down to ... 131–132

Compilation of financial statements under SSARS No. 8, process of ... 77

Compilation report
by accountant who is not independent ... 111–116
accountant's signature on ... 119, 128–129
addressing ... 129
changes under SSARS No. 9 to ... 128–129
country of origin referred to in ... 149–150
CPA required to compile financial statements in ... 108

Index **199**

date of ... 129
describing selected disclosures in ... 146–149
by employee ... 112–115
financial statements not
accompanied by ... 89
independence exception to ... 113, 115–116
issuance of ... 70, 83–84, 102
management omission of substantially all
disclosures required by GAAP in ... 122
not issued in management-use only
engagement ... 91, 102
for predecessor's compilation ... 144
reference to country of
origin in ... 149–150

Compilation requirement, general ... 73

Compliance test design ... 57–58

Comprehensive income
definition of ... 124
display of ... 127–128

**Consolidators, compilation engagement
charges reduced by ... 69**

**Controllership issues
for accountants ... 110–118**

**Controllership services,
examples of ... 111**

**Culture of management in smaller entities
to discourage fraud, ethical ... 57**

D

**Data mining among AICPA top 10
technologies ... 2**

**Database and application integration
among AICPA top 10 technologies ... 2**

**Databases, client, CPA
updates to ... 78, 79–80**

**Digital optimization among AICPA
top 10 technologies ... 2**

**Disaster recovery among AICPA
top 10 technologies ... 2**

Disclosures
financial statements
having selected ... 145–149
for management-use only
financial statements ... 95–96
substantially all ... 146

**Discounted cash flows method
to estate fair value ... 36**

E

Eldercare services ... 87, 88

**Electronic transactions, computer-
assisted techniques for testing ... 59**

Embezzlement ... 7

**Emerging technologies,
AICPA top 5 ... 2–3**

Employees
fraud by ... 7–9, 55
inquiries about risks of fraud to ... 53, 54

Engagement letter
converted to transmittal letter ... 90
description of management's
responsibility for fraud in ... 13
documentation of ... 85–86
for management-use only financial
statement engagement ... 84–86, 89,
91, 93–95, 102
material departures from GAAP or OCBOA
noted in ... 93–95
protective language about submission of
financial statements in ... 82
sample ... 86, 94
for write-up engagement and part-time
controllership ... 110

Estates, financial statements for ... 87, 88

Ethics Interpretation 101-3 ... 111

Ethics Ruling 10 ... 117

Ethics Ruling 65 ... 117

Ethics Ruling 203 ... 117, 118

**Evidence about appropriateness of fair
value measurement ... 39**
subsequent events and transactions
as providing ... 42

**Exemptions from SSARSs,
four ... 69, 103–110**
list of services applicable under ... 106–108

**Expectation gap between client and
auditor for fraud ... 12–13**
SAS No. 82 addressing ... 46

F

Fair value
changes in ... 30
disclosures about ... 43
risk of material misstatement
in determining ... 37

**Fair value estimates, developing
independent ... 42**

Fair value measurements
appropriateness of ... 36
basis for ... 39, 40
complexity of ... 37, 38
conformity with GAAP of ... 34–36
of derivative instruments ... 35
specialist engagement in auditing ... 37
testing entity's ... 37–39
understanding of entity's process for
determining ... 33–34
use of ... 30

FASB Interpretation 46 of ARB No. 51, Consolidation of Variable Interest Entities—An Interpretation of ARB No. 51 ... 30

FASB No. 57, Related Parties ... 97, 99

FASB No. 107, Disclosures about Fair Value of Financial Instruments ... 30

FASB No. 130, Reporting on Comprehensive Income ... 124, 127

FASB No. 142, Goodwill and Other Intangible Assets ... 30

FASB No. 144, Accounting for the Impairment or Disposal of Long-Lived Assets ... 30

FASB No. 150, Accounting for Certain Financial Instruments with Characteristics of Both Liabilities and Equity ... 30

FASB statements, comparative number of ... 103

Fieldwork, evaluating fraud risks around end of ... 65

Financial statements
adjustments not evidenced by journal entries to ... 60–61
audited, reviewed, or compiled by another accountant ... 109
certification of disclosures required for public company ... 14, 24
client's computer-generated ... 76
fraud not material versus material to ... 65–66
generation of ... 73–74, 78–80
historical ... 108, 139–140
included in consulting reports ... 108
included in personal financial plan, exemption from SSARSs of ... 108
internal use ... 71
internally generated ... 118
issued to third parties ... 94
management-use only ... 73, 83, 84–103
in Microsoft Word or Excel file ... 80
modification of ... 74–75, 136–137
percentages in ... 137
personal ... 87–88
preparation of ... 75–76, 82
prepared by client ... 108
preparing but not presenting ... 81–82
presenting ... 77–79, 83
reasonable assurance about lack of misstatements in ... 50
revising predecessor's ... 144–145
selected disclosures in ... 145–149
"shortcut" ... 70
trial balances differentiated from ... 107
unaudited, accountant's name in communication containing ... 119, 120 121

Forensic audits ... 47

Fraud
audit tests for ... 59
communicating statistics to clients about ... 13
concealing ... 49–50
definition and characteristics of ... 48–49
documenting auditor's consideration of ... 66–67
environmental conditions for ... 49
identification of risks of material misstatements due to ... 6, 46
incentives or pressures to commit ... 54–55
not material to financial statements ... 65
perpetuating ... 49
rationalizing ... 8–9, 55

Fraud detection ... 45–68
auditor's responsibility in ... 50–51, 67
management's responsibility for ... 48
under SAS No. 82 ... 46–47

Fraud risk factors
defined ... 54
for fraudulent financial reporting, SAS No. 99 examples of ... 46, 54–55
for misappropriation of assets ... 47, 55

Fraud risks
addressing, procedures to be performed in ... 59
evaluated around end of fieldwork ... 65
identifying ... 52–57
information gathering about ... 5
inquiries of audit committee and internal auditors about ... 53
inquiries of management about ... 53
responses to identified, SAS examples of ... 59–59–60
role of analytical procedures in identifying ... 52–53, 54
in small businesses ... 9–10

Fraud triangle (incentives, opportunities, and rationalizations) ... 8–9, 54–56

Fraudulent financial reporting ... 6–7
definition of ... 49
examples of ... 49
risk factors for occurrence of ... 46, 54–55

Future earnings in management assumptions, forecasts of ... 41

G

Gallup poll of public image of various professions ... 4–5

General Accounting Office (GAO) report, Public Accounting Firms: Mandated Study on Consolidation and Competition (GAO Report) ... 24–25, 28

General ledger software, generating financial statements using ... 78–79

Index 201

Generally accepted accounting principles (GAAP)
disclosures about fair value made in conformity with ... 43
disclosures required by ... 95–96, 122
fair value measurements under ... 30, 31–32, 34–36
material departures from, noted in engagement letter ... 93–95
missing disclosure as departure from ... 148
OCBOA statements not requiring some elements to ... 12
PCAOB responsibility for ... 14
statement of retained earnings not required by ... 121
titles for ... 94–95
types of ... 6–8. *See also* individual types
types of assets of transactions susceptible to ... 7–8

Generally accepted auditing standards (GAAS)
PCAOB responsibility for ... 14
SAS No. 99 guidance for audits complying with ... 47

Governmental entities, financial statements for ... 87, 88

Graphs in financial statements ... 137

H

Higher risk areas, focusing audit on ... 12

Historical financial information in developing management assumptions, reliance on ... 41

I

ID/authentication among AICPA top 5 emerging technologies ... 2

Independence, auditor
controllership issues with ... 110–112
Interpretation No. 21 of SSARS No. 1 for lack of ... 112–116
required to audit internal controls under Sarbanes-Oxley ... 23
write-up services as threat to ... 110

Information security among AICPA top 10 technologies ... 1

Institutional investors, preference for "Big 4" accounting firms of ... 26

Interim financial statements reviewed for fraud risk factors ... 55

Internal audit function
to constrain fraud ... 9
outsourced ... 25

Internal auditors, inquiries about risks of fraud to ... 53

Internal control reporting (Sarbanes-Oxley Section 404) ... 22–24
reportable conditions relating to ... 66

Internal controls
annual report by public companies of their ... 22–24
auditor's report on management's assessment of ... 23–24
components of ... 57
management's ability to override ... 49. *See also* Management override of controls
management's responsibility for establishing and maintaining ... 23
poor, opportunity for fraud provided by ... 8–9, 47, 55

Internal Revenue Code regulations, comparative number of ... 103

Interpretation No. 1 of SSARS No. 1 ... 149

Interpretation No. 14 of SAS No. 62, Special Reports ... 122

Interpretation No. 14 of SSARS No. 1, Differentiating a Financial Statement Presentation from a Trial Balance ... 107

Interpretation No. 20 of SSARS No. 1 ... 108

Interpretation No. 21 of SSARS No. 1, *Applicability of SSARS No. 1 When Performing Controllership or Other Management Services* ... 112–116
summary table of requirements of ... 113–114

Interpretation No. 22 of SSARS No. 1, *Use of "Selected Information—Substantially All Disclosures Required by Generally Accepted Accounting Procedures Are Not Included"* ... 145, 148–149

Interpretation No. 23 of SSARS No. 1, *Applicability of Statements on Standards for Accounting and Review Services When an Accountant Engaged to Perform a Business Valuation Derives Information from an Entity's Tax Return* ... 108

Interpretation No. 24 of SSARS No. 1, *Reference to Country of Origin in Review or Compilation Report* ... 149–150

Interpretation No. 25 of SSARS No. 1, *Omission of Display of Comprehensive Income in a Compilation* ... 127–128

Interpretations, SSARS, list of ... 105–106

Inventories
focusing audit on risks for ... 12
fraudulent financial reporting of ... 7
responses to identified risks with ... 60

Investment bankers, preference for "Big 4" accounting firms of ... 26

202 TOP AUDITING ISSUES FOR 2005 CPE COURSE

J

Journal entries
fraud perpetrated by
recording inappropriate ... 60
nonstandard ... 61
testing of ... 61

L

**Letterhead, printing accountant's
report on ... 129**

**Levels of service by
accounting firms ... 71–72, 101–103**

**Litigation services, exemption from
SSARSs of financial statements in ... 108**

M

**Malpractice insurance covering
controllership ... 110**

Management
auditor's inquires of ... 35
communicating possible fraud to client ... 66
not present in previous period ... 131
receipt of management-use only financial
statements by, requirements for ... 97–100

Management assumptions
auditor evaluation of ... 42
reasonableness of, in written management
representation letter ... 44
testing significant ... 38, 39–42

**Management disinterest,
fraud risk from ... 10**

Management estimates
estimates supported by audit evidence
differing from ... 61–62
in responding to identified fraud risks ... 60

**Management inquiries about risks
of fraud ... 53**

Management integrity, reliance on ... 87

Management override of controls
auditor's additional procedures
to assess ... 6
auditor's response to address risk of ... 60–61
documenting results of procedures
to address ... 67
employee inquiries to provide
examples of ... 54
in fraud triangle ... 8–9
in misappropriation of assets ... 55

Management representation letter
additional disclosures in ... 134
for all periods reported ... 130–132
date of ... 130, 132–134

designing effective ... 133–134
guidance for ... 43, 130
in litigation ... 134
new language in ... 6
representations included in ... 44, 119
responsibility for fraud assessment in ... 13
signature of
management on ... 131, 132, 133
SSARS No. 9 changes to ... 129–134

**Management services
by accountants ... 111–116**

**Management-use only financial
statements ... 73, 83, 84–103**
changes in level of service for ... 101–103
in compilation engagement without
report (Rule 1) ... 91
disclosures permitted but not
required for (Rule 6) ... 95–96
eligibility to receive, subsequent ... 100
engagement letter to document client's
understanding (Rule 2) ... 91–92
identification of supplementary
information in (Rule 7) ... 96
legends for (Rule 3) ... 92
material departures from GAAP or
OCBOA noted in engagement letter
for (Rule 5) ... 93–95
peer review considerations for ... 101
performance requirements in
SSARS No. 1 for (Rule 4) ... 93
restricted issuance of ... 100
third-party use of (Rule 8) ... 96–101
titles for ... 94–95

**Management's assertions, third party
confirmations of ... 58**

**Market shares of "Big 4"
accounting firms ... 25–28**

Material misstatements. *See also* **Risks of
material misstatement**
ascertaining whether
misstatements are ... 65
indicative of fraud, 65–66

**Message applications among AICPA
top 10 technologies ... 2**

**Microsoft Word or Excel file, presenting
financial statements in ... 80**

Misappropriation of assets
concealing ... 50
effect of ... 49
examples of ... 49
fraud risk factors for ... 47, 55
as fraud type ... 6, 7–8, 57
immaterial methods of company ... 7
responses to identified risks of
fraud from ... 60
risks resulting in, due to fraud ... 56–57
temporary ... 7

N

Name of accountant, improper
use of ... 120–121

Non-public company audits
as commodity to business owners ... 11
explanation of fraud
responsibilities in ... 11
implementation of
SAS No. 99 for ... 11–12

Not-for-profit or government entities
financial statements for ... 87, 88
management-use only financial
statements for ... 99

O

OCBOA in financial statements
disclosures required by ... 95–96, 122–123
material departures from, noted in
engagement letter ... 93–95
to reduce audit time ... 12

Off-balance sheet transactions,
disclosure of ... 14

Over-auditing ... 11

P

Payment for goods or services
not received ... 7

Peer review of compilation
engagements ... 70
covered by SSARS No. 1 ... 73

Personal financial plan, exemption
from SSARSs of financial
statements within ... 107

Plain paper engagement ... 71–72

Practical Guidance for Implementing
SSARS No. 8 (The Guide)
distinction between performing
bookkeeping and preparing financial
statements in ... 76, 79
guidelines for preparation and submission
of financial statements in ... 82–83
language for management-use only
engagement letter in ... 102
legends for financial statements
described in ... 92
members of management under ... 97–99
as nonauthoritative practice aid ... 72

Predecessor accountant
client communication with ... 144–145
communications between
successor and ... 130
definition of, SSARS No. 9
as modifying ... 142

Prepaid items, reducing
audit time for ... 12

Prescribed forms, exemption from SSARSs
of financial statements in ... 108

Public accounting firms
absorption of Arthur Andersen clients
by other ... 28
barriers to entry for smaller ... 26
"Big 4," percentage of audits
performed by ... 25–26
business opportunities for specialists
in Section 404 compliance in ... 24
concentration of industries
among "Big 4" ... 29
consolidation of ... 24–26
expansion of, effects of
state laws on ... 27
global operations of, largest firms for ... 27
nonlicensed, compilation reports by ... 69
PCAOB inspections of ... 15
revenues and staff of non "Big 4" ... 27, 28
switching, statistics for choices in ... 25
U.S. operations of, largest firms for ... 27–28

Public Company Accounting Oversight
Board (PCAOB) ... 14–16
annual report by ... 16
authority for GAAP and GAAS of ... 14
created by Sarbanes-Oxley ... 14
funding of ... 15
oversight by SEC of ... 14
purpose of ... 14
registered public accounting firms
inspected by ... 15
responsibilities of ... 15
SEC appointment of members of ... 15

Public company, insurance and litigation
costs of auditing large ... 26–27

Q

Quality control policies
and procedures ... 141

Quality control standards, relationship
of SSARSs to ... 140–141

Quality control system, requirement to
adopt ... 120

R

Radio frequency identification (RFID)
among AICPA top 5 emerging
technologies ... 2

Related party transactions,
disclosure of ... 14

Report to the Nation, Occupational Fraud
and Abuse, 2002 (ACFE) ... 7, 9

Requirements for audit committees (Sarbanes-Oxley Section 301) ... 22, 24

Retained earnings, disclosing change in ... 121–123

Revenue recognition
analytical procedures
performed for ... 64–65
focusing audit on ... 12

Revenue recognition in responding to fraud risks ... 59, 66

Review engagement
omission of substantially all
GAAP disclosures causing
nonacceptance of ... 149
rules for dealing with supplementary
information in ... 135

Review report
accountant's signature on ... 119, 128–129
addressing ... 129
changes under SSARS No. 9 to ...
128–129
country of origin referred to in ... 149–150
CPA requirement to review financial
statements in ... 108
date of ... 129
for interim periods ... 132
reference to country of
origin in ... 149–150

Risk
associated with issuing financial
statements with transmittal letter to
third party ... 118
attributes of ... 57

Risk assessment for fair value measurements ... 32–34

Risk factors, fraud
for misappropriation of assets ... 47, 55
for occurrence of fraudulent financial
reporting ... 46, 54–55

Risk management for management-use only financial statements ... 87

Risks of material misstatement
additional procedures to deal with ... 6
assumption of ... 57
auditor consideration of ... 5
auditor identification of, for fraud ... 6, 47
auditor's response to ... 58, 60
due to fraud, identifying ... 56–57
overall responses to ... 58

S

Sarbanes-Oxley Act of 2002
aftermath of ... 13–29
competition among audit firms
limited by ... 25

conflicts of interest and auditor
independence rules of ... 17
corporate disclosures under, new ... 19–20.
See also individual types
costs of compliance with ... 11
effects on corporate boards and audit
committees of ... 17–18
effects on corporate officers of ... 18–19
effects on investment bankers and
analysts of ... 20–21
effects on SEC company
auditors of ... 16–17
impact on accounting profession of ... 1
issuance of final or proposed rules
required under ... 22
overview of ... 13–14
passage in August 2002 of ... 13
penalties and criminal fraud provisions in
... 20
Public Company Accounting Oversight
Board created by ... 14–16. *See also*
Public Company Accounting Oversight
Board (PCAOB)
Section 301 of. *See* Audit committees and
Requirements for audit committees
(Sarbanes-Oxley Section 301)
Section 404 of. *See* Internal control
reporting (Sarbanes-Oxley Section 404)
Sections 302 and 906 of. *See* Certification
of disclosures in companies' quarterly
and annual reports (Sarbanes-Oxley
Sections 302 and 906)
trickle-down effect of ... 22

SAS No. 1, *Codification of Auditing Standards*
amendments to ... 67
professional skepticism required under ... 50

SAS No. 29, Reporting on Information Accompanying the Basic Financial Statements in Auditor-Submitted Documents ... 130

SAS No. 32, Adequacy of Disclosure in Financial Statements, disclosures of fair values under ... 43

SAS No. 55, Consideration of Internal Control in a Financial Statement Audit, understanding of internal control in ... 33, 34, 57

SAS No. 56, Analytical Procedures ... 42

SAS No 57, Auditing Account Estimates ... 32

SAS No. 61, Communication with Audit Committees, requirements for audit matters in ... 44

SAS No. 70, Service Organizations, requirements of ... 33

SAS No. 73, Using the Work of a Specialist ... 37

Index **205**

SAS No. 82, *Consideration of Fraud in a Financial Statement Audit*
expectation gap addressed in ... 46
SAS No. 99 as superseding ... 5, 46

SAS No. 84, Communication Between Predecessor and Successor Auditors ... 141, 145

SAS No. 85, *Management Representations*
amendment of ... 6, 67
guidance concerning representations to be obtained in ... 43, 53
guidance for auditors finding existing illegal acts in ... 47

SAS No. 93, Omnibus Statement on Auditing Standards—2000, audit report changed by ... 149, 150

SAS No. 99, *Consideration of Fraud in a Financial Statement Audit*
audit time to comply with ... 10–13
background of ... 46–47
communicating to client the standards of ... 13
costs of compliance with ... 10–11
fraud identification and client deliberations about fraud described in ... 1
Fraud Risk Factors Appendix to ... 54
impact on audits of nonpubli
c entities of ... 5–10
integration of the requirements into audit process for ... 48
scope of ... 47–48
understanding and applying ... 45–68

SAS No. 101, *Auditing Fair Value Measurements and Disclosures ... 29–45*
guidance on auditing fair value measurements in ... 30, 32
requirements of ... 30–34

SASs, comparative number of ... 103

Securities fraud, criminal penalties for ... 14

Segregation of duties in small businesses, poor ... 10

Simple Object Access Protocol (SOAP) among AICPA top 5 emerging technologies ... 2

Small businesses
effects of Sarbanes-Oxley on ... 14
fraud in ... 9–10, 13

Spam technology among AICPA top 10 technologies ... 2

Specialist engaged by auditor
auditor consideration of data used by ... 42
included in audit team discussions of possible fraud ... 52
for inventory fraud investigations ... 60
for substantive tests and evaluations ... 37

SQCS No. 2, *System of Quality Control for a CPA Firm's Accounting and Auditing Practice ... 55*

SSARSs
comparative number of ... 103
four exemptions from ... 69
interpretations of, list of ... 105–106
No. 1, *Compilation and Review of Financial Statements* ... 69, 70–71, 72–73, 75, 82–84, 103–104, 106–109, 112, 128, 137
No. 1, SSARS No. 9 changes to ... 119, 121, 124, 127, 128, 129–130, 134, 140–141, 145
No. 2, Reporting on Comparative Financial Statements ... 104
No. 3, Compilation Reports on Financial Statements Included in Certain Prescribed Forms ... 104, 108
No. 4, Communications Between Predecessor and Successor Accountants ... 104, 141
No. 5, Reporting on Compiled Financial Statements ... 104
No. 6, Reporting on Personal Financial Statements Included in Written Personal Financial Plans ... 104, 108
No. 7, Omnibus Statement on Standards for Accounting and Review Services ... 104, 129
No. 8, Amendment to Statement on Standards for Accounting and Review Services No. 169, 72–73, 75, 79–83, 91–100, 102, 106, 127–128
No. 9, Omnibus Statement on Standards for Accounting and Review Services 2002 ... 104–105, 119–130, 142
relationship of quality control standards with ... 140–141
relationship of SQCSs to ... 140–141

Statement of cash flows, omitting ... 146

Statement of Position 94-6, *Disclosures of Certain Significant Risks and Uncertainties ... 43, 148*

Statements of retained earnings and comprehensive income, reporting requirements for ... *119, 121–127*

Statements on Quality Control Standards (SQCSs) ... 119
relationship to SSARSs of ... 140–141

Stealing assets ... *7*

Submission of compilation, definition of ... 70, 72, 73
post-2000 ... 75–76
pre-2001 ... 73–74
services not covered under ... 106–107
SSARS No. 8 changes to ... 82–83, 103

206 TOP AUDITING ISSUES FOR 2005 CPE COURSE

Subsequent events and transactions after balance-sheet date ... 42

Substantive tests
of fair value measurements ... 38
timing of, during year ... 59

Successor accountant
communications between predecessor and ... 130, 141–145
definition of ... 142

Successor Accountant Acknowledgment Letter ... 144

Supplementary information
budgets presented with historic statements treated as ... 139–140
definition of ... 136–137
legends for each page of ... 138–139
mishandling reporting on ... 135–136
presenting ... 138–139
procedures for reviewing or compiling ... 138
separate report on ... 119, 134–135, 136
titles for pages of ... 139

T

Tax return information
as exempt from and subject to SSARS No. 1 ... 107
used to perform business valuation ... 108–110

Theft or defalcation. *See* **Misappropriation of assets and Stealing assets**

3G wireless
among AICPA top 5 emerging technologies ... 2
used for fraud ... 7

Third parties, definition of ... 97

Time savings
for audits ... 11–12
for management-use only financial statements ... 89

Timeline of ARSC consideration of levels of accounting services ... 71–72

Titles for pages of supplementary information ... 139

Top Ten Technology Issues of 2004 (AICPA) ... 1
list of technologies from ... 1–2

Trade payables, focusing audit on ... 12

Transaction approval procedures in small businesses, poor ... 10

Transmittal letter to third party
by accountant lacking independence ... 115–116
clear indication of employment title in ... 117
legal liability for ... 118

rules for ... 117–118

Trial balance
adjusting entries to ... 76
differentiating financial statements from ... 107
preparation of ... 73, 79

Trusts, financial statements for ... 87, 88

U

Unaudited information, accountant's name in communication containing ... 119, 120–121

Unpaid fees, predecessor accountant's refusal to respond to successor's inquiries due to ... 143, 144

Unusual transactions, evaluating business rationale for ... 62

V

Valuation by independent appraiser ... 38

Valuation methods
GAAP requirements for ... 31, 43
relevance of ... 36
selection of ... 35–36
significant assumptions underlying ... 40

Valuation model
auditor evaluation of assumptions used in ... 41
testing ... 38

Victims of fraud, types of ... 7

Virtual office among AICPA top 10 technologies ... 2

W

Wall Street Journal/NBC Poll of public view of accounting ... 3–4

Wireless technologies among AICPA top 10 technologies ... 2

Working papers, permission to review predecessor's ... 144
sample letter for ... 145

Write-up services, risks to accountants performing ... 110

Y

Year-end compilation engagement as separate from management-use only engagement ... 102

TOP AUDITING ISSUES FOR 2005 CPE COURSE
CPE Quizzer Instructions

The CPE quizzer is divided into two modules. There is a processing fee for each quizzer module submitted for grading. Successful completion of Module 1 is recommended for **8 CPE Credits.*** Successful completion of Module 2 is recommended for **5 CPE Credits.*** You can complete and submit one module at a time, or both modules at once for a total of **13 CPE Credits.***

To obtain CPE credit, return your completed answer sheet for each quizzer module to **CCH INCORPORATED, Continuing Education Department, 4025 W. Peterson Ave., Chicago, IL 60646**, or fax it to (773) 866-3084. Each quizzer answer sheet will be graded and a CPE Certificate of Completion awarded for achieving a grade of 70 percent or greater. A quizzer answer sheet is located after the quizzer questions for this course.

Express Grading: Processing time for your answer sheet is generally 8-12 business days. If you are trying to meet a reporting deadline, our Express Grading Service is available for an additional $19 per module. To use this service, please check the "Express Grading" box on your answer sheet, and provide your CCH account or credit card number and your fax number. CCH will fax your results and a Certificate of Completion (upon achieving a passing grade) to you by 5:00 p.m. the business day following our receipt of your answer sheet. **If you mail your answer sheet for express grading, please write "ATTN: CPE OVERNIGHT" on the envelope.** *NOTE:* CCH will not Federal Express Quizzer results under any circumstances.

Date of Completion: The date of completion on your certificate will be the date that you put on your answer sheet. However, you must submit your answer sheet to CCH for grading within two weeks of completing it.

Expiration Date: December 31, 2005

Evaluation: To help us provide you with the best possible products, please take a moment to fill out the course evaluation located at the back of this course and return it with your quizzer answer sheet(s).

One **complimentary copy** of this course is provided with all copies of the Miller Auditing Guides. Additional copies of this course may be ordered for $25.00 each by calling 1-800-248-3248 (ask for product 0-0912-100).

CCH INCORPORATED is registered with the National Association of State Boards of Accountancy (NASBA) as a sponsor of continuing professional education on the National Registry of CPE Sponsors. State boards of accountancy have final authority on the acceptance of individual courses for CPE credit. Complaints regarding registered sponsors may be addressed to the National Registry of CPE Sponsors, 150 Fourth Avenue North, Suite 700, Nashville, TN 37219-2417. Web site: www.nasba.org.

CCH INCORPORATED is registered with the National Association of State Boards of Accountancy (NASBA) as a Quality Assurance Service (QAS) sponsor of continuing professional education. State boards of accountancy have final authority on the acceptance of individual courses for CPE credit. Complaints regarding registered sponsors may be addressed to NASBA, 150 Fourth Avenue North, Suite 700, Nashville, TN 37219-2417. Web site: www.nasba.org.

Recommended CPE:	8 hours for Module 1
	5 hours for Module 2
	13 hours for all modules
Processing Fee:	$79.00 for Module 1
	$59.00 for Module 2
	$138.00 for all modules

* Recommended CPE credit is based on a 50-minute hour. Participants earning credits for states that require self-study to be based on a 100-minute hour will receive ½ the CPE credits for successful completion of this course. Because CPE requirements vary from state to state and among different licensing agencies, please contact your CPE governing body for information on your CPE requirements and the applicability of a particular course for your requirements.

TOP AUDITING ISSUES FOR 2005 CPE COURSE
Quizzer Questions: Module 1

1. Misappropriation of assets is accomplished in several ways, including all of the following *except:*

   a. Embezzling receipts
   b. Stealing assets
   c. Overstating revenue
   d. Causing the entity to pay for goods or services not received

2. Three conditions usually are present when a fraud occurs. These three conditions are commonly referred to by fraud examiners as the:

   a. Fraud triangle
   b. Fraud threesome
   c. Triple fraud factor
   d. None of the above

3. The three conditions of the fraud triangle include all of the following *except:*

   a. Incentive or pressure
   b. Opportunity
   c. Rationalization or attitude
   d. Timing and emotional intelligence

4. Smaller businesses have certain characteristics that make them more susceptible to fraud than their larger counterparts. Examples of such characteristics include all of the following *except:*

   a. Poor segregation of duties
   b. Disinterested management/owner
   c. Inadequate financing
   d. Informal approval process

TOP AUDITING ISSUES FOR 2005 CPE COURSE

5. The author provides several recommendations to reduce audit time that include all of the following *except:*

   a. Reduce the amount of work on inventories
   b. Increase use of analytical procedures in lieu of tests of account balances
   c. Focus your time in those areas where there is a high degree of inherent risk
   d. Consider using OCBOA (income tax basis) financial statements to reduce audit time.

6. Under the Sarbanes-Oxley Act, the new standards that registered firms must adopt include all of the following *except:*

   a. A seven-year workpaper retention policy
   b. A concurring or second partner review
   c. A five-year audit firm rotation
   d. Report on internal control

7. Under Sarbanes-Oxley Act, prohibited activities by accounting firms including all of the following *except:*

   a. Actuarial services
   b. Internal audit outsourcing services
   c. Management functions or human resources
   d. Tax return preparation

8. Under Sarbanes Oxley Act, Section 404 compliance requirement represents a significant challenge for public companies as they must do all of the following *except:*

   a. Assess their control environment, systems capabilities, and accounting principles and practices.
   b. Identify and document significant controls.
   c. Prepare an internal control report.
   d. Disclose all new accounting principles and their application.

9. According to the GAO report, of the former Andersen clients, only _____ switched to non-Big 4 firms.

   a. 13 %
   b. 20 %
   c. 5 %
   d. None of the above

10. The results of the GAO's Mandated Study on Consolidation and Competition in the Accounting Profession revealed that the GAO found empirical evidence that consolidation has impacted competition in the audit services market, the quality of audits, audit fees, and the capital markets. *True or False?*

11. Under present GAAP, fair value measurements are used in numerous GAAP statements, examples of which include all of the following *except:*

    a. FASB No. 107, *Disclosures about Fair Value of Financial Instruments*
    b. FASB No. 142, *Goodwill and Other Intangible Assets*
    c. FASB No. 144, *Accounting for the Impairment or Disposal of Long-Lived Assets*
    d. FASB No. 109, *Accounting for Income Taxes*

12. SAS No. 101 states that fair value measurements for which _____ are not available are inherently imprecise because those fair value measurements may be based on assumptions about future conditions, transactions, or events whose outcome is uncertain and will therefore be subject to change over time.

    a. Observable market prices
    b. Present value measurements
    c. Discounted cash flow measurements
    d. None of the above

13. In obtaining an understanding of the entity's process for determining fair value measurements and disclosures, the auditor should consider various factors, including all of the following *except:*

    a. The use of information technology in the valuation process
    b. The use of specialists, if any, in determining fair value measurements and disclosures
    c. The process used to monitor changes in management's assumptions
    d. The format of the disclosures included in the notes to financial statements

212 TOP AUDITING ISSUES FOR 2005 CPE COURSE

14. To be reasonable, the assumptions on which the fair value measurements are based (for example, the discount rate used in calculating the present value of future cash flows), both individually and taken as a whole, need to be realistic and consistent with all of the following *except:*

a. Existing market information
b. Assumptions made in prior periods, if appropriate
c. Management's best guess of future and past experiences, on a weighted basis
d. Past experience of or previous conditions experienced by the entity, to the extent currently applicable

15. SAS No. 85 requires that the auditor obtain written representations. With respect to fair value, depending on the nature, materiality, and complexity of fair values, management representations about fair value measurements and disclosures contained in the financial statements may include representations of all of the following *except:*

a. The appropriateness of the measurement methods and related assumptions used by management in determining fair value and the consistency in application of the methods
b. The completeness and adequacy of disclosures related to fair values
c. Whether subsequent events require adjustment to the fair value measurements and disclosures included in the financial statements
d. The amount by which fair value exceeds carrying value of the underlying investment

16. _____ is ultimately responsible for making the fair value measurements and disclosures included in the financial statements.

a. Management
b. The auditor
c. The audit committee
d. The board of directors

17. SAS No. 55, Consideration of Internal Control in a Financial Statement Audit, as amended, requires the auditor to obtain an understanding of each of the _____ components of internal control sufficient to plan the audit.

a. Five
b. Three
c. Seven
d. Ten

QUIZZER QUESTIONS — Module 1 **213**

18. Management often documents plans and intentions relevant to specific assets or liabilities and GAAP may require it to do so. While the extent of evidence to be obtained about management's intent and ability is a matter of professional judgment, the auditor's procedures ordinarily include inquiries of management, with appropriate corroboration of responses, such as all of the following *except:*

- **a.** Considering management's past history of carrying out its stated intentions with respect to assets or liabilities
- **b.** Reviewing written plans and other documentation, including, where applicable, budgets, minutes, and other such items
- **c.** Considering management's stated reasons for choosing a particular course of action
- **d.** Asking management for a written representation of its ability to carry out a particular course of action

19. When there are no observable market prices and the entity estimates fair value using a valuation method, the auditor should _____.

- **a.** Evaluate whether the entity's method of measurement is appropriate in the circumstances.
- **b.** Try to find an intrinsic valuation method that the auditor has used in the past.
- **c.** Conclude that a reasonable and relevant valuation method is not possible.
- **d.** None of the above.

20. When testing the entity's fair value measurements and disclosures, the auditor evaluates whether:

- **a.** Management's assumptions are reasonable and reflect, or are not inconsistent with, market information.
- **b.** The fair value exceeds the carrying value.
- **c.** Management is qualified to consider fair value and to evaluate it.
- **d.** None of the above.

21. Which of the following statements regarding the auditor's responsibility to detect fraud was evidenced in SAS No. 82?

- **a.** Responsibility for detecting material misstatements, if caused by fraud
- **b.** Responsibility for detecting all fraud, if material in amount
- **c.** Responsibility for detecting fraud, if caused by misappropriation of assets
- **d.** Responsibility for detecting all fraud, if caused by management

214 TOP AUDITING ISSUES FOR 2005 CPE COURSE

22. Fraudulent financial reporting includes all but which of the following?

   a. Alteration of the date of a sales invoice so that the sale could be recorded in an earlier period

   b. Deliberate double payment of purchase invoice to supplier who is related to the employee

   c. Omission from the footnotes disclosure that the company is being sued for patent infringement

   d. Postdating checks to improve the company's cash per books

23. An opportunity for fraud may exist when:

   a. Management's bonuses are based on book earnings.

   d. The company lacks a well-developed set of ethical guidelines.

   c. Perpetual inventory records are updated daily.

   d. Internal controls are not effective.

24. Professional skepticism is best defined as:

   a. Assuming that management's assertions are likely to overstate financial results

   b. Assuming that internal controls are inadequate, unless testing reveals otherwise

   c. Possessing a questioning mind and critically examining audit evidence

   d. Possessing the knowledge that fraud is not an unlikely occurrence

25. The audit team should "brainstorm" about the risks of fraud:

   a. Prior to gathering information about the risks of fraud

   b. Immediately after gathering information about the risks of fraud

   c. After completion of the fieldwork, but prior to writing the annual report

   d. Never, because assessing the risks of fraud is the responsibility of the in-charge audit person

26. Which of the following may increase the likelihood of fraud?

   a. An opportunity to commit fraud

   b. Incentives for management to commit fraud

   c. A culture that enables fraud

   d. All of the above

QUIZZER QUESTIONS — Module 1   215

27. A complex operating structure is an example of which of the following fraud risks factors?

   a. Incentives/pressures existing to commit fraud
   b. An opportunity to commit fraud
   c. Attitudes/rationalizations that allow or justify committing fraud
   d. None of the above

28. The pervasiveness attribute of the risks of fraud is:

   a. The possibility that it will lead to a material misstatement
   b. The possibility of creating material misstatements
   c. Whether the risk is of fraudulent reporting or misappropriation
   d. Whether it would affect the financial statements as a whole

29. An internal control requiring a second signature on checks in excess of $10,000 would be an example of:

   a. A management manipulation control
   b. A routine, batch level control
   c. A specific control
   d. A broad control

30. Which of the following responses to identified fraud risks would constitute a change in the extent of the procedures performed?

   a. Observing inventory at the end of the year instead of an earlier date
   b. Obtaining more third party confirmations
   c. Performing more analytical procedures
   d. Inspecting plant and equipment

31. Management override is least likely to occur with which of the following transactions?

   a. Batch transactions
   b. Journal entries
   c. Year-end transactions
   d. Highly complex transactions

216 TOP AUDITING ISSUES FOR 2005 CPE COURSE

32. If the auditor identifies a risk of fraud with respect to inventory, she is more likely to:

    a. Observe the taking of inventory at an interim date rather than at year-end

    b. Observe inventory at more locations than originally planned Obtain third party confirmations of all inventory

    c. Physically count the inventory herself

33. Which of the following would not lead the auditor to exercise professional skepticism over the business purpose of a transaction?

    a. The transaction is with a large customer

    b. The transaction is with an unconsolidated related party

    c. The transaction is extremely complex

    d. Parties to the transactions appear to lack the financial strength to engage in the transaction without assistance from the entity

34. Retrospective reviews of the prior year's accounting estimates are recommended so that:

    a. A test can be made of the auditor's previous professional judgments

    b. The ethical standards of management may be assessed

    c. Opportunities in the entity for committing fraud may be better estimated

    d. It can be determined if estimates reflect a possible bias on the part of management

35. Comparing net income to cash flow may be a helpful analytical tool in determining the risks of fraud because:

    a. It is more difficult to manipulate cash flow than net income.

    b. A decrease in cash balances may indicate misappropriation of assets.

    c. Pressures on management to achieve expectations of cash flow per share are greater than pressures to achieve net income per share.

    d. Cash presents the opportunity for fraud as well as incentive.

36. With respect to fraud, auditors are expected to inquire of management all but which of the following?

    a. Whether management is aware of allegations of fraud.
    b. Existence of specific controls to mitigate fraud risks.
    c. Management's assessment of the likelihood that fraud has occurred.
    d. How management communicates its views to employees of ethical behavior.

37. Causing an entity to pay for goods and services not received constitutes an example of fraudulent financial reporting. *True or False?*

38. Collusion among members of the entity make it more likely that the auditor will make false inferences about audit evidence. *True or False?*

39. The lack of a business purpose for an entity's transaction may be an indication that the transaction is fraudulent. *True or False?*

40. One likely response of the auditor to an identified risk of fraud is to conduct more tests of controls at the end of the audit. *True or False?*

218 TOP AUDITING ISSUES FOR 2005 CPE COURSE

TOP AUDITING ISSUES FOR 2005 CPE COURSE

Quizzer Questions: Module 2

---

41. SSARS No. 8 does which of the following?

   a. Changes the definition of *submission* used in SSARS No. 1
   b. Changes the definition of *financial statement* used in SSARS No. 1
   c. Changes the definition of *trial balance* used in SSARS No. 1
   d. None of the above

42. The definition of *submission* has how many elements?

   a. Three
   b. Four
   c. Two
   d. Six

43. To prepare financial statements, the accountant must use all of the following to create financial statements that would not have existed otherwise *except:*

   a. Knowledge
   b. Education
   c. Experience
   d. Expertise

44. If a CPA presents an updated general ledger to a client that also has financial statements embedded in the software, the CPA has also presented the financial statements to the client. **True or False?**

45. Which of the following is the SSARS No. 8 loophole?

   a. Having the CPA adjust numbers in general ledger software, prepare financial statements by revising account classifications, and sending the file to the client electronically
   b. Submitting financial statements on hard copies printed from adjusted general ledger software
   c. Presenting financial statements for a specific period in a Microsoft Word or Microsoft Excel file
   d. Preparing and presenting financial statements on hard copy or electronically without allowing the client to create financial statements

QUIZZER QUESTIONS — Module 2 **219**

46. For management-use only financial statements, the modes of communication that generally satisfy the definition of *present* include all of the following *except:*

 a. Handling or mailing a set of paper financial statements to the client or third party
 b. Giving the financial statements to the client or third party on a diskette or CD-ROM
 c. Sending the financial statements to the client or third party electronically
 d. Giving the client a trial balance

47. The second significant change in SSARS No. 8 is that it introduces:

 a. Third-party only financial statements
 b. Management-use only financial statements as an alternative to a review engagements
 c. Management-use only financial statements as an alternative to a traditional compilation report engagement
 d. None of the above

48. With respect to management-use only financial statements, the CPA must document a written understanding with the client using an engagement letter:

 a. That must be signed by management
 b. That is preferably signed by management
 c. That must be signed by both management and the CPA
 d. None of the above

49. The required items to include in an engagement letter for management-use only financial statements comprise all of the following *except:*

 a. Nature and limitations of the services to be performed
 b. No opinion or any other form of assurance on the financial statements will be provided
 c. The financial statements cannot be relied upon to disclose errors, fraud, or illegal acts
 d. The fact that a compilation report will be issued in accordance with SSARS No. 1

50. The general rule in SSARS No. 1 is that a CPA should not submit unaudited financial statements of a nonpublic entity to a client or third party unless the CPA complies with the provisions of SSARS No. 1. *True or False?*

220 TOP AUDITING ISSUES FOR 2005 CPE COURSE

51. Each page of a management-use only financial statement must include a limitation such as *Restricted for Management's Use Only.* **True or False?**

52. The performance requirements for a compilation engagement found in SSARS No. 1 are applicable to management-use only financial statements. The performance requirements state that the CPA must do all of the following *except:*

   a. Possess a level of knowledge of the accounting principles and practices of the industry in which the entity operates

   b. Obtain additional or revised information if he or she becomes aware that information supplied by the client is incorrect

   c. Read the financial statements and consider whether they are free from obvious material errors

   d. Prepare the financial statements and have them reviewed by an independent person to consider whether they are free from obvious material errors

53. Disclosures for management-use only financial statements are:

   a. Required

   b. Permitted but not required

   c. Not allowed

   d. None of the above

54. Which of the following persons is normally not included as a member of management under FASB No. 57?

   a. Chief executive officer

   b. Member of the board of directors

   c. Chief operating officer

   d. Bookkeeper

55. In order for the CPA to consider issuing management-use only financial statements, the CPA should consider several key factors that include all of the following *except:*

   a. The third-party need for financial information

   b. The integrity of management

   c. Risk management consideration

   d. Whether the CPA has adequate training in preparing such statements

QUIZZER QUESTIONS — Module 2   **221**

56. Which of the following is not a benefit to a CPA in saving time and maximizing profit in creating management-use only financial statements?

    a. Completing the engagement at the client's office
    b. Issuing management-use only financial statements that accompany tax returns
    c. Issuance of management-use only financial statements does not obligate the accounting firm to enroll in AICPA's Practice Monitoring Program
    d. None of the above

57. Which of the following is true relating to changes in the level of service?

    a. If the accountant has issued management-use only financial statements, he or she can subsequently issue compiled or reviewed financial statements for the same financial statement period.
    b. If the accountant has issued management-use only financial statements, he or she cannot subsequently issue compiled or reviewed financial statements for the same financial statement period.
    c. If the accountant has issued management-use only financial statements, he or she can subsequently issue compiled, but not reviewed, financial statements for the same financial statement period.
    d. None of the above.

58. A trial balance differs from a financial statement in all of the following ways *except:*

    a. A financial statement combines general ledger accounts to create account groups.
    b. Trial balances do not contain labels such as statement of income.
    c. Financial statements present the balance sheet in the order of liquidity.
    d. A trial balance is the same as a financial statement under the definition found in SSARS No. 1,

59. The exemptions from SSARS No. 1 include all of the following *except:*

    a. Financial statements included in a written personal financial plan
    b. Financial statements submitted to a third-party
    c. Financial statements involved in certain litigation services
    d. Financial statements included in certain prescribed forms

222 TOP AUDITING ISSUES FOR 2005 CPE COURSE

60. In considering whether a controller may issue compiled financial statements, which of the following is true?

   a. SSARS Interpretation No. 21 offers authoritative guidance as to the reporting responsibilities for accountants offering controllership services.

   b. SSARS Interpretation No. 21 offers nonauthoritative guidance as to the reporting responsibilities for accountants offering controllership services.

   c. SSARS Interpretation No. 21 does not address the issue of accountants offering controllership services.

   d. None of the above.

61. SSARS No. 9 amends SSARS No. 1 to state that a statement of retained earnings is_____.

   a. Not a required statement

   b. A required statement

   c. Required to be presented either in supplementary information or as a primary statement

   d. None of the above

62. The date of the compilation report is the _____.

   a. Date of completion of the compilation

   b. Last date of field work

   c. Date the report is mailed

   d. None of the above.

63. In designing an effective representation letter, an accountant may wish to consider all of the following *except:*

   a. Avoid the use of technical terms and, instead, use terms that are understandable to the client.

   b. If needed, soften the language in the letter.

   c. It is good practice to review the representation letter with the client before the letter is signed.

   d. Make the letter very technical in nature so that it will be binding in the event of litigation.

QUIZZER QUESTIONS — Module 2 **223**

64. SSARS No. 9 amends SSARS No. 1 to allow for a separate report on supplementary information in a _____.

   a. Review engagement
   b. Compilation engagement
   c. Attestation engagement
   d. None of the above

65. Supplementary information includes all of the following *except:*

   a. Operating expense schedule
   b. Schedule of cost of sales
   c. Statement of income
   d. Condensed financial statements for previous years

66. With respect to a review engagement, a successor accountant is:

   a. Not required to communicate with a predecessor accountant
   b. Required to communicate with a predecessor accountant
   c. May be required in certain cases to communicate with a predecessor accountant
   d. None of the above

67. With respect to referencing the country of origin in a review or compilation report, which of the following is true?

   a. SSARS do not require the reference to the country of origin.
   b. SSARS require the reference to the country of origin.
   c. SSARS are silent as to whether reference to the country of origin is required.
   d. None of the above.

225

TOP AUDITING ISSUES FOR 2005 CPE COURSE   (0744-2)

Module 1: Answer Sheet

NAME _____

COMPANY NAME _____

STREET _____

CITY, STATE, & ZIP CODE _____

BUSINESS PHONE NUMBER _____

DATE OF COMPLETION _____

SOCIAL SECURITY NUMBER _____

On the next page, please answer the Multiple Choice questions by indicating the appropriate letter next to the corresponding number. Please answer the True/False questions by marking "T" or "F" next to the corresponding number.

You will be charged a $79.00 processing fee for each submission of Module 1.

Please remove this Answer Sheet (both pages) from this booklet and return it with your completed Evaluation Form to CCH at the address below. You may also fax your answer sheet to CCH at 773-866-3084.

METHOD OF PAYMENT:

☐ Check Enclosed   ☐ Visa   ☐ Master Card   ☐ AmEx

☐ Discover   ☐ CCH Account* _____

Card No. _____ Exp. Date _____

Signature _____

* Must provide CCH account number for this payment option

EXPRESS GRADING: Please fax my Course results to me by 5:00 p.m. the business day following your receipt of this answer sheet. By checking this box I authorize CCH to charge an additional $19.00 for this service.

☐ Express Grading $19.00   Fax No. _____

SEND TO:

CCH INCORPORATED
Continuing Education Department
4025 W. Peterson Ave.
Chicago, IL 60646-6085
1-800-248-3248

TOP AUDITING ISSUES FOR 2005 CPE COURSE (0744-2)
Module 1: Answer Sheet

Please answer the Multiple Choice questions by indicating the appropriate letter next to the corresponding number. Please answer the True/False questions by marking "T" or "F" next to the corresponding number.

1. ___	13. ___	25. ___	37. ___
2. ___	14. ___	26. ___	38. ___
3. ___	15. ___	27. ___	39. ___
4. ___	16. ___	28. ___	40. ___
5. ___	17. ___	29. ___	
6. ___	18. ___	30. ___	
7. ___	19. ___	31. ___	
8. ___	20. ___	32. ___	
9. ___	21. ___	33. ___	
10. ___	22. ___	34. ___	
11. ___	23. ___	35. ___	
12. ___	24. ___	36. ___	

Please complete the Evaluation Form (located after the Module 2 answer sheet) and return it with this Quizzer Answer Sheet to CCH at the address on the previous page. Thank you.

TOP AUDITING ISSUES FOR 2005 CPE COURSE   (0745-2)

Module 2: Answer Sheet

NAME _____

COMPANY NAME _____

STREET _____

CITY, STATE, & ZIP CODE _____

BUSINESS PHONE NUMBER _____

DATE OF COMPLETION _____

SOCIAL SECURITY NUMBER _____

On the next page, please answer the Multiple Choice questions by indicating the appropriate letter next to the corresponding number. Please answer the True/False questions by marking "T" or "F" next to the corresponding number.

You will be charged a $59.00 processing fee for each submission of Module 2.

Please remove this Answer Sheet (both pages) from this booklet and return it with your completed Evaluation Form to CCH at the address below. You may also fax your answer sheet to CCH at 773-866-3084.

METHOD OF PAYMENT:

☐ Check Enclosed   ☐ Visa   ☐ Master Card   ☐ AmEx

☐ Discover   ☐ CCH Account* _____

Card No. _____ Exp. Date _____

Signature _____

* Must provide CCH account number for this payment option

EXPRESS GRADING: Please fax my Course results to me by 5:00 p.m. the business day following your receipt of this answer sheet. By checking this box I authorize CCH to charge an additional $19.00 for this service.

☐ Express Grading $19.00   Fax No. _____

SEND TO:

CCH INCORPORATED
Continuing Education Department
4025 W. Peterson Ave.
Chicago, IL 60646-6085
1-800-248-3248

231

TOP AUDITING ISSUES FOR 2005 CPE COURSE   (0745-2)

Module 2: Answer Sheet

Please answer the Multiple Choice questions by indicating the appropriate letter next to the corresponding number. Please answer the True/False questions by marking "T" or "F" next to the corresponding number.

41. _____	50. _____	59. _____
42. _____	51. _____	60. _____
43. _____	52. _____	61. _____
44. _____	53. _____	62. _____
45. _____	54. _____	63. _____
46. _____	55. _____	64. _____
47. _____	56. _____	65. _____
48. _____	57. _____	66. _____
49. _____	58. _____	67. _____

Please complete the Evaluation Form (located after the Module 2 answer sheet) and return it with this Quizzer Answer Sheet to CCH at the address on the previous page. Thank you.

PAGE 2 OF 2

233

TOP AUDITING ISSUES FOR 2005 CPE COURSE (0912-1)
Evaluation Form

Please take a few moments to fill out and mail or fax this evaluation to CCH so that we can better provide you with the type of self-study programs you want and need. Thank you.

About This Program

1. Please circle the number that best reflects the extent of your agreement with the following statements:

	Strongly Agree				Strongly Disagree
a. The course objectives were met.	5	4	3	2	1
b. This course was comprehensive and organized.	5	4	3	2	1
c. The content was current and technically accurate.	5	4	3	2	1
d. This course was timely and relevant.	5	4	3	2	1
e. The prerequisite requirements were appropriate.	5	4	3	2	1
f. This course was a valuable learning experience.	5	4	3	2	1
g. The course completion time was appropriate.	5	4	3	2	1

2. This course was most valuable to me because of:

____ Continuing Education credit 　　____ Convenience of format
____ Relevance to my practice/ 　　____ Timeliness of subject matter
　　　　employment 　　　　　　　　____ Reputation of author
　　　　　　　　　　　　　　　　　　____ Price
____ Other (please specify)

3. How long did it take to complete this course? (Please include the total time spent reading or studying reference materials, and completing CPE quizzer).

Module 1 ____　　　Module 2 ____

4. What do you consider to be the strong points of this course?

5. What improvements can we make to this program?

PAGE 1 OF 2

TOP AUDITING ISSUES FOR 2005 CPE COURSE   (0912-1)

Evaluation Form cont'd

General Interests

1. Preferred method of self-study instruction:
   ____ Text   ____ Audio   ____ Computer-based/Multimedia   ____ Video

2. What specific topics would you like CCH to develop as self-study programs? (Select more than one if appropriate.)

   ____ Accounting Standards   ____ Auditing
   ____ Compilation and Review   ____ Financial Reporting
   ____ Fraud   ____ Government Standards

3. Please list other topics of interest to you _____

   _____

   _____

About You

1. Your profession:

   ____ Accountant   ____ Auditor
   ____ Controller   ____ CPA
   ____ Enrolled Agent   ____ Risk Manager
   ____ Other (please specify) _____

2. Your employment:

   ____ Self-employed   ____ Public Accounting Firm
   ____ Service Industry   ____ Non-Service Industry
   ____ Banking/Finance   ____ Government
   ____ Education   ____ Other _____

3. Size of firm/corporation:

   ____ 1   ____ 2-5   ____ 6-10   ____ 11-20   ____ 21-50   ____ 51+

4. Your Name _____

   Firm/Company Name _____

   Address _____

   City, State, Zip Code _____

5. I would like to be informed of new CCH Continuing Education products by electronic message. My e-mail address is: _____
   _____. If you prefer, send your e-mail address to CCH.CPE@cch.com.

THANK YOU FOR TAKING THE TIME TO COMPLETE THIS SURVEY!

PAGE 2 OF 2

NOTES

NOTES

NOTES

NOTES

NOTES

NOTES

NOTES

NOTES

NOTES

NOTES